LESSONS AND LEGACIES IV

LESSONS AND LEGACIES IV

Reflections on Religion, Justice,
Sexuality, and Genocide

*Edited and with an introduction
by Larry V. Thompson*

NORTHWESTERN UNIVERSITY PRESS   EVANSTON, ILLINOIS

Northwestern University Press
Evanston, Illinois 60208-4210

Copyright © 2003 by Northwestern University Press. Published 2003.
All rights reserved.

Printed in the United States of America

10 9 8 7 6 5 4 3 2 1

ISBN 0-8101-1989-7 (cloth)
ISBN 0-8101-1990-0 (paper)

Library of Congress Cataloging-in-Publication data are available from the Library of Congress.

The paper used in this publication meets the minimum requirements of the
American National Standard for Information Sciences—Permanence of Paper for
Printed Library Materials, ANSI Z39.48-1992.

*In memory of
Irving and Beatrice Mills
Alexander and Sylvia Reiff*

*And in honor of
the Mills family*

Contents

Acknowledgments	ix
Theodore Zev Weiss Foreword	xi
Larry V. Thompson Introduction	xiii

I. Propriety

Lawrence L. Langer
Preempting the Holocaust — 5

Robert Melson
Problems in the Comparison of the Armenian Genocide and the Holocaust: Definitions, Typologies, Theories, and Fallacies — 24

II. Morality

Doris L. Bergen
Religion and the Holocaust: Some Reflections — 41

Michael Phayer
The Holocaust in the Shadow of the Cold War: Moral Questions about Papal Policy — 66

Robert A. Krieg
To *Nostra Aetate:* Martin Buber and Romano Guardini — 81

III. Legality

Ruth Bettina Birn
War Crimes Prosecutions: An Exercise in Justice?
A Lesson in History?   101

Randolph L. Braham
The National Trials Relating to the Holocaust
in Hungary: An Overview   128

Piotr Wróbel
Hitler's Helpers? The *Judenräte* Controversy   152

IV. Sexuality

Marion Kaplan
Gender: A Crucial Tool in Holocaust Research   163

Atina Grossmann
Trauma, Memory, and Motherhood: Germans
and Jewish Displaced Persons in Post-Nazi
Germany, 1945–1949   171

V. Proximity

Tomasz Kranz
Between Planning and Implementation:
The Lublin District and Majdanek Camp
in Nazi Policy   215

Geoffrey J. Giles
Confirming Their Prejudices: German University
Students and Himmler's Resettlement Program   236

Jeffrey Lesser
Visions of the Other: Stereotypes, Survival,
and the Refugee Question in Brazil   250

Notes on Contributors   267

Acknowledgments

Lawrence L. Langer's essay has appeared in Lawrence L. Langer, *Preempting the Holocaust* (Yale University Press, 1998), pp. 1–22.

Atina Grossmann's essay has appeared in *Archiv für Sozialgeschichte* 38 (1998): 230–54.

Theodore Zev Weiss

Foreword

THIS IS THE FOURTH VOLUME OF SCHOLARLY PAPERS PUBLISHED AS AN outgrowth of the Lessons and Legacies Conferences that the Holocaust Educational Foundation sponsors in partnership with major centers of higher learning. As with its predecessor, Lessons and Legacies III, our partner is Northwestern University, and we are pleased to acknowledge the help of its academic officers, as well as Northwestern University Press. These conferences sponsored by the foundation have become an ongoing tradition. The two Northwestern University conferences of 1990 and 1992 were followed by the Dartmouth College conference in 1994. We are pleased to acknowledge the University of Notre Dame for hosting Lessons and Legacies IV in 1996, and we are very grateful to Professor Robert Wegs for all his help in planning a successful conference.

The success of the Lessons and Legacies Conferences is only one of the areas in which the work of the Holocaust Educational Foundation has made gratifying strides in recent years. The number of colleges and universities teaching courses on the Holocaust with the foundation's help has grown from twenty at the beginning of the 1990s to more than two hundred today. Moreover, the foundation has established the biannual summer seminar trip to Holocaust sites in Central and Eastern Europe, enabling, to date, some one hundred scholars who teach courses on the Holocaust to acquaint themselves firsthand with the "topography of terror" that the Nazi regime established. Finally, by establishing the annual Summer Institute on Holocaust and Jewish Civilization held at Northwestern University, the foundation has begun a program of educating current and future college and university professors about the history, faith, and culture of the Jewish people, whom Nazism targeted for extinction. All of these efforts have brought us into ever more fulfilling contact with a growing "family" of decent and dedicated academicians who share our conviction that learning remains the best antidote to humanity's most inhumane impulses.

I want to take this opportunity to express my deep gratitude to the board members who have contributed so generously to the foundation's work and who made all this possible.

Finally, as always, my strongest sense of gratitude is to my wife, Alice, and my children, Danny and Deborah, who have encouraged the work of the foundation at every juncture and replenished my energies at every step.

Larry V. Thompson

Introduction

ISSUES OF PROPRIETY, MORALITY, LEGALITY, SEXUALITY, AND PROXIMITY are the focus of this *Lessons and Legacies* volume. The topical breadth of these thirteen essays adheres closely to the thematic emphasis selected for a conference held at the University of Notre Dame in the fall of 1996 in which earlier versions of these essays were presented. That conference focused on issues of religion, gender, and genocide within the Holocaust experience, and it generated scholarship that reaffirms the continuing eclecticism of Holocaust studies while also featuring essays showcasing what in the mid-1990s were emerging areas of research. Accordingly, this volume's organization seeks to blend contributions in established fields of Holocaust research, such as religion and justice, with scholarship breaking new ground in areas of concern, such as propriety, sexuality, and proximity.

Individually and collectively these essays do not directly engage the "why" or the "how" behind the Final Solution. While we now know a great deal about how the Holocaust evolved, a similar certitude about why it happened is lacking. Indeed, controversy continues to surround works attempting to "explain" what many insist is the inexplicable. This volume does not seek to be controversial, although a number of essays address topics, such as Christianity and the Holocaust or the efficacy of postwar efforts at retributive justice, that are and have been contentious. With few exceptions the essays offer no redemptive message of consolation that despite everything something good emerged from evil. Furthermore, no "lessons" to be learned from the Holocaust are embedded in them. Rather, they are reflections on aspects emanating from the Holocaust or directed at elements attached to it. Thus, the volume revisits some topics central to the Holocaust, such as the stance of the papacy or concern about the uses to which the Holocaust has been put, while presenting research on those less-examined areas mentioned above.

In part I, from very different disciplinary perspectives, Lawrence Langer and Robert Melson wrestle with the always potentially explosive issue of Holocaust use. Both authors offer admonitions of what is and what is not appropriate use, or what may be abuse, of the Holocaust. Langer explores the ambiguities and unintended consequences surrounding some intellectual, artistic, and clerical efforts to extract positive lessons from so monstrously negative an event. Melson asserts that efforts to claim uniqueness for the Holocaust restrict its usage in developing models and theories that promote understanding of why the phenomenon happened. Indeed, Melson argues that the Holocaust and the Armenian Genocide, while different in some respects, share some important similarities and are, therefore, comparable. In both essays the continuing search for Holocaust meaning for either inspirational or educational uses remains the crucial issue over which the authors disagree.

The role of religion in promoting, condoning, or mitigating the Holocaust continues to inspire interpretive treatments that remain highly controversial. Part II provides some refreshing assessments to this ongoing debate. Catholic-Jewish relations are the focus of all three essays, although each chooses subject matter of decidedly different scale. Doris Bergen examines the centrality of religion to the Holocaust, reminding us that religion and not race determined destiny. Analyzing Catholics, Jews, or Protestants in the aggregate, Bergen offers insights as to why some Christians helped Jews while others were committed Nazis. She also explores a neglected aspect of the Jewish response to the Holocaust by assessing the apparently minimal role played by religion in promoting Jewish resistance.

Michael Phayer, on the other hand, opts for a micro approach and concentrates on only one individual—Pope Pius XII. He insists that the pope's anticommunism, a pivotal factor in his behavior toward Nazism before and during the war, proved an obstacle to Jewish-Christian relations after the conflict. Phayer argues that the postwar cold warrior mentality of the papacy enabled German Catholics to avoid confronting their guilt for the regime's crimes, crippled indemnification and restitution efforts for survivors, sanctioned and protected regimes in Eastern Europe with fascist pasts, and strained Vatican relations with Israel.

Robert Krieg also takes a minimalist tack when evaluating the professional-*cum*-personal friendship between Martin Buber and Romano Guardini. He demonstrates that what began as scholarly awareness and curiosity about one another's work became a friendship based on mutual respect. The course of their relationship parallels in microcosm the history of Catholic-Jewish relations over the same era. Guardini kept aloof from Buber during the Third Reich, but actively pursued contact with him after the war. Where Buber had sought to maintain contact in the 1930s only to be rebuffed, Guardini eagerly became Buber's patron in Germany in the postwar era. Krieg suspects that moral remorse may explain Guardini's belated behavior, but he also suggests that the intellectual and theological benefits ultimately derived from the friendship played a subtle role in promoting the Second Vatican Council's 1965 Declaration on the Relation of the Church to Non-Christian Religions *(Nostra Aetate)*. Clearly, Krieg believes that something good subsequently resulted from evil.

Part III contains three essays that examine postwar efforts aimed at bringing to justice individuals accused of participating in or cooperating with Nazi criminality. Bettina Birn assesses proceedings held in the Soviet Union, Germany, and North America that took place after the Nuremberg trials ended and that extend into the present. She concludes that judicial structures and procedures in all three locales seriously affected verdicts and sentencing, generally freeing or granting undue leniency to the accused. Birn agrees that Germany's prosecutorial record is especially lamentable and believes that it reflects the continuing existence of pro-Nazi feelings overtly or subconsciously held. While the trials produced mixed judicial results at best, Birn argues that they have brought us greater historical truth concerning the Holocaust. Both Randolph Braham and Piotr Wróbel agree with her.

Braham examines the track record of retributive justice in the national trials held in postwar Hungary and elsewhere when Hungarian nationals were defendants. He finds the results depressingly meager in terms of justice received and believes that the cold war was responsible for the leniency exhibited almost everywhere. Most recently, Hungarian reversals of guilty judgments reached shortly after the war have inspired revisionist and denial efforts aimed at rehabilitating a fascist past. These efforts persuade Braham of anti-Semitism's continued durability.

Piotr Wróbel views the combined results of all postwar efforts at retributive justice aimed at individuals who belonged to the wartime Jewish Councils *(Judenräte)* as equally disappointing. Wróbel focuses on attempts made in Holland, Israel, and Poland, as well as in the postwar displaced persons and survivor camps in Germany and Italy, to punish Jews who had cooperated with, served, or assisted the Nazis. Almost everywhere persecution motivated by desire for vengeance gave way to politics, apathy, and indifference. When punishment came to individual Jews, it took the form of exclusion, the loss of office-holding and voting rights, or denial of material assistance. The message emanating from these three studies is consistent: whether the miscreants were Germans, Hungarians, East European sympathizers, or Jews caught up in the destruction process, retributive justice achieved little success. Cold war politics, the difficulty of prosecuting individuals for state-sponsored violence, collective pangs of guilt and complicity, and the accidents of time and place inspiring a sense of "there but for the grace of . . ." all contribute to the dismal statistics.

The emphasis shifts in Part IV from perpetrators or tarnished bystanders to the different layers of victimization within the Holocaust. Gender and sexuality concerns create different perspectives for experiencing or remembering the barbarism. As Marion Kaplan observes, gender mattered not only in terms of survival—women were far more vulnerable than men, and if pregnant, mothers, or old, they were certain of death—but also when coping, suffering, and anticipating. Kaplan demonstrates that women, simply because they were women, needed strategies for these and other circumstances. The kinds of strategies women ultimately adopted and followed made the Holocaust qualitatively different for them—a reality only recently noted or appreciated.

Atina Grossmann's essay extends the issue of gender and sexuality to the immediate postwar era. Her focus is on motherhood and on the contrastive attitudes toward it exhibited by Germans and Jews in Berlin as well as by Jewish survivors, who as displaced persons inhabited the DP camps. Grossmann demonstrates that both Germans and Jews were traumatized either through defeat or the Holocaust, but she stresses that the Germans quickly identified themselves as innocent victims, while the Jews in the camps viewed themselves as fortunate survivors. Germans, thus convinced they were confronting a bleak future, viewed pregnancy as both a personal and national liability. Abortions soared. Jews, on the other hand, welcomed pregnancy and celebrated motherhood confident, with Zionist encouragement, that a brighter future awaited them and their offspring in Palestine. Grossmann's motherhood prism enables us to view Berlin, the camps, and the postwar era from an entirely new perspective. In addition, she proves that something positive unexpectedly emerged from the genocidal nightmare: a renewed Jewish affirmation of life.

Part V features the importance of proximity when experiencing or viewing the Holocaust. Two essays deal with events taking place at the epicenter of destruction—Poland—while a third offers a glimpse from the periphery through an analysis of Brazilian refugee policy concerning European Jews. Tomasz Kranz details why the Lublin District of Poland (then part of the rump area known as the General Government) became the focal point for Nazi population policies as well as the extermination center for Polish and European Jews. Kranz points out that the total number of Jews murdered in the Lublin region is comparable with the number murdered at Auschwitz-Birkenau, and he provides a poignant overview of Polish suffering in consequence of the spectrum of Nazi actions that included expropriation, resettlement, forced labor, and concentration camp servitude. Kranz demonstrates the centrality of place when he reminds us that the Lublin region became the center for extermination because its proximity to the large Jewish populations of Poland and Ukraine made it attractive to Nazi population experts.

German university students sent to the *Warthegau* region of western Poland in 1940, for what was called an "eastern deployment" to renew German *Kultur* there, experienced firsthand the consequences of being close to the Holocaust's epicenter. As Geoffrey Giles demonstrates, the students gained an opportunity to confirm prejudices previously drummed into them at school and from party propaganda. Indoctrination in racism clearly surpassed even the most exacting expectations of party ideologues or professors. Giles provides some damning student commentary concerning Poles and Jews drawn from their observation of the Lodz ghetto and work experience in isolated Polish villages. He points out how remarkably similar their comments were to those made by the SS executors of the resettlement and extermination programs. Taking into consideration the students' awareness that their reports would be read by others, their racism nevertheless offers yet another example of how "ordinary" Germans behaved under extraordinary circumstances.

Opportunism, perhaps masquerading as pragmatism, describes Brazilian refugee policy toward Jews before and during the war. Jeffrey Lesser argues that Brazilian stereotypes of Jews living in Brazil as well as elsewhere shifted from negative images of urban, cosmopolitan, and culturally barren individuals to positive views of them as the capitalists, industrialists, and managers Brazil needed for economic progress. Eventually casting aside another negative image dear to the heart of pro-Axis nationalist sympathizers—Jewish leadership of international communism—Brazil's diplomats and politicians seemingly restricted Jewish immigration while actually turning a blind eye to the numbers entering the country. The economic development boost anticipated from relaxing restrictions on Jewish refugees helped overcome ingrained domestic prejudices. As Lesser makes clear, Brazil's small Jewish population proved surprisingly influential and persuasive in promoting this policy shift, but external pressures from international refugee organizations as well as the United States and Great Britain also convinced Brazil's political elite to offer a haven for Jews escaping the Holocaust. Lesser demonstrates that Brazilian support for the creation of Israel in the United Nations after the war was a continuation of the refugee policy turnaround begun during it. In this instance, support gained from the periphery eased, however slightly, the horrific pressures closer to the Holocaust's epicenter.

Inevitably, these Holocaust reflections variously are preoccupied with issues of guilt and victimization. The retributive judicial proceedings examined by Birn, Wróbel, and Braham, sought to prove the guilt of perpetrators. Michael Phayer and Robert Krieg touch upon the individual guilt of bystanders like Pius XII and Romano Guardini, while Doris Bergen probes the institutional guilt of organized religion. And, in his subtle critique of Holocaust representation, Lawrence Langer suggests that guilt often plays a decisive role in works promoting, consciously or not, redemptive closure.

These essays also reveal that victimization within the Holocaust experience is surprisingly open-ended. As Marion Kaplan indicates, their gender victimized Jewish women at every turn, making their treatment markedly more lethal, while Atina Grossmann notes that postwar Germans, wallowing in defeat and self-pity, viewed them-

INTRODUCTION • xix

selves, rather than Jews, as the greatest victims of the epoch. Tomasz Kranz reminds us that Poles, Jewish or not, were among the Holocaust's most numerous victims simply because of where they resided. Piotr Wróbel demonstrates the victimization of the *Judenräte* given their untenable position as liaisons between Germans and Jews. And, as Geoffrey Giles illustrates, German university students were also victims—victims of ideological inculcation and racist propaganda that skewed their education and made them willing bystanders, if not, later, willing participants.

As noted above, these reflections offer no comforting "positive lessons" to be learned, nor do they provide any assurances that such an abomination cannot happen again. However, they add to the ongoing examination of Holocaust consequences, and they offer insightful analyses to facets of it previously minimized or neglected. They also illustrate that matters of gender, sexuality, and proximity are crucial for shaping perceptions of a Holocaust reality that remains elusive.

For Professor Marshall Lee, whose initial efforts helped make this volume possible.

LESSONS AND LEGACIES IV

I. P·R·O·P·R·I·E·T·Y

Lawrence L. Langer

Preempting the Holocaust

THE UNSHAKABLE CONVICTION THAT THE HOLOCAUST CONTAINS A positive lesson for all of us today unites the three figures whose ideas I plan to examine here. The intellectual, the artist, and the cleric, whom I will identify shortly, each unfolds a vision of that event consonant with his or her worldview. When I speak of preempting the Holocaust, I mean using—and perhaps abusing—its grim details to fortify a prior commitment to an ideal of moral reality, community responsibility, or religious belief that leaves us with space to retain faith in their pristine value in a post-Holocaust world.

Although I find this strategy both misleading and presumptuous, I have no corrective vision of my own to provide, other than the opinion that the Holocaust experience challenged the redemptive value of all moral, community, and religious systems of belief. A life more shrouded by darkness than radiant with light—one inevitable bequest of the mass murder of European Jewry—is not necessarily a hopeless one, but only the least sensitive among us could celebrate a return to absolute normalcy after such chaos. Indeed, another major legacy of that event is the defeat of the words that try to describe it, since after such *ab*normalcy our very definitions of the normal seem flaccid and weak, while a generic term like "chaos" cannot begin to portray the moral and spiritual anarchy of those grievous times.

Let me begin with a concrete detail, because I am convinced that all efforts to enter the dismal universe of the Holocaust must start with an unbuffered collision with its starkest crimes. Recently I was watching the testimony of a survivor of the Kovno ghetto. He spoke of the *Kinderaktion,* when the Germans rounded up all the children (and many elderly) and took them to the nearby Ninth Fort for execution. The witness was present in the room when an SS man entered and demanded from a mother the one-year-old infant she was holding in her arms. She refused to surrender it, so he seized the baby by its ankles and tore the body in two before the mother's eyes.[1]

Whenever I hear stories like these, which unfortunately are not exceptional but illustrative of hundreds of similar incidents, I react with the same frozen disbelief, partly because of the intrinsic horror of the episode but also because it violates my sense of how life should and might be lived. I try to imagine the response of those in attendance—the mother, the witness, and the killer—but even more, I ask myself what we can do with such information, how we can inscribe it in the historical or artistic narratives that later will try to reduce to some semblance of order or pattern the spontaneous defilement implicit in such deeds? Where shall we record it in the scroll of human discourse? How can we enroll such atrocities in the human community and identify them as universal tendencies toward evil inherent in all humankind?

Well, we can't: we require a scroll of *in*human discourse to contain them; we need a definition of the *in*human community to coexist with its more sociable partner, and in their absence, we turn by default to more traditional forms of expression. The results may be comforting, but what price must we pay for such ease? The alternative is to begin by accepting a reality that escapes the bounds of any philosophy or system of belief that we have cherished since our beginnings, and to pursue the implications of this unhappy admission wherever they may lead. Consider, for example, this fragment of testimony from a former inmate of Auschwitz and Plaszow:

> We never knew . . . who would come back from roll call. Those who were "selected" for the "action" had to first dig their graves, then after stripping and placing everything they were wearing on the ground (in proper order: clothes on one side, underwear on the other), they had to kneel at the edge of the ditch and wait for the bullets in the back. Bullets that the Germans made the Jewish "leaders" of the camp pay for. Economizing on ammunition meant that the work was often botched, and cries rose from the ditches for hours after the execution. During large "actions" things moved too fast. There was no question of burying the bodies, they were simply covered with sand, so you could no longer tell whether you were walking on bones that were old or recent. Everything happened so fast that you didn't even have time to see your mother or sister van-

ish. We were no longer capable of suffering, or of being scared or surprised. Death is only frightening to the living. We hadn't been that for a long time.²

It is fearful enough to have to outlive the death, or more exactly the murder, of those one loves, some of whom have been buried while still breathing. But it is equally agonizing to have to outlive one's *own* death, as this witness insists she did, embracing an anguish beyond suffering that lifts her experience out of the realm of the familiar and deposits it in a limbo whose boundaries have yet to be clearly defined. We have the option of accepting the Holocaust as an event in quest of a concept to contain it or a language to express it, a phenomenon alien to our usual patterns of speech or belief; or we can assume that it only threatens but does not subvert the virtue, the vision, and the loving-kindness that my intellectual, my artist, and my cleric affirm. They do so as they venture to face the Holocaust with a universalizing vocabulary and imagery that never troubles to ask what it might mean to be dead while still alive. Which path we choose to follow depends on a complex tension between the stable instincts of our nature and a reality that tramples on those instincts with a contemptuous disdain.

"If we fail to master the past," writes Tzvetan Todorov in *Facing the Extreme: Moral Life in the Concentration Camps,* echoing both a famous German formulation and an overquoted aphorism of George Santayana, "it may master us." But it is not some abstract force called "the past" that the Holocaust challenges us to master; it is the mass murder of European Jewry. It is an SS man tearing a Jewish infant in two, or the German and Lithuanian murderers at the Ninth Fort in Kovno not even bothering to learn whether their victims were all dead before they ordered them to be covered with sand. How one goes about "mastering" such atrocities, as one of the murderers, or as a surviving member of the burial detail, or even as a detached reader today, I have no idea; I don't even know what "mastering" means in this context. But I suspect it doesn't help much to secrete such moments beneath a blanket of bland and evasive phrasing. *What* one faces when one faces the "extreme" of genocide is less important to Todorov than the assurance that moral life was still possible in the camps for both victims *and* murderers in spite of what went on there. He is not much interested in the specific agonies of the victims or the precise brutalities of their killers. He prefers instead to rescue both from the precincts of extremity and return them to the landscape of what he calls ordinary situations.

Todorov admits that many who outlived the camps and ghettos have written and spoken eloquently if bitterly about the selfish ways of behaving forced on them by the need to stay alive. But he is unwilling to accept this as a prevailing or even a requisite norm. It may seem odd that as recently as 1991 an intellectual as renowned as Todorov still finds it necessary to confirm the possibility of moral life even in the concentration camp (especially after Terrence Des Pres had defended the same idea so eloquently in *The Survivor* fifteen years earlier); I suppose, given the history of our indecent century, the impulse to defend the decency of the human species must surface periodically as ballast against the darker view.

But when such an effort is based on a dubious opposition between ordinary virtue on one hand and what Todorov calls "the principles of immorality expressed by the survivors" on the other, the resultant dichotomy leads us astray and blurs the tangled issue of who behaved how and why. Polarities, of which Todorov is unduly fond, quickly disintegrate in the atmosphere of a place like Auschwitz. For example, I have never heard a single survivor refer to the "principles of immorality" that governed his or her conduct in the camps. This locution is Todorov's invention, designed to emphasize a contrast between moral and immoral that may never have existed. He admits—and he really gives the game away through this admission—that "as a project, interpreting evil appeals less to me than understanding goodness."[3] As a result, he devotes most of his considerable intellectual energy to recovering the human, in both victims and their oppressors, from the midst of the inhuman, and then expanding the circle of those reassured to include his readers, and himself.

Todorov's book is one of three recent examples of universalizing the Holocaust that I am addressing in this inquiry. What happened in Nazi Germany and Stalin's Russia—Todorov speaks of them interchangeably—might have been done to, or done by, all of us. Experience, he says, is a contest between ordinary virtues—he labels them decency, caring, and the life of the mind—and ordinary vices: fragmentation, depersonalization, and the enjoyment of power. The Holocaust was little more than a drastic example of this modern conflict, and once we understand that, we will be in a better position to combat the totalitarian form of suppression of which the Holocaust was a not-so-singular example. This is a concise summary of Todorov's argument.

And where does all of this lead us—or lead Todorov? Well, it leads him to some extraordinary statements, and some even more extraordinary conclusions. Imagine their impact on the uninitiated reader, in search of authoritative accounts of the Holocaust. For example: "It is worth noting that the great majority of survivors have fallen victim to depression or trauma. The rate of suicide among this group is abnormally high, as is the prevalence of mental and physical illness." Or: "Life in the camps had been arduous in the extreme, and precisely because of this there had been something exalting in it [*elle a quelque chose d'exaltant*]. After the intensity of this experience, everything seemed colorless, futile, false" (263, 266). If the unexamined life is not worth living, what are we to say of these unexamined obiter dicta?

"Camp inmates," Todorov asserts—he seldom refers to Jews—"were made to know the far limits of human experience; it became their duty to humanity to report, in all honesty, what they saw and what they felt, for even in the most horrible experience there is some possibility for mankind's enrichment [*un enrichissement*]; only total oblivion calls for total despair."

Because many victims were still alive at the end of the war, obviously we are not dealing with total oblivion. Hence the truth of their ordeal as they transmit it should not only enlighten and instruct but also enrich. One truth of their ordeal is as follows: a doctor at Mauthausen, in training as a physician for the front with an SS unit, liked to amputate the arms or legs of Jews to see how long it would take them to bleed to death. After all, this would be useful medical information for his subsequent military career. And once, when he was not thus professionally engaged, showing admirable initiative, because he clearly was not ordered to do this, he took two young Jews from an arriving transport, killed them, cut off their heads, then boiled the flesh from the skulls, which he used as desk trophies for himself and a colleague. After the war, he married another doctor, and together they set up a gynecological practice in Germany. How this confirms Todorov's theoretical conviction that even in the most horrible experience, there is some possibility for humankind's enrichment must forever remain a mystery to most of us—though in a gruesome sense, it does ratify his opinion that "no life is lived in vain if it leaves behind some trace of itself" (96).

I suppose anyone can excavate from the rubble of mass murder a piece of testimony to support his or her philosophy or system of belief or critical point of view. Many of us who explore the terrain of atrocity are occasionally guilty of that. But not at the price, one hopes, of distorting the truth. Nothing is more threatening to the integrity of the historian than to allow facts to play him or her false for the sake of a thesis. Yet this is the trap Todorov succumbs to through his unempirical approach to the Holocaust. "To know, and to let others know," he proclaims, "is one way of remaining human" (97). But the rhetorical force of this idea so consumes his energy that he neglects the accuracy of the details that presumably lead to such knowledge.

So committed is Todorov to the notion that a bureaucratic system was responsible for the murder of the Jews rather than a collection of individuals who were enthusiastically pledged to destroying them that in one crucial but damning instance the forest blinds him to the real contribution of the separate trees. He designs a chain image to suggest the fragmentation of the killing process in Auschwitz. Each link leads impersonally to the next, beginning with Hitler, who of course makes the initial decision; followed by Reinhard Heydrich, "who never sees a single suffering fact"; next comes the policeman, "who merely carries out a routine order to arrest and expedite" (but never, presumably, to tear Jewish babies in two); then we have the turn of Adolf Eichmann, whose "purely technical job" is to see that the trains leave and arrive on time; after him is Rudolf Höss, the commandant, who oversees the emptying of the trains and the transfer to the gas chambers; and finally, Todorov concludes, "the last link: a group of inmates, a specialized commando that pushes the victims into the gas chambers and releases the lethal gas [*et verse dedans le gaz mortel*]." Before we have recovered from this breathtaking and infamous error, the author feels obliged to add to our knowledge: "The members of this commando are the only people who kill with their own hands." And now that we have been enlightened with the information that the only people *literally* involved in the murder of Jews in the gas chambers of Auschwitz were Jews themselves, we are relieved to learn that "they quite obviously are victims themselves, not executioners" (153).

Now how was this mistake possible, and what lies behind it? Certainly no malice, overt or covert: Todorov's tone is compassionate throughout. But the most elementary student of the Holocaust knows how Zyklon B was introduced into the gas chambers; how could Todorov have been guilty of such a lapse? If his aim had been to *represent* atrocity during the era of the Third Reich, he would have been more scrupulous in his research. But his intent from the beginning has been to *universalize* the event we call the Holocaust, implicating all of humanity as potential participants in genocide. There is a bizarre logic to his blunder that highlights the danger of any effort to schematize mass murder; it fits in with his earlier admission that "what interests me are the banal sources of exceptional actions, the ordinary attitudes that could make 'monsters' of us, too, were we to have to work in a concentration camp" (140). Primo Levi felt that such issues were irrelevant; we were victims, he said, and the Germans killed us. The rest was distracting speculation. History is not written about what other men and women might have done but did not.

One of the guilty parties in this confusion about truth is language itself. As long as we regard the Holocaust as an "exceptional action" instead of naming its specific inhuman content, we face the danger of losing contact with its reality. Todorov does not traffic in atrocities but is devoted to the ideal of "the common membership of all in the human community." This in turn leads to a reverse principle, which he offers with equally fervent conviction: "the fear one can feel in discovering that evildoers are not radically different from oneself" (225, 279). If by evildoers we mean the Germans and their collaborators who tore babies in half, buried (or burned) human beings alive, or, as in the case of the Mauthausen doctor, "operated" them to death, then one may be excused for believing that in some dimension they *are* radically different from oneself, though this need not be a statement about personal virtue or an explanation of a kind of behavior we may never understand. Indeed, the humble admission that we may never understand the conduct of the people we hide behind the name of perpetrators could turn out to be the most exasperating legacy of all from the multitude of crimes clustered under an abstract rubric like genocide.

Exasperation, of course, is not a very fruitful legacy, and perhaps this is why in the end Todorov chooses to distinguish between literal and exemplary memory. Having exhausted the historical roles of the functionalists and intentionalists, we may now turn to their successors, the literalists and the exemplarists. For Todorov, literal memory of the atrocities of the Holocaust, narratives of the unique painful ordeal of individual survivors, spreads "the consequences of the initial trauma over all the moments of existence." The results may be "true," but they are not very useful, in the sense that they create no new unity, no avenues for pursuing the future with fresh vigor and hope. Thus, Todorov confesses, literal memory is a "potentially risky endeavor" (258).

But there is another way of approaching the "recovered event," as Todorov calls it: paradigmatically, through exemplary rather than literal memory. This, he insists, is "truly liberating." Since it is a view of the Holocaust shared by my artist and cleric too, it is worth dwelling on for a moment. Why literal memory is a potentially risky endeavor Todorov does not say, but presumably he means that it may lead us into a dark cave of disenchantment from whose shadows we may never entirely escape. This is not a cheerful prospect—but neither was the murder of European Jewry. He is much more explicit, however, about the value of exemplary memory, which goes by the name of justice and involves "generalizing from the particular and applying abstract principles to concrete offenses." Anyone reading his book will see how easily this definition allows him to gloss over the concrete offenses for the sake of a higher principle. The exemplarists can tolerate the Holocaust only if it can be used as "an instrument that informs our capacity to analyze the present.... Only then can we tell ourselves that, at least from the viewpoint of humanity, the horrible experience of the camps will not have been in vain, that it contains lessons for us, who think we live in a completely different world" (258, 259).

Todorov has given me a label: in the sphere of memory, I am a literalist, not an exemplarist. I feel no impulse, not the slightest, to reclaim meaning from Holocaust atrocity or to embrace a Lincolnesque rhetoric seeking to persuade us that "the horrible experience of the camps will not have been in vain." There is nothing to be learned from a baby torn in two or a woman buried alive. But Todorov does unwittingly provide some helpful insight into the motives and strategy of my second example of preempting the Holocaust: Judy Chicago, the title of whose work—*Holocaust Project: From Darkness into Light*—gives us an unsubtle glimpse of the trajectory of her thought.

Chicago, too, is an exemplarist; she could not conceive of a Holocaust project subtitled "From Light into Darkness." But her antecedent agenda is quite different from Todorov's. "My interest in issues of gender certainly prefigured my interest in the Holocaust," she admits, following this with a more dubious pronouncement that nonetheless gives us a further clue about what led her to venture into the realms of mass murder: "Most people," she writes, "have not paid any attention to the fact that the architects of the Third Reich were *all* men."[4] Any inquiry that begins with a fixed premise and then seeks evidence to support it risks lapsing into a blinkered view of history. We shall have to see whether Chicago's belief in a link between patriarchy and mass murder, masculinity and Nazi ideology, entices us into further darkness, or greater light.

Judy Chicago's Holocaust education is enormously instructive, since she is perfectly frank about the tabula rasa of her mind as she began her investigation. It may surprise us to learn that a grown woman, an artist, was "ignorant" of the Holocaust as recently as 1985, but because she was not alone in her oblivion—millions of Americans share her unawareness—it would not be fair to charge her with anything more than a negligence of history. And her procedure for trying to remedy the defect is commendable: she watches Claude Lanzmann's *Shoah* and survivor testimonies, reads a library of standard Holocaust works (though her judgment here is sometimes questionable), and together with her photographer husband visits many sites of the disaster. Her initial response is far from trivial; indeed, to anyone who has tried to initiate students into the subject, it is both honest and familiar:

> After a while, I realized that some of my basic assumptions about people and the world were being profoundly challenged by the information I was encountering. I had always trusted people and believed the world to be a relatively fair and just place. Of course, I knew that terrible events happened, but I tended to see those as isolated phenomena. Confronting the Holocaust brought me face to face with a level of reality beyond anything I'd experienced before: millions of people murdered, millions more enslaved, millions made to suffer, while the world turned its back on the implementation of the Final Solution. I couldn't take it all in; it was too painful, and I was a long way from understanding what it meant about human beings and the world in which we live. (8)

We seem to be encountering the incipient deconstruction of a natural idealist. At this point, two roads diverge in a yellow wood, one the potentially risky path of the literalists, the other planted by the exemplarists with what Todorov calls lessons that "can all be evaluated according to certain universal rational criteria that underlie human dialogue."[5] Judy Chicago hardly hesitates in her decision, pursuing the latter with an evolving enthusiasm that betrays her unwillingness to surrender a prior commitment to universal criteria and human dialogue.

Instead of considering the possibility of disjunction, of rupture between familiar forms of violence and the explosive savagery of the Final Solution, Chicago intuitively seizes on connections—a true exemplarist. "I began to perceive," she admits, "that the unique Jewish experience of the Holocaust could be a window into an aspect of the unarticulated but universal human experience of victimization." Now this is a perfectly admissible analytical approach, but it creates a problem to which exemplarists have found no satisfactory solution: how to express the universal human experience of victimization while honoring, in Chicago's words, "the particularity of the Holocaust as a historical event." The answer is that in this respect exemplarism is a self-defeating strategy. You *cannot* honor the particularity of the Holocaust in its uniquely Jewish features if your basic intention is to use it to illustrate the universality of suffering and evil, and make it into a bridge toward the creation of "a new global community based on shared human values." Distinctions evaporate amid the ardor of reformist zeal: "To me," Chicago confesses rather early in her investigation, "one of the most important aspects of the Jewish experience of the Holocaust is that it provides us with a graphic demonstration of the vulnerability of all human beings and, by extension, of all species and our fragile planet as well."[6] There are those, however, who might find more than a touch of the trivial in linking the fate of the spotted owl or the ozone layer to the doom of European Jewry.

Perhaps visionaries like Todorov and Chicago who have programs for "creating a more peaceful and equitable world" should resist the temptation to include the Holocaust in their agenda—but the fashion is upon us, and no effort to co-opt mass murder for noble ends can be simply dismissed. Do we ignore, or at least distort, history when we agree with Chicago that the "fact of patriarchy" made the Holocaust possible? She admits frankly that feminism is the philosophical framework "that provides the underpinnings for the *Holocaust Project,*" and we need now to ask where this leads and what insights into the Jewish catastrophe it supplies.

As it turns out, Chicago's education in Holocaust matters only assumes the formality of impartial historical inquiry, because her feminist beliefs color her conclusions from the beginning. There is absolutely nothing wrong with regarding "reverence for the feminine as an essential step toward the humanization of the world," but when the price we pay is a reductive misrepresentation of everything that doesn't agree with this position, then analysis becomes a matter of finding the proper file drawer and label for Holocaust discourse, and commentary withers into a mere system for classification. Citing only Elie Wiesel as an example, Chicago concludes that "most Holocaust literature written by men . . . almost invariably stresses the uniqueness and mystery of the Holocaust," whereas, in the opinion of a single woman survivor whom she quotes, "focusing on the female experience of the Holocaust helps us move toward, rather than away from, an understanding of our human connectedness and helps repair the human fabric of community" (10, 11). The notion that "connectedness" in representing Holocaust experience is primarily the property of a single sex and not a dual-gendered thing ignores the familiar male bonding between Primo Levi and Alberto, Elie Wiesel and his father, Vladek Spiegelman (in *Maus*) and various camp inmates, and Viktor Frankl and his barracks-mates when he restores their flagging spirits with an all-night reassuring harangue. I am speaking not of a dispute between patriarchy and feminism but of the need to multiply the voices we hear, and to go on multiplying them, before we conjure up gender differences that will withstand authoritative scrutiny. And this Judy Chicago has not done.

The aesthetic stance of the *Holocaust Project* also requires appraisal, because it reflects a problem that Chicago shares with many others who enter the realm of Holocaust darkness in pursuit of light. Responding to a reading of Jerzy Kosinski's *The Painted Bird,* she writes, "Being so graphic scares me, as it has to do with letting go on a level beyond what I've ever done before. Moreover, I'm afraid that what I'll create will be ugly." Mass murder is never pretty, so this would not be a problem for an artist willing to be guided by her material instead of needing to examine it selectively for data to verify her thematic concerns. As part of her scholarly investigation, Chicago also reads Yitzhak Arad's study of the Operation Reinhard death camps, *Belzec, Sobibor, Treblinka: The Operation Reinhard Death Camps,* but can manage only forty-five minutes a day. Then she takes a furlough: "I've stopped reading for a while; that book on the Nazi killing operating at the extermination camps really depressed me" (26, 89). This retreat is characteristic of the exemplarist position, and we encounter it again and again; apparently, woman's search for meaning in the Holocaust, like man's, must surmount the merely depressing if it is to transcend the literal horrors and leave us with a more consoling vision.

Chicago's demurral is an honest admission; not many can tolerate a daily diet of atrocity. But Arad's work does not deal with moral life in the concentration camps any more than it furnishes evidence for a rivalry between patriarchy and sisterhood in Treblinka. Its theme is the murder of Jews in mobile killing vans and gas chambers, and even the most stalwart among us might find it depressing. Nor is Chicago alone in responding by needing—not only wanting, but needing—to find a way out of its darkness back into light. Exemplarism was born of this psychological impulse to uncover in the spiritual economy of the world some reassuring lesson to neutralize the depressing fact of mass murder.

If Jewish experience in the Holocaust can be made to "stand for" something else, some "larger human experience," whether a testimony to the integrity of the moral self, as in Todorov, or, in the case of Judy Chicago, a positive statement about the human condition in general, then the intolerable might seem more tolerable through the sheer invocation of patterns or analogies. Whatever the intention, the result is to dilute or diffuse the particularity of mass murder. And indeed, the quest for connections is an essential ingredient of the *Holocaust Project,* though some might question the worth of the comparisons it leads to: "I began to wonder about the ethical distinction," Chicago writes, "between processing pigs and doing the same to people defined as pigs." A moment of reflection on how the German military cherished their horses and dogs might have forestalled this effort to establish a link between animal rights and human slaughter. But her view grows more all-encompassing as she continues: "What is the relationship, for example, between what happened to the Jews and the extermination of the Aborigines in Australia or the Native Americans?" (58, 96). The drift toward the universal is anything but accidental; its sources lie in the fear and depression that the material itself initiates.

Perhaps with a certain amount of naïveté, Chicago discovers what the creative imagination has to face when it enters the vestibule of Holocaust atrocity: "Making art about a subject as overwhelming as this one is turning out to be is going to take an exceedingly long time. But I don't want to spend too many years on such dreadful material—it takes all the joy out of life!" (62–3). This is in fact a genuine challenge to anyone crossing the frontier that separates Holocaust landscapes from ordinary space. We all find our own beacon to guide us into this eclipsed terrain. But like Todorov, Chicago seems willing to complete the journey only if she can return exalted—and able to exalt us—by the adventure. And this she resolves to do through her vision in the *Holocaust Project*.

The technique Chicago and her husband devised for presenting this vision is ingenious, and if her talent as a painter had been greater and her universalizing impulse more restrained, the effect might have been truly impressive. She knows that Holocaust art must be rooted in the veracity of the subject, so the decision to include photographs of places like Treblinka in the final panels reflects an original and potentially powerful design. But her goal is not the kind of insight into the enigmas of atrocity that art can generate; "painting," she insists, "can provide a means of transformation." Why so much Holocaust commentary must have a cause to plead or a campaign to launch is not entirely clear to me, but I suspect it has something to do with the dreadful nature of the subject. For Chicago, what begins as a Holocaust project ends up as a philanthropic scheme: to be included, photographs may not be too horrific, and the measure becomes "what the aesthetic limits are in terms of what I can and cannot transform" (50, 135).

Art thus plays hostage to humanitarian zeal: the culminating work in the series, painted on vividly colored stained glass, is called "Rainbow Shabbat" and depicts the beginning of a Sabbath meal. At one end of the table, a Jewish woman is about to bless the candles; at the other end, a Jewish man raises the kiddush cup. The seated guests, most with an arm on a neighbor's shoulder and a smile on their faces, include a white priest, an African, an Asian, an Arab, and some children. Beneath the table, a cat and dog lie peacefully together, reminding us that animal abuse is one of the many atrocities in contemporary society for which the Holocaust is a precedent. If we have ever been uncertain about the agenda of the project, small panels containing Stars of David at either end of the tableau cement its intent; they contain Yiddish and English versions of a prayer to embrace us all: "Heal those broken souls who have no peace and lead us all from darkness into light." No one could quarrel with this sentiment, but for a context like the Holocaust, it does not begin to address the question of how to heal. In my copy of Chicago's text, the Yiddish is printed upside down (it was corrected in subsequent printings), as if some mischievous spirit of contradiction afloat in the Holocaust universe wished to sabotage her plan to, in her words, "transform these images of intense human struggle into a visual atmosphere of hope and integration" (163). That life goes on after death is by now a platitude; that *death* may also go on after death seems a plight beyond the range of the exemplarist imagination.

I turn now to the last advocate for an exemplarist position, and in many ways the most difficult one to deal with—the Christian theologian Franz Jozef van Beeck. In 1992 he delivered a talk at Cornell University called "Two Kindly Jewish Men: A Sermon in Memory of the Shoa," which initiated a Jewish-Christian dialogue whose echoes will close my analysis—and, I hope, clarify some of the distinctions I have been examining. In a letter before delivering the sermon, van Beeck admitted to his friend the Jewish theologian and scholar Eugene Borowitz—one of the two men to whom he eventually dedicated his talk—"that my sermon was the first piece I have ever written on the Holocaust myself, and that I had hardly ever discussed it in depth with anybody, Jew or Gentile."[7] This does not necessarily mean that his comments are superficial, because they emerge from years of silent pondering on the subject. Yet they also spring from years of eloquent speaking on Christian issues, and the influence of that kind of discourse, the particular idiom that verbalizes its convictions, testifies to the deficiency of certain language for analyzing the Holocaust when it is imposed on the topic with little consideration for its adequacy.

Like Todorov, who confessed to being more interested in good than in evil, and Judy Chicago, who admitted that her universalist tendencies determined her approach to the Holocaust, van Beeck has a fixed initial position that colors his response to the murder of European Jewry: "I have never," he concedes, "been able to feel raw rage or indignation at the Holocaust and its atrocities; I often used to wonder why." Perhaps this attitude is a consequence of his genuinely kind nature; perhaps it is a failure of imagination. In any event, when Father van Beeck speaks of Hitler as "a little man with a shrill voice and a large ego and a murderous theory," one begins to wonder whether a failure of imagination may not indeed be part of the problem.[8] Monstrous deeds require monstrous words to conjure up, if not the inhuman monsters who did not create them, then at least the inhuman human beings who did. A commitment to personal restraint and decency, however admirable, is a powerful antidote to both.

There is an imagery that dramatizes the assault of mass murder on the integrity of the individual self, and one that universalizes the impact of that assault and transforms it into what Father van Beeck calls "the fellowship of the suffering and the long suffering." Maybe a sermon is an inappropriate form of discourse for approaching the Holocaust, since its style seems consciously tailored to minimize atrocity. Is it either consoling *or* illuminating to hear that we live in a world "where goodness and virtue will never quite succeed in being victorious"? Is it unfair to inquire whether we have moved one inch beyond Job when we are told that we also live in a world "in which unjust suffering borne in patience is not infrequently a sign of intimacy with God"? Radical division is simply impermissible to the kind of thinking that, as this particular form of Christian discourse does, wants to see spring from the ruins of the Holocaust "hope for a humanity renewed by kindness" (178, 182).

Different imagery, however, leads in different directions. Through an odd coincidence, the other person to whom Father van Beeck dedicates his sermon is named Paul Davidowits, a Holocaust survivor whose story I happen to know well because I have written about it in *Holocaust Testimonies*. Paul D.—the name under which his testimony is classified—tells of a Greek Orthodox priest in his native Slovakia who agreed to supply false certificates verifying that certain Jewish families had converted to Christianity before 1938 (thus exempting them temporarily from deportation), provided parents were willing to have any children in the family baptized into the Greek Orthodox faith. Paul D.'s parents agreed to his baptism and received the false certificates.

This part of his narrative rouses in Paul D. the memory of a dream or vision he had shortly afterward, which he recalls in vivid detail: "I'm on a meadow, and there are Jewish kids playing around me. And at one point they move away from me, and I am alone on this meadow. And God appears before me. And he's a mountain. And God holds in his hands an axe. And he just goes [raising his hands], takes the axe over his head, and with a full swing splits me in half. And I just break [gesturing] into two." At this juncture the interviewer, obviously an exemplarist in training, inquires, "Jew and Christian?" to which Paul, a confirmed literalist, replies: "I think it's more like killing me. Like punishment. It doesn't feel like Jew and Christian. It feels like annihilation." Then he adds, "I tried to be Christian, but it didn't work."[9]

Paul D.'s parable of a cosmic rift that throbs with division rather than union or communion reflects a further split within his self. Filtered through his awareness of future events, his dream foretells the fate of the Jewish children playing nearby (for whom being a Jew didn't help any more than trying to be a Christian did), as well as of his own shattered identity in its futile task of finding a "self" that might help him to survive. His memory of his dilemma during those critical years accents killing and annihilation, not reconciliation—in himself, with his fellow Jews, or the God of Jews and of Christians.

It is a bitter bequest from a threatened life, and it sits uneasily on the consciousness as we return to Father van Beeck's plea to his Jewish brothers to close "the cosmic gap between the death-camp operators and their Jewish and other victims." Does Eugene Borowitz point to an imperishable breach between attitudes, two ways of approaching the legacy of the Holocaust, when he insists that he cannot speak "of compassion and mercy without an equal emphasis on the imperative of pursuing justice"? Justice here is more than an abstract concept, because it invokes crimes in the past that will not tolerate amnesia. Compassion and mercy, by contrast, summon us into a future harmony, what van Beeck envisions as "the actual embracing of all human persons, even if we have to overcome deep, deep revulsion to do so."[10] His position is not that different from Tzvetan Todorov's or Judy Chicago's: all three seek an affinity between what van Beeck calls "humanity acquired by enduring human cruelty and humanity acquired by experiencing human compassion."[11]

Nowhere is the poverty of words more evident than in the attempt to portray the deeds of the Germans and their collaborators through expressions like "deep revulsion" and "human cruelty." The impulse toward universalization here infiltrates vocabulary itself, and the best way to puncture its pretensions is by juxtaposing it with an episode of atrocity and asking ourselves what "enduring human cruelty" can possibly mean, for the victims or ourselves, in its presence. Near the end of his exhaustive re-creation of his ancestral village in Poland, the shtetl of Konin, Theo Richmond uncovers some testimony that describes the fate of the Jews of that town and its vicinity. It is in a protocol taken by the Soviets a few months after war's end from an eyewitness to the slaughter, a Polish Catholic and member of the underground who was forced by the Gestapo to gather the clothing and belongings of the victims. I am convinced that any analysis of a promising moral and spiritual condition, both in the camps and in post-Holocaust society, remains flawed unless it works *through* and not around the details of such moments as these, refusing to preempt them for the sake of a larger ideal. They may leave us aghast, but they support the belief that voyagers to the haven of exemplary behavior risk running aground unless they set sail in the vessels of Holocaust atrocity.

The witness, who after his gruesome task in the woods of Kazimierz Biskupi, was sent to Mauthausen and its subcamp at Gusen, describes two pits in a clearing, the larger one covered on its bottom by a layer of quicklime. Then he continues:

> [The Gestapo] ordered the assembled Jews to strip—first those who were standing near the large pit. Then they ordered the naked people to go down into both pits and jump into the larger pit. I could not describe the wailing and the crying. Some Jews were jumping without an order—even most of them—some were resisting and they were being beaten about and pushed down. Some mothers jumped in holding their children, some were throwing their children in, others were flinging their children aside. Still others threw the children in first and then jumped in. . . . This lasted until noon and then a lorry came from the road and stopped on the path by the clearing. I noticed four vat-like containers. Then the Germans set up a small motor—it was probably a pump—connected it with hoses to one of the vats and two of them brought the hoses from the motor up to the pit. They started the motor and the two Gestapo men began to pour some liquid, like water, on the Jews. But I am not sure what the liquid was. While pumping, they were connecting hoses to the other containers, one by one. Apparently, because of the slaking of the lime, people in the pit were boiling alive. The cries were so terrible that we who were sitting by the

piles of clothing began to tear pieces of stuff to stop our ears. The crying of those boiling in the pit was joined by the wailing and lamentation of the Jews waiting for their perdition. All this lasted perhaps two hours, perhaps longer.[12]

Nothing we hear from well-intentioned commentators like Tzvetan Todorov about moral life in the concentration camps, or from Judy Chicago about the light of human community emerging from Holocaust darkness, or from Franz Josef van Beeck about the "fellowship of the suffering and the long suffering" or closing "the cosmic gap between the death-camp operators and their Jewish and other victims" can silence the cries of those hundreds of Jews being boiled to death in an acid bath. There is simply no connection between our ordinary suffering and their unprecedented agony, nor do our trivial inclinations toward sin resemble in any way the minds that devised such terminal torture. Literalist discourse about the Holocaust—and I must stress that I am speaking *only* about the Holocaust—leads nowhere but back into the pit of destruction. At least it has the grace to acknowledge that we learn nothing from the misery it finds there.

NOTES

This essay has appeared in Lawrence L. Langer, *Preempting the Holocaust* (Yale University Press, 1998), pp. 1–22.

1. Tape T-662, testimony of Charles A., Fortunoff Video Archive for Holocaust Testimonies at Yale University.

2. Ana Novac, *The Beautiful Days of My Youth: My Six Months in Auschwitz and Plaszow,* trans. George L. Newman (New York: Henry Holt, 1997), pp. 158–9.

3. Tzvetan Todorov, *Facing the Extreme: Moral Life in the Concentration Camps,* trans. Arthur Denner and Abigail Pollak (New York: Henry Holt, 1996), pp. 36–7, 121.

4. Judy Chicago, *Holocaust Project: From Darkness into Light* (New York: Viking, 1993), p. 5.

5. Todorov, p. 258.

6. Chicago, pp. 11, 9, 10.

7. Eugene Borowitz and Frans Jozef van Beeck, "The Holocaust and Meaning: An Exchange," *Cross Currents* 42 (fall 1992): 420.

8. Frans Jozef van Beeck, "Two Kind Jewish Men: A Sermon in Memory of the Shoa," *Cross Currents* 42 (summer 1992): 180, 181.

9. Tape T-48, testimony of Paul D., Fortunoff Video Archive.
10. Borowitz and van Beeck, pp. 421, 423.
11. Van Beeck, p. 176.
12. Theo Richmond, *Konin: A Quest* (New York: Pantheon, 1995), pp. 479–480.

Robert Melson

Problems in the Comparison of the Armenian Genocide and the Holocaust
Definitions, Typologies, Theories, and Fallacies

INTRODUCTION

IN HIS CLASSIC STUDY *THE PROTESTANT ETHIC AND THE SPIRIT OF Capitalism,* Max Weber wished to discover the driving forces making for industrialization and capitalism, and to this end he compared northern to southern Europe. He noted that the north was more industrialized and capitalist than the south, and he wished to explain the reasons for the difference. He then arrived at his stunning thesis that it was Protestant belief that infused the spirit of capitalism and accounted for the greater industrialization of the north. It was not that Protestantism as a religious system was somehow superior to Catholicism on moral, aesthetic, or ontological grounds. The difference, claimed Weber, was that Protestantism gave religious sanction to the realm of work and economic activity in a way that Catholicism did not.

Those of us who study genocide comparatively should keep Max Weber's example in mind. For purposes of scholarship it is not enough to list similarities and differences or to make claims that one genocide was superior, or inferior, or equal to the other. As scholars we seek theories, underlying patterns that explain events.[1] Such explanations should be able to shed light on particular instances of genocide as well as on the process of genocide itself. After all, some of the central questions attending any genocide, including the Holocaust and the Armenian Genocide, are: Why did it happen? How did it happen? And what can be learned from it to prevent similar occurrences in the future? A comparative scholarly approach might be helpful in providing some answers.

My own work has centered on the comparison of the Armenian Genocide to the Holocaust.[2] However, before I could make such a comparison I had to deal with four problems whose solution might be useful to other scholars examining other instances. These four problems concerned:

    1. *Definition:* What is genocide, and how do the Armenian Genocide and the Holocaust fit this definition?

    2. *Typology:* How do other destructions of peoples in the past and in the present compare to the Armenian Genocide and the Holocaust?

    3. *Theory:* Are there valid explanations for the Armenian Genocide and the Holocaust? Can there be a theory of genocide the way there are theories of capitalism and revolution, for example?

    4. *Fallacy:* It has been suggested that the very attempt at comparing genocides is misleading. Indeed, certain scholars of the Holocaust have argued that the Holocaust is unique and thus cannot be compared to any other genocide, including the Armenian Genocide. This brings us to the fourth and last question: "Is it a fallacy to compare the Armenian Genocide to the Holocaust?"

In this essay I touch on each problem in the hope that my formulations, even though they are provisional, might advance the scholarly comparison of genocide. I should add that what follows is not presented as dogma—after all, problems can have more than one solution—but as suggestions that might clear up confusions and prompt further research. Before proceeding to the four problems, however, allow me first to sketch out a brief comparison of the Armenian Genocide and the Holocaust. In this sketch I mean to point out some of the similarities as well as the differences between these two instances of genocide.

THE ARMENIAN GENOCIDE AND THE HOLOCAUST

The Armenian Genocide and the Holocaust[3] were the quintessential instances of total genocide in the modern era. Four reasons may be cited for this claim. First, both mass murders were the products of state-initiated policies. These policies were intended, respectively, to eliminate the Armenian community from the Ottoman Empire and to eliminate Jews from Germany and Europe, and even beyond Europe. These were unmistakable instances of what the United Nations has called "genocide-in-whole," or "total genocide," to distinguish such instances from "genocide-in-part" or "partial genocide." Examples of partial genocide from which both differ are the destruction of Overseas Chinese in Indonesia in 1965, Ibos in Northern Nigeria in 1967, and Muslims in Bosnia in 1992–1996.

Second, both victimized groups were ethnoreligious communities that had been partially integrated and assimilated into the larger society, the Ottoman Empire and European society respectively. Their destruction was not only a war against foreign strangers. It was a mass murder that commenced with an attack on an internal domestic segment of the state's own society. Thus the Armenian Genocide and the Holocaust were instances not only of "total genocide," but of "total domestic genocide"—to differentiate these two cases from the genocide of foreign groups, that is, foreign with regard to the borders of the state. For example, the Armenian Genocide and the Holocaust differ from the destruction of foreign peoples such as the men of Melos by the Athenians, Carthage by Rome, and a host of native communities by the Europeans in the New World and Africa.

Third, Armenians and Jews were unmistakably communal or ethnic groups, not classes or political groups whose inclusion under the UN definition of genocide has generated some controversy. Although Armenians and Jews may have occupied certain strata in the social structures of the Ottoman Empire, Germany, and Europe, they were not social classes like, for example, the Kulaks of the Soviet Union and the urban Cambodians that were destroyed by the Stalinists and the Khmer Rouge respectively.

Fourth, both the Armenian Genocide and the Holocaust were the products of modern ideologies and the circumstances of revolution and war. The Armenian Genocide occurred under the circumstances of the Young Turk Revolution and World War I, while the Holocaust was a product of the Nazi revolution and World War II.

To elaborate this last point it can be noted that for centuries Armenians had been tolerated as a minority *(dhimmi)* millet in the Ottoman Empire. They welcomed the Young Turk Revolution of 1908, hoping that it would improve their situation, which had become increasingly desperate under the regime of Sultan Abdul Hamid II. However, following the Ottoman military disasters of 1908–1912, the Young Turks abandoned Ottomanism, a worldview that tolerated religious and ethnic differences, for Pan-Turkism, a variant of contemporary integral or ethnic nationalism. By 1915, under the circumstances of World War I, they deported and destroyed the Armenian community.

The Jews of Imperial Germany had been emancipated by 1871, and despite the rise of the anti-Semitic movement, they hoped to be assimilated and accepted in the wider German and European society. Following the disasters of World War I, the inflation of the 1920s, and the Great Depression, the democratic Weimar Republic collapsed and the Nazis rose to power. The Nazis were motivated by a worldview that fused radical anti-Semitism with racism, and under the circumstances of World War II they committed total genocide against the Jews and Gypsies and partial genocide against other groups, like the Poles.

Although there are striking similarities between the Armenian Genocide and the Holocaust, there are differences as well. Three may be briefly listed. These touch on issues of status, of territory or land, and on the scope of the destruction. First, the Armenian millet in the Ottoman Empire, like the Jews of Europe, occupied a distinctively inferior status; however, Armenians, unlike the Jews, were never stigmatized as killers of God. Their being viewed as deicides, on the one hand, and their demands for inclusion, on the other, may explain why Jews were met by a racialist anti-Semitic movement that demonized and excluded them in a manner quite distinct from treatment of the Armenians in the Ottoman Empire.

Second, Armenians were largely a peasant society living on its own lands in Cilicia and the eastern provinces of Anatolia, while the Jews were largely an urban community scattered throughout Germany and Europe and not concentrated on its ancestral lands. The result was that in the period of nationalism, there existed among Armenians nationalist political parties demanding territorial autonomy and self-administration; conversely, with the exception of the Zionist movement, the Jews of Europe were hoping for assimilation and inclusion in their countries of domicile. The Armenian Genocide and deportations, in contrast to the Holocaust, included not only a destruction of the Armenian community, but also the loss of ancestral Armenian lands dating back to the pre-Christian era.

Third, in contrast to the Young Turks, who had nationalist and imperial aspirations, the Nazis were a totalitarian movement whose racialist anti-Semitic ideology had global scope.[4] Consequently the Holocaust, in contrast to the Armenian and other genocides, was global in its intentions and scope. For example, the Nazis demanded that their Japanese allies hand over their Jews for destruction. Although the Japanese refused, this example illustrates the difference in ideological intentions between the Nazis and the Young Turks. The former saw themselves in a global war against the Jews, while the latter wished to eliminate the Armenians from Anatolia and the rest of their Pan-Turkic realm. Unlike the Nazis, the Young Turks did not aspire to exterminate their victims the world over.

I make this last point not to claim that the Holocaust was more murderous than was the Armenian Genocide, or indeed any other genocide, but to illustrate the distinct mentality of the Nazis. This is an observation to which I shall return below. Having briefly compared the Armenian Genocide and the Holocaust, stressing both some of their similarities and differences, I turn to the four problems raised above.

DEFINITION

The UN defines "genocide" as acts *committed with intent to destroy in part or in whole a national, ethnic, racial, or religious group as such.*[5] However, without amendment, the UN definition is both too broad and too narrow for scholarly comparative purposes. It is too broad because it does not distinguish between massacre and pogrom and partial genocide, and it is too narrow because it limits its scope to communal groups and excludes economic classes and political movements.

For example, in 1953 in Kano, a city in Northern Nigeria, some one hundred Ibos were massacred by thugs drawn from the local Hausa and Fulani. I call this a massacre and not a genocide because the number of victims was small relative to the total Ibo population, and there was no apparent intent to destroy the Ibos or their culture.

However, by 1967 the Ibos were not only being killed by the thousands all over Northern Nigeria, they were driven out en masse and their institutions were destroyed. Following the UN definition, I would call the killings of 1967 a genocide-in-part, or a partial genocide, differentiating these both from the massacre of 1953 and from the genocide-in-whole or total genocide that occurred in the Armenian case and in the Holocaust.

Here is another example: during the Stalinist collectivization of the countryside, it is estimated that between eleven and twenty million "Kulaks" perished. According to a narrow reading of the UN definition, this would not be a genocide because the Kulaks, an ideologically constructed economic category, were not an ascriptive communal group such as a nationality, ethnicity, race, or religion. Nevertheless, Kuper has shown that it was Soviet pressure on the UN that had prevented classes and political groups from being included under the purview of the genocide convention.[6] It would seem to me that this is not a valid reason for excluding the case of the Kulaks from a discussion of genocide.

There is an apparent tension between a moral and legal definition of genocide that would condemn and punish all kinds of mass killings, and a definition useful for comparative scholarly purposes that would make distinctions between types and levels of genocide. One solution to the problem might be to introduce the notion of *genocidal continuum* on which massacre, partial genocides, and total genocides could be located. Acts lying on the genocidal continuum could then be morally and legally condemned and punished in a manner proportional to the crime.

To get around these problems I would suggest the following definition of genocide: *actions intended to destroy in small part (massacre), in large part, or in whole a social collectivity or category, including its culture and identity.*[7] This definition makes explicit the distinctions between "genocidal massacre," "genocide-in-part," and "genocide-in-whole."

By "collectivity" I mean a human group that has a self-conscious identity, and by "category" I mean a subset of society like an age cohort or a gender that might be singled out for victimization but lacks a self-conscious identity and exists as a group mainly in the mind of the perpetrator. According to my definition, the destruction of the

Kulaks would be a genocide because the Soviet state put into effect a policy of destroying a whole category of persons, even though the victims were not strictly speaking a communal collectivity.[8]

This definition allows me to subsume both the Armenian Genocide and the Holocaust under the rubric of genocide-in-whole, which I call "total genocide." Moreover, it broadens the scope of the definition, which then allows me to include both the destruction of the Kulaks and the Cambodian "Autogenocide," as additional instances for comparative purposes.

TYPOLOGY

Armenians and Jews were segments of the very states and societies that attacked them. They were not foreign enemies living in distant lands. They were not like the men of Melos that the ancient Athenians put to death during the Peloponnesian War. Nor were they in the path of some invading Genghis Khan. Nor were they even the native peoples of America, Africa, and Australia, who were labeled by their European conquerors as "heathen savages" and therefore as inhuman. The Jews of Europe and the Armenians of the Ottoman Empire were familiar communities, often one's neighbors. That they were killed as if they had been suddenly transformed into a rampaging horde of aliens begs for an explanation. Indeed, it links their case to more recent slaughters in the Soviet Union, Cambodia, Yugoslavia, and most recently, Rwanda; while at the same time it distinguishes these mass murders from the destruction of native Americans and colonial peoples in Africa and Asia.

The observation that Jews and Armenians had been domestic parts of the very societies that destroyed them allows us to make a distinction between *foreign* and *domestic* genocides. Jews and Armenians were domestic components of Germany and the Ottoman Empire, while the victims of colonial and imperial genocide were foreign to the peoples and states that attacked them. Indeed, it may be pointed out here that modern genocides have increasingly been domestic partial or total genocides, while, with some exceptions, in the ancient world most mass killings were directed at strangers living abroad.

Distinguishing, therefore, between domestic and foreign genocide and recalling the distinction between genocide in part and in whole, it is possible to arrive at a simple fourfold typology:

TABLE I. TYPES OF GENOCIDE

1. total domestic genocide
2. total foreign genocide
3. partial domestic genocide
4. partial foreign genocide

In the absence of a global theory of genocide, I would suggest that we first follow a strategy of trying to discover patterns or explanations for each of the four types. For example the massacres of Overseas Chinese in 1965, of Ibos in Northern Nigeria in 1967, and the campaign against the Kurds of Iraq in 1988 and 1991 are instances of partial domestic genocide (cell 3). The colonial mass murders of native peoples in Africa, Asia, and the Americas are examples of partial and total foreign genocide, although in some instances native peoples were murdered after they had been incorporated as component units of the state (cells 2 and 4). For the most part, however, these types are distinct from total domestic genocide (cell 1) as happened in the Holocaust and the Armenian Genocide, and they may call for different kinds of explanations.

Finally, it should be noted that although the Holocaust started with the victimization of the German Jews, a domestic minority, once the war began and European Jews fell under Nazi domination, the Final Solution proceeded to become both a total domestic and total foreign genocide (cells 1 and 2). Indeed, its global scope differentiates the Holocaust from the Armenian Genocide and the other examples subsumed under "total domestic genocide" and makes it distinctive in that sense. I shall return to this point later when I discuss the problem of fallacies.

THEORY

None of us has a general theory of genocide, nor does space permit discussing theories for the four types of genocide. However, there are a number of explanations for the phenomenon I have called "total domestic genocide" that we might consider. Among these can be listed the ideology of the perpetrators; the provocations of the victims; the functional needs of organizations; social, political, and economic crises; and the dynamics of totalitarian states. My own explanation stresses both the intentions of the killers and the circumstances of revolution and war. I present a sketch of it here as an example of a scholarly explanation derived from a comparative analysis of the Holocaust and the Armenian Genocide.

No doubt the intentions of the killers, as expressed in their ideology, are essential for an understanding of the causes of genocide. Indeed, how could we begin to understand the Holocaust without an analysis of Nazism, or the Armenian Genocide without Pan-Turkism? However, in any society, including liberal peaceful democracies, there are persons who harbor murderous thoughts against national, ethnic, religious, racial, and other groups, but since they do not have the power to act on their intentions their murderous projects are mostly stillborn. The question therefore arises: what are the circumstances under which genocidal killers might be able to gain power in order to act on their intentions? In some important cases the circumstances of revolution and war made it possible for genocidal killers to come to power and to implement their policies.

The Nazis came to power in 1933 after the destruction of the old regime of Imperial Germany and the collapse of the Weimar Republic. They put into effect their "Final Solution" in the context of World War II. The Young Turks came to power in 1908 in the midst of a disintegrating Ottoman Empire. They tried to implement radical changes, and started the deportations of the Armenians in the context of World War I. In these two instances the killers came to power during a revolutionary period; the revolutionary regime was governed by an ideology that identified certain groups as the enemies of society; this regime was at war with foreign and domestic enemies—some of them of its own making—and in that context it sought to destroy what it called "the enemies of the revolution."

This is not to suggest that all revolutions lead to genocide, nor that all genocides are the products of revolution. Indeed, the British and the American revolutions did not lead to total genocide; moreover, as noted above, invasions, colonialism, and religious revivals are among some other contexts, besides revolutions and wars, that can promote genocide. It is to suggest, however, that revolution and war may provide the necessary but not the sufficient circumstances for total domestic genocide.

Why are revolutions and wartime circumstances conducive to genocide? When revolutionary vanguards come to power, in a situation where most institutions have been undermined and the identity of the political community is in question, they need to reconstruct society, revitalize support for the state by way of a new system of legitimation, and forge new identities. In a revolutionary context they will redefine the identity of a subset of the political community as "the people," "the nation," "the race," "the religion," or "the class." These are the group or groups that are celebrated by the ideology of the revolutionaries and from whom they hope to draw their support. Groups that are not included and are singled out as racial, national, religious, or class enemies, run the danger of being defined as "the enemies of the revolution and the people." And it is such groups that may become the victims of repression or genocide.

At its founding a revolutionary regime seeks not only to reshape the domestic social structure and redefine the identity of its people; it also aims to alter the state's international situation. Indeed, for many revolutionaries it was their country's relative weakness in the international arena that prompted them to challenge the old regime in the first place. Thus revolutions are often the products of war and lead to further war. It is in the circumstances of revolution that lead to war that genocide is most likely to be committed.

Revolutionary war is closely linked to genocide in three ways. First, it gives rise to feelings of vulnerability and to paranoid fears that link supposed domestic enemies to external aggressors. The victims of all of the major genocides were said to be in league in a nefarious plot with the enemies of the revolutionary state: Jews with the communists, Armenians with the Russians, the Cambodian bourgeoisie with the American imperialists. Second, war increases the autonomy of the state from internal social forces, including public opinion, public opposition, and its moral constraints. Third, war closes off other policy options of dealing with "internal enemies." The expulsion of "internal enemies" may not be possible, while their assimilation or segregation may take too long and may not be feasible in a wartime situation. Thus revolutions, and especially revolutions that lead to wars, can provide the circumstances for genocide.

Some confirming cases of the proposition that revolutions may provide the circumstances for genocide are the destruction of the Kulaks by the Stalinist regime, the Cambodian genocide, and the recent events in Burundi and Rwanda.[9]

FALLACY

The comparison of instances of genocide is of course essential for the development of theory. Regrettably, however, such comparisons can also be misleading and fallacious. This can be most clearly observed in the comparative treatment of the Holocaust, wherein two fallacies often occur.

The first, which I shall call the "equivalence" fallacy, suggests that because the Holocaust may be similar to another instance of genocide it is therefore equivalent to it. The second, which I shall call the "uniqueness" fallacy, claims that because it was unique, the Holocaust is incomparable. The first is a fallacy, of course, because a thing or an instance can be similar on some dimensions without being equivalent in all. The second is a fallacy because a thing or an instance can be distinctive in one or more important ways without being distinctive in all. These fallacies appear so frequently that one suspects that behind each of these may lie hidden moral and political agendas that should be briefly discussed.

Since the Holocaust has become a standard by which to measure the extremity of genocide and radical evil, at least in the West, some writers have drawn a spurious equivalence between the Holocaust and some other events that they deplore. Thus it is said, for example, that the drug problem or the AIDS epidemic are instances of "Holocaust." This is the misuse of the Holocaust for hyperbole, exaggeration, and propaganda.

More seriously, because they wish to undermine the significance of the Holocaust, some writers have drawn a false equivalence between it and other seemingly similar events. They discover Holocaust-like events throughout history and the world over, not to understand them or even to exaggerate their import but to relativize and therefore make less exceptional the enormity of the Holocaust.

When I read a comparative study of genocide, especially if it includes the Holocaust, I apply a very simple test to detect the equivalence fallacy. I look to see if in addition to similarities, the study stresses differences. If it does not, I suspect that the equivalence fallacy may be at work.

The recent controversy among German historians, the *Historikerstreit,* is a case in point.[10] Some German historians have argued that the Holocaust was essentially equivalent to the Armenian Genocide and the Stalinist destruction of the Kulaks in the 1930s, and that indeed the latter crime set a precedent and had indirect consequences for the Holocaust itself. Other German historians vigorously oppose this view. They detect in it a thinly veiled attempt to relativize the Holocaust in order to lift the stigma and relieve the burden of the past from German history.

I have already commented on some of the similarities and differences between the Armenian Genocide and the Holocaust. Moreover, a comparison between the Holocaust and the destruction of the Kulaks is not necessarily wrong. Indeed, above, I refer to the destruction of the Kulaks as a confirming case linking total domestic genocide to revolution. The two instances were mass murders on a vast scale, and they did eliminate collectivities and categories from their respective societies, an ethnoreligious community in one case and an ideologically invented class in the other. However, comparison does not imply equivalence. A failure to stress some of the distinctive features of the Holocaust, especially the Manichean racialist theodicy of the Nazis, which divided the world into the Aryan "sons of light" and the Jewish "sons of darkness," and the global scope of the mass murder, overlooks the distinctive mentality and project of the Nazis. This suggests either historical incompetence or an insensitivity to the moral and legal significance of the events attending the Holocaust.

Finally, let me turn to the uniqueness fallacy. It may be that in order to combat the trivializers and the relativizers, some scholars have insisted on the uniqueness of the Holocaust, with the implication that it is simply incomparable. Other scholars, holding religious views, may find in the uniqueness and incomparability of the Holocaust a validation of their claim that all of Jewish history is distinctive and providential. To be more precise, they do compare the Holocaust to other mass murders but only to show that these are categorically different from the Holocaust and that the Shoah, like all of Jewish history, is sui generis. Indeed, one writer plainly argues that only the Holocaust fits his narrow definition of "genocide."

Steven T. Katz defines genocide as "the actualization of the intent, however successfully carried out, to murder in its totality any national, ethnic, racial, religious, political, social, gender, or economic group, as these groups are defined by the perpetrator by whatever means."[11]

Katz departs from the widely accepted UN definition by excluding the partial destruction of groups (genocide in part) while widening the scope of the definition to include other than communal categories. Since he previously noted that only in the Holocaust did the perpetrator intend physically to murder every Jew in the world, it follows from his definition that only the Holocaust is truly a genocide. Other mass murders may be tragic events, argues Katz, but the term "genocide" can be applied only to the Holocaust. He then sets out to prove his case by demonstrating that every other event once claimed to be a genocide does not come up to his exacting standards. Neither the destruction of natives in Africa, Asia, and the Americas, nor the Armenian Genocide, nor the Cambodian, nor any other event fits his narrow perspective. None are instances of genocide according to him.

Katz may indeed be right that only in the Holocaust did the perpetrators intend to kill every single member of the targeted group the world over, and his definition of genocide is not illogical. What then is the problem? The problem is that the Holocaust, or any other genocide, cannot be reduced only to the ideological intentions of the perpetrators. The Holocaust was a process that included the Nazis' coming to power, their decision to destroy the Jews, and the implementation of that decision. Nazi intent does not explain how and why they came to power, nor how they were able to mobilize the various institutional spheres of German society to implement the Final Solution, nor how they carried out the mass murder.

In effect, Katz's definition prevents him and other scholars from making valid comparisons to other aspects of the Holocaust by reducing the Holocaust to the intentions of the Nazis. In this way he misses the opportunity to derive meaningful theoretical insights that might have shed some light on the Holocaust itself. It would be as if Max Weber, after having compared northern to southern Europe, had declared that northern Europeans are uniquely capitalist and had neglected to suggest that the Protestant ethic produced the spirit of capitalism!

I am afraid that Katz's solution by fiat will stop neither the trivializers nor the relativizers nor, indeed, those like me and my colleagues who wish to compare the Holocaust in order to understand it better. Beyond wishing to understand the Holocaust better, I too have a hidden agenda or a moral position on the subject. I believe that, far from undermining the terrible significance of the Shoah, by stressing its uniqueness as well as its comparability I have helped to keep the historical and moral lessons of the Holocaust relevant and alive. By better understanding the common causes of genocide, among which the Holocaust and the Armenian Genocide stand out as extreme examples, we are called upon to aid in its abolition from human history.

NOTES

Parts of this essay were presented at an international colloquium, L'actualité du Génocide des Armeniens, Sorbonne, Paris, 18 April 1998. Earlier versions were presented at the Lessons and Legacies Conference IV, Notre Dame University, South Bend, Indiana, 4 November 1996, and at the International Colloquium on Genocide in Modern History, Bibliothek für Zeitgeschichte, Stuttgart, Germany, November 1997. I am grateful to my friends and colleagues, Professors Richard S. Levy and Jacques Kornberg, for their astute comments. The views presented in this essay are my own.

1. Charles S. Maier, a perceptive critic of Holocaust research, makes this point very clearly: "Comparison is a dual process that scrutinizes two or more systems to learn what elements they have in common, and what elements distinguish them. It does not assert identity; it does not deny unique components. The issue to be resolved is under what circumstances comparison adds to knowledge. First it must have a plausible basis in fact. Just as important, however, comparison should go beyond taxonomy and offer perspectives that the single case might not suggest. Then it can reveal a wider historical process at work." See his *The Unmasterable Past: History, Holocaust, and German National Identity* (Cambridge: Harvard University Press, 1988), p. 69. For theoretical discussions of comparative history and sociology see among others, S. N. Eisenstadt, *The Political Systems of Empires* (New York: Free Press, 1963); Raymond Grew, "The Case for Comparing Histories," *American Historical Review* 85, no. 4 (1980): 763–78; Theda Skocpol, ed., *Vision and Method in Historical Sociology* (Cambridge: Cambridge University Press, 1984); and the works of George M. Fredrickson, including his *White Supremacy: A Comparative Study in American and South African History* (New York: Oxford University Press, 1981) and *The Comparative Imagination: On the History of Racism, Nationalism, and Social Movements* (Berkeley and Los Angeles: University of California Press, 1997).

2. Robert Melson, *Revolution and Genocide: On the Origins of the Armenian Genocide and the Holocaust* (Chicago: University of Chicago Press, 1992). See also Vahakn N. Dadrian, *The History of the Armenian Genocide: Ethnic Conflict from the Balkans to Anatolia to the Caucasus* (Providence, R.I.: Berghahn Books, I-A.W, 1995); Helen Fein, "A Formula for Geno-

cide: A Comparison of the Turkish Genocide (1915) and the German Holocaust (1939–1945)," in *Comparative Studies in Sociology*, vol. 1, ed. Richard F. Tomasson (Greenwich, Conn.: JAI Press, 1978), pp. 271–9; and Yves Ternon, *L'état criminel* (Paris: Editions du Seuil, 1995).

3. This section of the essay relies on my article "Revolution, War, and Genocide: The Armenian Genocide and the Holocaust Compared," in *Encyclopedia of Genocide*, vol. 2, ed. Israel W. Charney (Denver, Colorado: ABC Clio, 1999), pp. 499–501.

4. Stephan Astourian has noted that the Young Turks were indeed affected by nineteenth-century racialist and social Darwinist influences. He also made the point, however, that Turkish racism was distinct from the absolutist scientific "bio-medical vision" of the Nazis. Remarks made at the International Colloquium on the Armenian-Genocide, "L'actualité du Génocide des Armeniens," Sorbonne, Paris, 18 April 1998.

5. United Nations, *Yearbook of the United Nations, 1948–49* (New York, 1949), pp. 959–60.

6. See Leo Kuper, *Genocide: Its Political Uses in the Twentieth Century* (New Haven: Yale University Press, 1981), pp. 19–39, 138–60.

7. This definition differs from the one in my book and emphasizes more clearly the cultural dimension of genocide. See Melson, p. 32. For other approaches to the problem of definition see, for example, Israel W. Charny, "Toward a Generic Definition of Genocide," in *The Conceptual and Historical Dimensions of Genocide*, ed. George Andreopoulos (Philadelphia: University of Pennsylvania Press, 1994), pp. 64–94; Helen Fein, "Genocide: A Sociological Perspective," *Current Sociology* 38, no. 1 (spring 1990): preface–126; and Frank Chalk and Kurt Jonnasohn, eds., *The History and Sociology of Genocide* (New Haven: Yale University Press, 1990), p. 23.

8. I included the definition of identity and culture in this definition because except in the rare case of extermination, as happened in the Shoah, the intention of most genocides is not necessarily to kill every member of a targeted group. The purpose is to murder a sufficient number of persons and to destroy the entity's cultural institutions such that the group ceases to exist in a social, cultural, and political sense and is eliminated from the social structure, culture, and polity of the larger society.

9. See for example René Lemarchand, *Burundi: Ethnic Conflict and Genocide* (New York: Cambridge University Press, 1994), and Gérard Prunier, *The Rwanda Crisis: History of a Genocide* (New York: Columbia University Press, 1995).

10. For a masterful treatment of the topic, see Maier.

11. Steven T. Katz, *The Holocaust in Historical Context*, vol. 1 (New York: Oxford University Press, 1994), p. 131.

II. M·O·R·A·L·I·T·Y

Doris L. Bergen

Religion and the Holocaust
Some Reflections

HOW MIGHT A FOCUS ON RELIGIOUS ISSUES ENRICH OUR UNDERstanding of the history of the Holocaust?[1] This essay explores that question.[2] In the first part, I address a matter that attention to religion may help resolve: what was unique and what was shared about the Jewish experience of the Holocaust? Part 2 offers reflections on complicity and resistance, areas where awareness of religion can open up new and potentially productive avenues of investigation. I conclude with some thoughts about how keeping religion in mind might deepen and humanize our work as Holocaust educators.

WHAT IS UNIQUE AND WHAT IS SHARED ABOUT THE JEWISH EXPERIENCE OF THE SHOAH?

Anyone who studies the Nazi era and World War II in Europe encounters a terrifying array of people who suffered. Jews, Gypsies, the "asocial," those deemed handicapped, Soviet prisoners of war, Polish intellectuals, Communists, homosexual men, Afro-Germans, Jehovah's Witnesses—members of these groups and people defined as among them were starved, persecuted, tortured, and murdered by Nazi Germans and their collaborators, by the thousands, tens of thousands, and in some cases, millions. People who study these events have defined "victims of the Holocaust" in varying ways. Some assert Jewish singularity, others include Gypsies and the handicapped, and still others posit a broadly inclusive definition.[3]

Each of those positions raises questions and carries risks. Claims of uniqueness can establish destructive hierarchies of suffering, but attempts to be all-encompassing can reduce those who experienced Nazi atrocities to an undifferentiated mass of "victims." How can we grasp the Nazis' wide-ranging brutality yet make the distinctions that honesty and respect require? What explains the particular thoroughness and zeal of the attack on Europe's Jews? Is it possible to acknowledge the unique nature of each assault yet see the links, ideological and practical, between and among the Nazis' target populations?

Answering these questions requires us to seek the delicate balance between difference and similarity that lies at the heart of historical inquiry. To begin to understand the Jewish case, we need to address religion, the factor that distinguished Jews from the European Christian majority in the first place. "No Christianity, no anti-Semitism," Leonard Dinnerstein, among others, has claimed.[4] That formulation may overstate the argument, but attention to religion does indicate some unique aspects of the Nazi murder of the Jews.

Only in the case of Jews did religion play a crucial role in both defining and identifying those marked for destruction. In Nazi policy toward Jews, religious distinctions masqueraded as racial, as evidenced in the Nuremberg Laws of 1935. That legislation described German citizenship as based on something called Aryan blood, but the fundamental criterion was religion. Under the terms of Nuremberg, it was the religious membership of one's grandparents, not any quantifiable characteristics of blood or physical appearance, that determined who counted as a Jew.[5] Racial differences existed only in the sphere of myth. The centrality of religion in turn gave the Christian churches a crucial role in providing the documentation—from baptismal records—on which the legal definitions of "Aryan" and "Jew" rested.[6]

Of the groups Nazis targeted for destruction, only the Jews felt the full force of European Christian tradition against them. So-called scientific racism did not replace old religious hatreds; it just added new layers on top of them.[7] Thus, prejudice toward Jews—genocidal prejudice—took on the metaphysical dimensions of a battle between "good" and "evil."[8] The charge that Jews had killed Jesus, the conviction that atonement comes through blood—these notions, almost instinctual to European Christians, shaped the Shoah.[9] Even Raul Hilberg, whose magisterial *Destruction of the European Jews* spends little time on religion, begins with discussion of Christian anti-Semitism and the anti-Jewish writings of Martin Luther.[10]

How did Christian anti-Jewishness and secular, genocidal hatreds connect? After all, many top Nazis like Hitler and Propaganda Minister Joseph Goebbels, ideologues like Alfred Rosenberg, and "ordinary" German perpetrators among the SS, *Einsatzgruppen,* and camp guards were not practicing Christians; indeed, some were openly hostile and perceived Christianity as a devious extension of Judaism.[11] In fact, Nazi racial anti-Semitism was suspicious of traditional Christian attitudes toward Jews even as it drew from them. According to one neopagan, the concept of "National Socialist Christians" was just as ludicrous as the notion of "SS-Semites."[12]

Those Christians in Germany who supported National Socialism resisted that tension, claiming Christianity and Nazism not only could but must coexist. Their strategy was defensive; they denied accusations that Christianity was a Jewish religion and turned those very denials into an affirmation of their own "true," anti-Jewish Christianity. For example, throughout the 1930s and 1940s, Protestant Reich Bishop Ludwig Müller asserted repeatedly that Christianity "did not grow out of Judaism but developed in opposition to it."[13] By his logic, Christians were quite naturally the strongest anti-Semites there could be.

Paradoxically, one link between the new "racial" anti-Semitism and the old religious anti-Judaism was the Bible itself, or at least a particular reading of it. Even secular, anti-Christian ideologues in Germany came from a world steeped in the stories, language, and images of the Christian Bible, Old and New Testaments. Biblical allusions, sometimes distorted and watered down but nevertheless identifiable, formed part of the shared legacy to which Nazi propaganda appealed, part of the culture with which its specific stereotypes resonated.[14] For example, a 1938 German regulation required those defined by the Nuremberg Laws as Jews to take on another name if their given names were not sufficiently "Jewish." Women were to add "Sara," men "Israel."[15] In the context of Nazi measures against Jews, those biblical names took on a brutal irony: Sara, mother of a people? Israel, founder of a nation? Indeed, Hitler's repeated references in *Mein Kampf* to Jews as the "Chosen People" echo that mockery.[16]

In the Nazi setting, the story of Jesus' crucifixion provided a meeting point for religious and secular hatreds of Jews. Germans from the Protestant pastor Martin Niemöller to Hitler and Martin Bormann pointed to the gospel accounts as evidence of Jewish perfidy in their own times.[17] A 1939 flier of the pro-Nazi, Protestant, German Christian Movement *(Glaubensbewegung Deutsche Christen)* numbered "destructive Jews" in their own age among "the same Jewish criminal people who nailed Christ to the cross!"[18] Against the backdrop of Nazism, the Oberammergau Passion Play became a propaganda pageant with no need even to change the text.[19] A noble, blond Jesus, villainous Pharisees, and swarthy, treacherous Judas fitted perfectly into an allegory of modern-day "Aryans" and Jews. In Nazi eyes, Jews were devils, the embodiment of evil.[20]

The legacy of Christian anti-Judaism, as well as its residue in the form of anti-Jewish biblical images, made Jews even more vulnerable than they would have been given racial ideology alone. A comparison of Christian responses to Nazi oppression of other target groups with reactions to persecution of Jews illustrates this point. Throughout the 1930s and 1940s, pro-Nazi Protestants said almost nothing about abuse of the handicapped.[21] But those publicists produced a torrent of literature endorsing National Socialist actions on the "Jewish Question."[22] German church leaders, Catholic and Protestant, publicly protested the so-called Euthanasia Program, the murder of those deemed handicapped.[23] Many of the same men remained silent when it came to the Jews.[24] German clergymen sometimes disobeyed regulations to offer pastoral services to Eastern European slave laborers and POWs, and some faced great danger to help converts from Judaism to Christianity.[25] But very few risked their safety to assist Jews. Bernhard Lichtenberg, the Catholic priest in Berlin who prayed openly for the Jews and died en route to Dachau in 1943, is a notable exception.[26]

By no means does Christian anti-Semitism explain the murder of six million Jews, nor does it alone account for the motivations of the ideologues and the killers. As Christopher Browning has shown, careerism and peer pressure were important factors.[27] And as Gerhard Weinberg asserts, cowardice and self-preservation were significant too; especially by the last stages of the war, many of the perpetrators much preferred brutalizing half-dead, enslaved populations to facing soldiers at the front who had weapons of their own.[28] Greed, sadism, fear, disorientation, moral numbing, and eventually even habit all played a part. But religion made the Jews identifiable as a target for aggression, and Christian anti-Semitism helped make the notion of genocide—a "final solution of the Jewish question"—comprehensible to those who carried out the crimes.

Attention to issues of religion highlights aspects of Jewish uniqueness, but it also suggests ways that the murder of Jews was linked to the Nazis' broader genocidal project. Popular sources for stereotypes of Jews, Gypsies, and people considered handicapped differed, but in each case, attacks drew on established hatreds and used familiar cultural codes. Preexisting prejudices seem to be a necessary, although not sufficient, condition for genocide. And in the Nazi case, such prejudices connected and reinforced each other in vicious ways. European folklore did not accuse Gypsies of killing Jesus, but it charged them with forging the nails that pierced his flesh.[29] Images of deformity and parasitism served propagandistic purposes against the handicapped, but they could also be transferred to purported racial enemies: Gypsies and Jews.[30] The centuries-old paranoia about homeless, predatory outsiders could be mobilized against both those groups as well.[31] Anxieties about the future of Christianity fueled hatred of Communism, and religious and sexual deviance blurred in imaginary worlds where Jews murdered Christian children for Passover and homosexuals preyed on pure "Aryan" boys.[32] Epithets such as "godless, Bolshevik Jews" and "effeminate, degenerate Jews" reveal how prejudices overlapped and underscored each other.[33]

Attention to religion and Christian anti-Judaism can help alert us to both the arbitrariness and the cultural rootedness of the process by which ideologues and practitioners of genocide selected and defined their victims. Nazi Germans may have "constructed" their targets as outsiders, but they did so with the tools that their culture—their religion, education, literature, folklore, and history—placed at their disposal. Awareness of the shared and distinct sources of prejudice allows us to see Nazi crimes as an interlocking system of specific assaults. Perhaps it can also alert us to cultural factors in contemporary hatreds. The tradition of warrior ballads and passion plays in the Balkans is one example;[34] myths about the "Semitic origins" of the Tutsis in Rwanda are another.[35] The ubiquitousness of cultural references suggests that even mass killers need to rationalize their actions, to cast them in familiar terms. Even murderers, it seems, want God— or at least tradition—on their side.[36]

RELIGION, RESISTANCE, AND COMPLICITY

Attention to religion can change the way we ask important questions about resistance and complicity, even if definite answers remain elusive. What motivated resistance to the Holocaust? What blocked resistance or shaped the forms it took? Such questions are relevant, although in very different ways, for the study of both Christians and Jews during World War II.

Some social scientists and historians have already explored religious motives for Christian resistance against Nazism.[37] Much less has been done to address religious factors in Christian silence and participation in Nazi crimes. Yet a look at European Christianity during the Holocaust highlights an important question. Why did loyalty to aspects of Christian tradition lead some Europeans to become pro–National Socialist syncretists yet prompt others to risk everything to save Jews?

The German Christian Movement is an instructive example of the first possibility.[38] From its formation in Germany in 1932, members sought to transform Christianity into the spiritual expression of the "pure Aryan" nation. They urged removal of everything from Christian scripture, tradition, and ritual that was connected to Judaism. Still they refused to abandon Christianity altogether, even defending the Old Testament in cases as an "anti-Jewish text"![39] They worked hard to retain Jesus for their faith and recast him as an "Aryan" warrior; meanwhile the gospels needed only some editing and highlighting to become a handbook of hatred toward Jews. On the basis of their non-Jewish, anti-Jewish version of Christianity, members of the German Christian Movement became enthusiastic supporters of Nazi policies toward Jews in their own world. They took the initiative to eject converts from Judaism from the Protestant clergy; they applauded the deportation of German Jews to unknown destinations in the East.[40]

The behavior of these German Christians hardly merits the label "Christian." It is important to keep in mind, however, that well into World War II, members of the group numbered approximately six hundred thousand.[41] And, moreover, their influence far outweighed their size: they controlled all but three regional church governments, dominated departments of theology at most German universities, and most important, remained part of the official Protestant church.

No mere marginalized oddity, they gave voice to a task that faced every Christian in Germany who supported the Nazi regime: how to reconcile their religious tradition with the demands of Nazism? That question in turn concerned the vast majority of Germans; as late as 1940, over 95 percent of the population remained baptized, tax-paying members of a Christian church.[42]

Germans had no monopoly on Christian anti-Semitism, nor were they unique in using and abusing biblical texts for various purposes. But at least some other Christian communities in Europe had very different responses to Nazi genocide. Dutch Calvinists and French Huguenots also belonged to cultures steeped in scripture. In their cases, however, fierce loyalty to the text and its authority served as a check on anti-Jewish (re)interpretations. Jews, many of them remained convinced, were the "people of the book," God's chosen ones. Associating the Old Testament with Jews in this way could inspire rescue operations, as it did for the Huguenots of Le Chambon-sur-Lignon in southern France. Pierre Sauvage's film *Weapons of the Spirit* shows how some of the villagers even referred to the Jews they sheltered as "Old Testaments."[43] Like Nazi Germans, those French Protestants perceived a link between the Hebrew Bible and living Jews. But in contrast to the Germans, they understood that connection as a call to solidarity and rescue, not exclusion and murder.

How do we explain religious impulses producing one outcome in the case of the "German Christians" and the opposite one among the Huguenots of Le Chambon? The answer is doubtless complicated, involving historical, national, and cultural factors. Certainly an old tradition of philo-Semitism within French, Dutch, and English Calvinism played a role in those societies.[44] But other theological issues entered the equation as well. Probably no other culture shared Germany's particular combination of a popular tradition rich in biblical images, a theological legacy of scriptural liberalism, and a tendency toward biblical academicism. Germans heard biblical allusions at home and from the pulpit. Proverbs and sayings brought the Bible into everyday language,[45] and children learned Bible stories in school.[46] Yet instead of efforts to live the word, we find attempts among Germans in the Third Reich to pick and choose from scripture, often on the assumption that Bible stories were simply mythological narratives, interchangeable with fairy tales.[47]

Such tendencies had at least some of their roots in German theological traditions. Martin Luther, Friedrich Schleiermacher, and Adolf von Harnack, arguably the most influential Protestant theologians in Germany before Karl Barth, had all contributed to removing scripture from the theological center to a sphere of academic discourse.[48] That process in turn facilitated selective readings to anti-Semitic ends. Thus Nazi German revisionists of the Old Testament could cite Luther as an authority on how to separate its "gold and jewels" from the "litter, stubble, and straw" it contained.[49] As one Protestant author claimed, Luther proved it was possible to hate Jews but still accept the Old Testament.[50] Leaders of the Confessing Church, often described as the Protestant bulwark against Nazism, practiced biblical anti-Judaism as well. Confessing Church publicists, Uriel Tal has shown, criticized the pro-Nazi German Christians and racist neo-pagans by comparing them to Jews.[51] Even Christians engaged in helping Jews and so-called non-Aryans retained anti-Jewish readings of biblical texts. In *After Auschwitz,* Richard Rubenstein describes his 1961 meeting with Heinrich Grüber, a prominent Protestant churchman whose work on behalf of German Jews and Christians of Jewish background had landed him in Dachau. When Rubenstein asked whether the murder of the Jews had been God's will, Grüber read from Psalm 44:22: "For Thy sake are we slaughtered every day." Like Nebuchadnezzar and other "rods" of divine anger, he insisted, Hitler had been sent by God to smite His people.[52]

In Nazi Germany, a selective, presentist reading of the Bible, combined with widespread suspicion of Jews, produced a situation where biblical notions reconciled easily with popular stereotypes.[53] The idea of the chosen people connected to paranoia about a Jewish world conspiracy; Jacob's purchase of his brother's birthright for "a mess of pottage" fit in with notions of Jewish trickery; accusations that Jews had crucified Jesus dovetailed with the popular stab-in-the-back myth that blamed treacherous Jews for the loss of the war in 1918.[54] Reading Bible stories through an anti-Semitic lens in turn helped make the fantastic and often contradictory claims of Nazi propaganda against Jews seem familiar and legitimate.

Linking religion and Christian involvement in the Holocaust raises a whole range of related questions. Why did an effort to preserve the integrity of the Catholic Church lead some priests and laypeople in Germany to risk imprisonment to protest removal of crucifixes from schools and public buildings,⁵⁵ yet contribute to the Vatican's silence on German atrocities, first against Polish Catholic priests, and then against the murder of millions of European Jews?⁵⁶ Why were military chaplains with the Wehrmacht willing to defy orders to give Christian burials to soldiers, yet they tacitly and sometimes actively endorsed Nazi war aims and said nothing about atrocities toward civilians?⁵⁷ In her book *Accounting for Genocide*, Helen Fein makes a provocative claim. "The majority of Jews evaded deportation," she indicates, "in every state occupied by or allied with Germany in which the head of the dominant church spoke out publicly against deportation before or as soon as it began."⁵⁸ Surely that view merits detailed investigation.

We know that Nazi assaults targeted the sites of Jewish religious practice and often took place on Jewish holidays.⁵⁹ The so-called *Kristallnacht*—the November Pogrom of 1938—brought mass destruction of synagogues all over the German Reich. During the Blitzkrieg against Poland, Germans torched synagogues, Torah scrolls, and other sacred objects, and prior to deportation of Polish Jews for killing, they singled out Orthodox Jews for acts intended to torment and humiliate.⁶⁰ But what do we know of Jewish responses, as they were organized or structured by religious teachings, practices, and rituals? In what ways did Judaism as a religion shape resistance?

When it comes to scholarly studies of Jewish resistance, religious issues often seem to have been bracketed out.⁶¹ Notable exceptions are Yaffa Eliach's collection of eyewitness accounts, *Hasidic Tales of the Holocaust*, and Yehuda Bauer's brief overview, *They Chose Life: Jewish Resistance in the Holocaust*.⁶² Even the phrase "spiritual resistance," which one might assume had to do with religion, usually refers more generally to unarmed forms of resistance, such as writing poetry, recording history, or creating art and music.⁶³ Indeed, when one considers religion in the context of what is generally called spiritual resistance, some paradoxes and ironies emerge. What could be more an act of spiritual resistance than the performance of Verdi's *Requiem* in Terezin in 1944?⁶⁴ For the Jews in the camp who performed that dramatically beautiful work, the music itself was a vehicle to assert life, to wrest control of their fantasies and their creativity away from their tormentors.⁶⁵ And the words of the mass themselves must have provided an intense and satisfying experience. With what defiance, what resistance must the musicians have thundered out the Latin text of the sequence "Dies Irae," "Day of Wrath," their eyes on the audience of Nazi murderers:

> Lo! The book exactly worded,
> Wherein all hath been recorded.
> Thence shall judgment be awarded.
> When the judge his seat attaineth
> And each hidden deed arraigneth,
> Nothing unavenged remaineth.[66]

Yet what could be more Christian—and less Jewish—than a requiem, a Roman Catholic mass for the dead? How did religious Jewish sensibilities factor into this and other acts of spiritual resistance?

We still know so little about the daily life of Jewish religious observance and the role it played in resistance. I was surprised to discover that at least one rabbi served as a chaplain with the Polish Jews who were organized militarily in the Soviet Union during the war. How many others played comparable roles? Were observant Jews more or less likely than their secular counterparts to engage in resistance of specific kinds? Fragmentary evidence suggests a wealth of possibilities. Some eyewitnesses, such as Primo Levi, criticize Jews in the camps who insisted on praying, and suggest that they not only wasted their energies but insulted fellow inmates.[67] Others, like Judith Magyar Isaacson, mention that at particular moments they found expressions of religious faith profoundly inspiring.[68] Many of the Hasidic Jews interviewed by Yaffa Eliach attribute their survival to their faith. Hannah Arendt is well known for her castigation of the European Jewish leadership,[69] but Elie Wiesel has observed that in all his reading and encounters with people who lived through the Holocaust, he has never found evidence of a rabbi who served as a Kapo.[70]

Emmanuel Levinas has given us one of the most evocative reflections on what genuine spiritual resistance could mean in the context of living Judaism. Levinas tells the remarkable story, "true," his commentator Richard I. Sugarman tells us, "as only fiction can be," of Yossel ben Yossel Rakover of Tarnopol, a man who witnessed all the horrors of the Warsaw ghetto. In the hours before his own death, Yossel, the last member of his family alive, "tests the certainty of God with a new force, under a heaven that is void." He experiences this

"God who obscures His face" as both "immanent and intimate" in a particularly Jewish way: through the "intermediary of a teaching, the Torah." Yossel son of Yossel loves God, he concludes, but he loves God's Torah even more. "To love the Torah more than God," Sugarman explains: "it is precisely this which means access to a personal God against whom one may revolt—for whom one can die."[71]

Why teach and learn about the Holocaust? How do we live in a world where humans inflict such pain on others? Where can we find meaning in the face of so much terrible suffering? These questions vex my students, and me too. It can be uncomfortable and even inappropriate for a historian to address such issues in class. Often we are tempted to leave these matters entirely to others, outside the discipline of history, in theology perhaps, or psychology. Yet what would it mean to offer a course on the Holocaust that left these questions out altogether? That kind of teaching could disintegrate into a retelling of horror stories, a cheap sensationalism at the expense of millions of dead, bereaved, anguished people. Can an awareness of religious issues—broadly defined as related to a search for meaning, for some hope outside ourselves—help us avoid a voyeuristic, titillating approach to the history of the Holocaust?

I venture a cautious "yes." It is not our task as teachers or scholars of the Holocaust to train good Catholics, Protestants, Jews, Mennonites, Buddhists, humanists, or atheists. But perhaps it is part of our job to alert our students to the fact that the Holocaust poses a challenge to them, as it does to all of us, to people of every faith, as well as those outside a faith tradition. It calls all of us to do what we can to face the past honestly, both to accept and resist despair, to continue our efforts in the hope that in some way this work has meaning.

NOTES

1. Many Christian and Jewish thinkers have addressed the connections between religion and the Holocaust. Some of the most important of their writings—by Richard L. Rubenstein, Elie Wiesel, Emil Fackenheim, and others—have been excerpted and published in the anthology edited by John K. Roth and Michael Berenbaum, *Holocaust: Religious and Philosophical Implications* (New York: Paragon House, 1989). See also Franklin H. Littell, *The Crucifixion of the Jews* (New York: Harper and Row, 1975); John Pawlikowski, *When Catholics Speak about Jews: Notes for Homilists and Cat-*

echists (Chicago: Liturgy Training Publications, 1987); *Faith and Freedom: A Tribute to Franklin H. Littell* (Oxford: Pergamon Press, 1987); Richard L. Rubenstein and John K. Roth, eds., *Approaches to Auschwitz: The Holocaust and Its Legacy* (Atlanta: John Knox Press, 1987); David Tracy, "Christian Witness and the Shoah," in *Holocaust Remembrance: The Shapes of Memory*, ed. Geoffrey H. Hartman (Oxford: Blackwell, 1994), pp. 81–90; and Carol Rittner and John K. Roth, eds., *From the Unthinkable to the Unavoidable: American Christian and Jewish Scholars Encounter the Holocaust* (Westport, Conn.: Greenwood Press, 1997). Nevertheless, many standard—and excellent—histories of the Holocaust have little to say about religion. See, for examples, Léon Poliakov, *Harvest of Hate: The Nazi Program for the Destruction of the Jews of Europe* (New York: Holocaust Library, 1979); Raul Hilberg, *The Destruction of the European Jews*, rev. ed., 3 vols. (New York: Holmes and Meier, 1985); Michael Marrus, *The Holocaust in History* (Hanover, N.H.: University Press of New England, 1987); and Leni Yahil, *The Holocaust: The Fate of European Jewry*, trans. Ina Friedman and Haya Galai (New York: Oxford University Press, 1987). A number of these works do acknowledge in significant ways the importance of religious issues: Poliakov begins with the assumption that Nazism itself was "primarily a religion" (p. 5); and Hilberg starts his analysis with a section on "Precedents" that addresses Roman and Christian hostility toward Jews from the time of Constantine. Yahil includes some discussion of Jewish religious practices during the war. Yehuda Bauer, *A History of the Holocaust* (New York: F. Watts, 1982) spends more time on both Christianity and Judaism than do most surveys. Rita Steinhardt Botwinick's *A History of the Holocaust: From Ideology to Annihilation* (Upper Saddle River, N.J.: Prentice Hall, 1996) probably goes furthest in the attempt to integrate attention to religion into a historical survey. John Weiss, *Ideology of Death: Why the Holocaust Happened in Germany* (Chicago: Ivan R. Dee, 1996) links religious factors, notably Christian anti-Judaism, to Nazi ideology. Theoretically informed, postmodern approaches to the Holocaust are at least as likely to neglect religion as are more traditional studies. As Dominick LaCapra has suggested, "There is an obvious sense in which we secular intellectuals are more comfortable with the notion of the aesthetic, even when we criticize its putative role, than we are with the idea of the continued importance of religion and its relations to secularization." LaCapra, *Representing the Holocaust: History, Theory, Trauma* (Ithaca: Cornell University Press, 1994), p. 221.

2. Many of the ideas in this essay were sparked by my participation in a panel on the churches and the Holocaust at the inaugural conference of the Research Institute of the United States Holocaust Memorial Museum in December 1993. The other panelists were Franklin Littell and John Pawlikowski; John Roth moderated, and Gerhard Riegner responded. I would

like to thank those speakers and everyone in the audience whose urgent questions and thoughtful remarks have continued to stimulate my thinking about religion and the Holocaust. I am also grateful to my colleague James Turner for his comments on a draft of this essay.

3. For an explicit and exclusive focus on Jews as victims of the Holocaust, see Daniel Jonah Goldhagen, *Hitler's Willing Executioners* (New York: Knopf, 1996). Henry Friedlander and Sybil Milton make compelling cases for analyzing Nazi genocide against Jews, Gypsies, and people deemed handicapped together: see Friedlander, *The Origins of Nazi Genocide: From Euthanasia to the Final Solution* (Chapel Hill and London: University of North Carolina Press, 1995), and Milton, "The Context of the Holocaust," *German Studies Review* 13, no. 2 (1990): 269–83. In the same camp are Michael Burleigh and Wolfgang Wippermann, *The Racial State: Germany 1933–1945* (New York: Cambridge University Press, 1991); and Burleigh, *Death and Deliverance: "Euthanasia" in Germany c. 1900–1945* (New York: Cambridge University Press, 1997). Michael Berenbaum makes a distinction between Jews as victims of the Holocaust and "other victims": "non-Jews persecuted and murdered by the Nazis"—Serbs, Poles, Slavs in general, POWs, Jehovah's Witnesses, gays, and Gypsies. Introduction to Berenbaum, ed., *A Mosaic of Victims: Non-Jews Persecuted and Murdered by the Nazis* (New York: New York University Press, 1990), pp. xi–xv. For a broad definition that includes Gypsies, Poles, Slavs in general, and POWs, see Bohdan Wytwycky, *The Other Holocaust: Many Circles of Hell* (New York: Novak Report, 1980). Richard C. Lukas, *The Forgotten Holocaust: The Poles under German Occupation, 1939–1945* (Lexington, Ky.: University Press of Kentucky, 1986), makes a special case for Polish gentiles.

4. See comments by Dinnerstein on papers by Glenn Sharfman and Doris L. Bergen at Duquesne History Forum, Pittsburgh, fall 1991. Dinnerstein's position echoes the influential work of Richard Rubenstein, *After Auschwitz: History, Theology, and Contemporary Judaism*, 2nd ed. (Baltimore: Johns Hopkins University Press, 1992), pp. 43–4: "Without Christianity, the Jews could never have become the central victims."

5. Raul Hilberg discusses development of a definition of "Jews" in Nazi Germany in *The Destruction of the European Jews*, rev. ed., vol. 1 (New York: Holmes and Meier, 1985), pp. 65–80. A first step was the Interior Ministry regulation of 11 April 1933 that defined as of "non-Aryan descent" anyone with a parent or grandparent of the Jewish religion. As Hilberg points out, that definition was "in no sense based on racial criteria" (p. 67). A definition of "Jews" followed two years later, in the First Regulation to the Reich Citizenship Law, 14 November 1935 (RGBl I 1333). The basis of distinction remained the religious status of the grandparents. In *Mein Kampf,* Hitler called it the "first and greatest lie, that the Jews are not

a race but a religion." Quoted in Benjamin Sax and Dieter Kuntz, *Inside Hitler's Germany: A Documentary History of Life in the Third Reich* (Lexington, Mass.: D. C. Heath, 1992), p. 201. Nazi insistence on this point collapsed racial and religious distinctions to create a category that was simultaneously neither and both.

6. The issuance of such certificates required a good deal of time and energy on the part of clergymen and their subordinates. In some cases extra staff needed to be hired specifically for that task. See, for example, circular "Beschwerde des Kirchmeisters Schröer," 1 August 1935, in Landeskirchenarchiv Bielefeld (hereafter cited as LKA Bielefeld) 4,55/B/22,4. See also Pastor Walter Vogler to Superintendent Clarenbach, 26 May 1940, Welver-Hamm (Westphalia), LKA Bielefeld 4,55/A/46.

7. Donald Niewyk and others have shown how, in the nineteenth and twentieth centuries, "new" racial forms of hatred built on top of and drew from "old" religious hostilities. See Niewyk, "Solving the 'Jewish Problem'—Continuity and Change in German Antisemitism, 1871–1945," *Leo Baeck Yearbook* (1990), p. 369; also Yehuda Bauer, "Vom christlichen Judenhaß zum modernen Antisemitismus—Ein Erklärungsversuch," *Jahrbuch für Antisemitismusforschung* 1, ed. Wolfgang Benz (Frankfurt and New York: Campus Verlag, 1992), pp. 77–90. Also useful is Wolfgang Benz, ed., *Antisemitismus in Deutschland: Zur Aktualität eines Vorurteils* (Munich: DTV, 1995). Some recent works emphasize the importance of Christian prejudices against Jews in laying the foundations for the Shoah: Gavin I. Langmuir, *History, Religion, and Antisemitism* (Berkeley: University of California Press, 1990); Wolfgang Stegemann, "Christliche Judenfeindschaft und Neues Testament," in *Kirche und Nationalsozialismus,* 2nd ed., ed. Stegemann (Stuttgart: W. Kohlhammer, 1992); and Weiss, *Ideology of Death.* Also of interest is Zvi Bacharach, *Anti-Jewish Prejudices in German-Catholic Sermons* (Lewiston, N.Y.: Edwin Mellen, 1993). Saul Friedländer has introduced the important concept of "redemptive anti-Semitism," a specific variety of hatred that had religious, cultural, and political dimensions: Friedländer, *Nazi Germany and the Jews,* vol. 1, *The Years of Persecution* (New York: HarperCollins, 1997).

8. On this point, see Richard L. Rubenstein, *The Cunning of History: Mass Death and the American Future* (New York: Harper and Row, 1975).

9. Again, see Rubenstein, *After Auschwitz,* especially pp. 20–4 on notions of sacrifice and how Christians have "condemned Jews to the sacred."

10. Hilberg, *Destruction,* vol. 1. In his memoir, Hilberg dates his attitudes toward religion back to his childhood: "Already I was contrary-minded, turning away from religion, which at first became irrelevant to me and then an allergy." *The Politics of Memory: The Journey of a Holocaust Historian* (Chicago: Ivan R. Dee, 1996), p. 37. But the beginning of *The De-*

struction of the European Jews and the dedication of the German edition of *Perpetrators, Victims, Bystanders* to Bernhard Lichtenberg reveal his awareness of the importance of religious issues in the Holocaust: Hilberg, *Täter, Opfer, Zuschauer: Die Vernichtung der Juden 1933–1945,* trans. Hans Günter Hull (Frankfurt am Main: S. Fischer, 1992), p. 7.

11. Even members of the staunchly pro-Nazi German Christian Movement complained about anti-Christian attitudes in the SA, SS, and army. See, for example, Walter Schultz to Hitler, 30 April 1941, and attached, untitled report, relevant sections titled "Bekämpfung und Verächtlichmachung des Christentums und der Kirche" and "Angriffe auf Geistliche," pp. 4–5, Bundesarchiv Koblenz (hereafter cited as BA Koblenz) R 43 II/172/fiche 1, pp. 3–6. For neopagan logic that denounced Christianity as disguised Judaism, see Friedrich Oberschilp, "Meine Antwort an Herrn Pfarrer Brökelschen," *Drehscheibe: Das Blatt der denkenden Menschen,* no. 42 (13 Gilbhard [September] 1935): 165–7, Archiv der Evangelischen Kirche im Rheinland, Düsseldorf (hereafter cited as AEKR Düsseldorf), Nachlaß Superintendent Dr. Wilhelm Ewald Schmidt, no. 17, pp. 50–2.

12. See legal complaint about neopagan derision of Christianity, Pastor Kittmann to public prosecutor, Tilsit, 1 April 1937, Tilsit, p. 1, Bundesarchiv Potsdam (hereafter cited as BA Potsdam), Deutsche Glaubensbewegung files, DG III 1937–39, p. 345. Kittmann, a pastor in Westphalia and member of the German Christian Movement, laid charges against a speaker from the neopagan German Faith Movement for public blasphemy. The speech in question had ridiculed attempts to reconcile National Socialist views of race and Christianity. "It cannot be proven whether or not Christ lived," the neopagan speaker had said. "If he were to be accepted into the National Socialist Party, he would need to bring along the Aryan certificate. If he could not do so, we would be rid of him. If Christ, as some people claim, was the product of a liaison between a Roman man and a Jewish woman, the Nuremberg Laws would apply to him. Thank God he was killed on the cross, so we are saved from him." The speaker denounced the Bible as a "dirty book of whore stories"; National Socialist Christians, he scoffed, was as absurd a notion as "SS-Semites." A copy of Pastor Kittmann's complaint was sent by the Reich minister of justice to the minister of church affairs, 10 May 1937, BA Potsdam, DG III 1937–39, p. 343. Information on the formal charge against the German Faith Movement speaker for blasphemy is in the same file: see public prosecutor to Reich minister of justice, 5 June 1937, Bochum, BA Potsdam, DG III 1937–39, pp. 351–3. According to a newspaper clipping in the same file, p. 360, from *Durchbruch,* no. 35 (2 September 1937), the accused was acquitted on the grounds that he did not realize his speech on the occasion in question was

a "public" event. These materials have been recatalogued since I first used them in what was then the Zentrales Staatsarchiv Potsdam. Translations are my own unless otherwise specified.

13. The theme of Christianity as the polar opposite of Judaism was a recurring one in utterances of the pro-Nazi German Christian Movement *(Glaubensbewegung Deutsche Christen)*. This example comes from Reich Bishop Ludwig Müller's speech of 28 February 1934, in "Der Reichsbischof spricht im Sportpalast," no author, *Evangelium im Dritten Reich,* no. 10 (11 March 1934): 115–20; quotation on p. 118; clipping in LKA Bielefeld 5,1/ 289,1.

14. Wolfgang Gerlach and others have pointed out the challenge to Christian theology of an analysis of Nazi anti-Semitism that takes seriously its religious components. See Gerlach, *Als die Zeugen Schwiegen: Bekennende Kirche und die Juden* (Berlin: Institut Kirche und Judentum, 1987). On the failure of Christianity in the Nazi era more generally, see Hans Prolingheuer, *Wir sind in die Irre gegangen: Die Schuld der Kirche unterm Hakenkreuz, nach dem Bekenntnis des "Darmstadter Wortes" von 1947* (Cologne: Pahl-Rugenstein, 1987).

15. Regulation Requiring Jews to Change Their Names, August 1938, signed by Dr. Stuckart for the Reich minister of the interior and Dr. Gürtler, Reich minister of justice, in Yitzhak Arad, Yisrael Gutman, and Abraham Margaliot, eds., *Documents of the Holocaust: Selected Sources on the Destruction of the Jews of Germany and Austria, Poland, and the Soviet Union* (New York: Yad Vashem/Pergamon Press, 1981), pp. 98–9.

16. Adolf Hitler, *Mein Kampf* (New York: Reynal and Hitchcock, 1940), ed. John Chamberlain et al., e.g., pp. 75, 251, 412.

17. See for examples the following: Martin Niemöller's explanation in a sermon of the "manifest penal judgment" against the Jews: "The Jews have caused the crucifixion of God's Christ. . . . They bear the curse, and because they rejected the forgiveness, they drag with them as a fearsome burden the unforgiven blood-guilt of their fathers." Quoted in Ruth Zerner, "German Protestant Responses to Nazi Persecution of the Jews," in *Perspectives on the Holocaust,* ed. Randolph L. Braham (Boston: Kluwer-Nijhoff, 1983), p. 63; Bormann's reference to the Jews' crucifying Jesus in a note to Hitler, conversation, Werwolf, evening 25 July 1942, in *Hitlers Tischgespräche im Führerhauptquartier 1941–1942,* ed. Henry Picker (Stuttgart: Seewald, 1965), p. 475; Hitler's reference to the crucifixion can be found in Gordon William Prange, ed., *Hitler's Words* (Washington: American Council on Public Affairs, 1944), p. 72.

18. See flier, "Juda in der Kirche!" 13 May 1939, no signature [Thuringian German Christians], United States Holocaust Memorial Museum

Archive (hereafter cited as USHMM), RG 11.001M.11, reel 80, fond 1240, opis 1, folder 55.

19. Saul S. Friedman, *The Oberammergau Passion Play: A Lance against Civilization* (Carbondale and Edwardsville: Southern Illinois University Press, 1984), especially pp. 114–30.

20. Already in the 1940s, Joshua Trachtenberg explored the powerful parallels between Nazi stereotypes and medieval religious visions of Jews: Trachtenberg, *The Devil and the Jews: The Medieval Conception of the Jew and Its Relation to Modern Antisemitism* (New Haven: Yale University Press, 1943).

21. In fact, I have found no publications from even the enthusiastically pro-Nazi German Christian Movement that were dedicated entirely to issues of eugenics and killing of the handicapped. A 1936 booklet titled "Blood and Race in View of the Bible" was unusual in devoting even twenty pages to the subject. The author affirmed the Sterilization Law, "under the terms of which a minor surgical intervention prevents criminals from producing a harmful line of descendants." But within a few pages, that writer abandoned the discussion of eugenics per se and returned to the more familiar—perhaps safer—ground of anti-Jewish racial policy. Max Slawinsky, *Blut und Rasse im Licht der Bibel*, 3rd ed. (Kassel: J. G. Oncken, 1936), pp. 2, 4, 6. For discussion, see Doris L. Bergen, *Twisted Cross: The German Christian Movement in the Third Reich* (Chapel Hill: University of North Carolina Press, 1996), pp. 38–43.

22. On German Christian publications condemning Jews and Judaism, see Bergen, and Susannah Heschel, "Nazifying Christian Theology: Walter Grundmann and the Institute for the Study and Eradication of Jewish Influence in German Church Life," *Church History* 64, no. 4 (December 1994): 587–605.

23. See, for example, documents regarding opposition to the so-called Euthanasia Program, in J. Noakes and G. Pridham, eds., *Nazism: A History in Documents and Eyewitness Accounts, 1919–1945,* 2 vols. (New York: Schocken, 1988), 2:1035–40. As Noakes and Pridham point out, the protests made were by individuals; for the most part, the official churches, Protestant and Catholic, remained silent.

24. On church leaders' attitudes toward the Jews, see Gerlach; also Beth Pollele, "A Pure Soul Is Good Enough: Bishop von Galen, Resistance to Nazism, and the Catholic Community of Münster" (paper presented at the Conference on Genocide, Religion, and Modernity, United States Holocaust Memorial Museum, May 1997).

25. Examples in Theodore N. Thomas, *Women against Hitler: Christian Resistance in the Third Reich* (Westport, Conn.: Praeger, 1995); Ruben-

stein's discussion of the work of Heinrich Grüber, in *After Auschwitz*, pp. 3–13; and John J. Delaney, "Defying Hitler: Clerical Opposition to Religious Apartheid in Nazi Germany" (paper presented at the American Catholic Historical Association meeting, Indianapolis, March 1998). See also Wolfgang Benz and Juliane Wetzel, eds., *Solidarität und Hilfe für Juden während der NS-Zeit* (Berlin: Metropol, 1996).

26. Hilberg, *Perpetrators, Victims, Bystanders: The Jewish Catastrophe, 1933-1945* (New York: HarperPerennial, 1992), p. 268.

27. Browning, *Ordinary Men: Reserve Police Battalion 101 and the Final Solution in Poland* (New York: HarperPerennial, 1992), especially pp. 159–89.

28. Weinberg, comments on paper by John Fout, German Studies Association annual meeting, Chicago, 1995.

29. This point was made by Ian F. Hancock in his address to the Annual Scholars' Conference on the Holocaust and the Churches, Minneapolis, March 1996; now published as "The Roots of Antigypsyism: To the Holocaust and After," in *Confronting the Holocaust: A Mandate for the 21st Century,* ed. C. Jan Colijn and Marcia Sachs Littell, Studies in the Shoah, vol. 19 (Lanham: University Press of America, 1997), pp. 19–49. See also Charles Godfrey Leland, *Gypsy Sorcery and Fortune Telling* (New York: University Books, 1962), p. ix; and poem, "The Gypsy and the Jew," referring to accusations that the two groups shared a part in the crucifixion of Jesus, quoted in Dennis Reinhartz, "Damnation of the Outsider: The Gypsies of Croatia and Serbia in the Balkan Holocaust, 1941–1945," in *The Gypsies of Eastern Europe,* ed. David Crowe and John Kolsti (Armonk, N.Y.: M. E. Sharpe, 1991), p. 82. Donald Kenrick and Grattan Puxon quote a Greek Easter carol as follows: "And by a Gypsy smith they passed, / a smith who nails was making. / 'Thou dog, thou Gypsy dog' said she, / 'What is it thou art making?' / 'They're going to crucify a man / And I the nails am making. / They only ordered three of me / but five I mean to make them. / The fifth the sharpest of the five, / within his heart shall enter.'" Kenrick and Puxon, *The Destiny of Europe's Gypsies* (New York: Basic Books, 1973), p. 27.

30. For example, one public speaker warned that a future Germany infiltrated by Judaism and its offspring, Christianity, would be a nation of "epileptics and idiots, bred through incest." See remarks of neopagan quoted in Pastor Kittmann to public prosecutor, Tilsit, 1 April 1937, p. 1, BA Potsdam, DG III 1937–39, p. 345.

31. For an example of anti-Gypsy propaganda based on the idea of the wandering people, see "Fahrendes Volk: Die Bekämpfung der Zigeunerplage auf neuen Wegen," *NS-Rechtsspiegel* (Munich), 21 February 1939, in *Archives of the Holocaust: An International Collection of Selected Documents,*

ed. Henry Friedlander and Sybil Milton, vol. 1, *Bildarchiv Preussischer Kulturbesitz, Berlin,* ed. Sybil Milton and Roland Klemig, pt. 1, 1933–1939, fig. 151. In the case of Gypsies as well as Jews, the notion of wandering as a curse is linked to charges of crimes against Christ: some legends maintain that Gypsies are "haunted by a red-hot nail that never cools and must ever wander." Kenrick and Puxon, p. 27. The reference is to the nails supposedly forged by Gypsy smiths for the crucifixion of Jesus.

32. For an example of collapsing of anti-Semitic and anti-Communist rhetoric, see German Christian sermon circulated to soldiers in 1942: "Judaism has been dashed to pieces on the person of Christ. And the Soviet state too will shatter on Christ: this state that crucified Christ for a second time, that erected a monument to Judas Iscariot—and has demanded the blood of thousands upon thousands of martyrs." Niemann, "Christentum und Deutschtum: Predigt im Reformationsmonat," *Theologischer Arbeitsbrief,* 1 October 1942, pp. 10–13, LKA Bielefeld, 5,1/295/2.

33. Nazi publications provide numerous examples of the conflation of categories of assumed enemies. Hitler's *Mein Kampf* repeatedly linked Marxists and Jews; articles in the *Völkischer Beobachter* blamed Jews for sowing gender confusion in German society. See, for examples, excerpts in Sax and Kuntz, pp. 203, 263.

34. See Michael Sells, "Religion, History, and Genocide in Bosnia-Herzegovina," in *Religion and Justice in the War Over Bosnia,* ed. G. Scott Davis (New York: Routledge, 1996), pp. 23–43. Sells analyzes how Serbian nationalists have used myths such as the martyrdom of the Serb prince Lazar in 1389 at the Battle of Kosovo. In passion plays depicting the event, Lazar is shown as a Christ figure, complete with disciples, one of whom is a traitor (p. 24). See also Paul Mojzes, *Yugoslavian Inferno: Ethnoreligious Warfare in the Balkans* (New York: Continuum, 1994); and Sabrina P. Ramet, *Balkan Babel: Politics, Culture, and Religion in Yugoslavia* (Boulder: Westview Press, 1992).

35. Tim Longman, "Christian Churches and the Genocide in Rwanda" (paper presented at the Conference on Genocide, Religion, and Modernity, United States Holocaust Memorial Museum, May 1997); see also Hugh McCullum, *The Angels Have Left Us: The Rwandan Tragedy and the Churches* (Geneva: WCC Publications, 1995).

36. Jonathan Steinberg makes a similar point in his discussion of Jasenovac, the infamous camp where Croatian fascists slaughtered Serbs, Jews, and Gypsies. Vladko Macek, the leader of the Croatian Peasants Party, who was arrested and sent to Jasenovac in October 1941, described an Ustaša officer who used to make the sign of the cross each night before going to sleep. Steinberg, "The Roman Catholic Church and Genocide in

Croatia, 1941–1945," in *Christianity and Judaism: Papers Read at the 1991 Summer and the 1992 Winter Meeting of the Ecclesiastical History Society,* ed. Diana Wood (Oxford: Blackwell, 1992), p. 463.

37. On motivations among Christian rescuers of Jews, including religious factors, see Philip P. Hallie, *Lest Innocent Blood Be Shed: The Story of the Village of Le Chambon and How Goodness Happened There* (New York: Harper and Row, 1979); also film by Myriam Abramowicz and Esther Hoffenberg, *Comme si c'était hier* (As if it were yesterday) (New York, 1980); Nechama Tec, *When Light Pierced the Darkness* (New York: Oxford, 1985); Eva Fogelman, *Conscience and Courage: Rescuers of Jews during the Holocaust* (New York: Doubleday, 1994), especially pp. 161–80 on "Morality as Motivation"; Samuel P. Oliner and Pearl M. Oliner, *The Altruistic Personality: Rescuers of Jews in Nazi Europe* (New York: Free Press, 1988); and Eva Fleischner, "Motivation of Catholic Rescuers in France" (paper presented at the Conference on Genocide, Religion, and Modernity, United States Holocaust Memorial Museum, May 1997). On Christian motives for the actions of German resisters, such as those associated with the 20 July 1944 plot, see Peter Hoffmann, *German Resistance to Hitler* (Cambridge, Mass.: Harvard University Press, 1988), and Hoffmann, *Stauffenberg: A Family History, 1905–1944* (New York: Cambridge University Press, 1995); also Beate Ruhm von Oppen, *Religion and Resistance to Nazism* (Princeton: Center of International Studies, 1971); and Ruhm von Oppen's edition of Helmuth James von Moltke, *Letters to Freya: 1939–1945* (New York: Knopf, 1990). For some discussion of issues surrounding Christian resistance, see Victoria Barnett, *For the Soul of the People: Protestant Protest against Hitler* (New York: Oxford University Press, 1992), especially "Reflections on Resistance," pp. 197–208. An intriguing, if complex, individual case is presented in Saul Friedländer, *Kurt Gerstein: The Ambiguity of Good,* trans. Charles Fullman (New York: Knopf, 1969).

38. On the German Christian Movement and its synthesis of National Socialism and Christianity, see Bergen, *Twisted Cross,* especially pp. 82–100 and 142–71; and Hans-Joachim Sonne, *Die politische Theologie der Deutschen Christen* (Göttingen: Vandenhoeck und Ruprecht, 1982).

39. Bergen, *Twisted Cross,* p. 145; also Susannah Heschel, "When Jesus Was an Aryan: The Protestant Church and Antisemitic Propaganda" (paper presented at the Conference on Genocide, Religion, and Modernity, United States Holocaust Memorial Museum, May 1997).

40. In the words of one German Christian publicist in 1944: "There is no other solution to the Jewish problem than this: that one day the whole world will rise up and decide either for or against Judaism, and they will keep on struggling with each other until the world is totally Judaized or completely purged of Judaism. We can say with an honest, pure conscience

that we did not want this war and did not start this war. But we can proudly profess before all the world—the world of today as well as of tomorrow—that we took up the gauntlet with the firm resolve to solve the Jewish question forever." In "Wesen und Entstehung der Judenfrage—Auszug aus einem Vortrag von K. F. Euler," Deutsche Christen Nationalkirchliche Einung *Informationsdienst,* no. 4 (29 April 1944), p. 6, Evangelische Zentralarchiv Berlin (hereafter cited as EZA Berlin) 1/A4/566.

41. Supporters and opponents accepted six hundred thousand as a reasonable estimate of the German Christian Movement's size in the mid-1930s, its weakest phase: circular, "An alle Mitarbeiter der DC!" Dresden, 9 July 1934, LKA Bielefeld, 5,1/290,2; Confessing Church view, "Evangelische Kirche im Kampf unserer Tage," *Reichsbote,* 28 Octover 1934, BA Potsdam, Reichlandbund clippings 1862, p. 31; state view: Reichskanzlei, "Vermerk: Betrifft: Fragen der evang. Kirche," 26 October 1934, p. 2, BA Koblenz, R 43 II/163/fiche 2, p. 54.

42. See data from the Ministry of Church Affairs, "Zusammenstellung über Kirchenaustritte und Kirchenrücktritte bezw. Übertritte, ermittelt nach den von den Kirchen veröffentlichten Zusammenstellungen," no author, [1940], in BA Koblenz, R 79/19.

43. Pierre Sauvage, *Weapons of the Spirit* (New York: First Run/Icarus Films, 1986). See also Hallie, *Lest Innocent Blood Be Shed,* especially reference to Deuteronomy 19:7–10 on p. 109.

44. For some background, see Alan Edelstein, *An Unacknowledged Harmony: Philo-Semitism and the Survival of European Jewry* (Westport, Conn.: Greenwood Press, 1982).

45. On biblical allusions in German proverbs, see Wolfgang Mieder, *Deutsche Sprichwörter in Literatur, Politik, Presse, und Werbung* (Hamburg: Helmut Buske, 1983). Mieder says that Hitler used biblical quotations to give his speeches "eine volkssprachliche Bildlichkeit," p. 7. See also Carl Schulze, *Die biblischen Sprichwörter der deutschen Sprache,* ed. Mieder, vol. 8, *Sprichwörterforschung,* ed. Mieder (Bern: Peter Lang, 1987). Schulze's book was first published in 1860. A fascinating analysis of Hitler's rhetoric, including attention to its "theological conceits," is J. P. Stern, *Hitler: The Führer and the People* (Glasgow: Fontana, 1975), especially pp. 51 and 88–91, where Stern describes the "astonishing montage of biblical texts" in Hitler's address to party political leaders at the 1936 Nuremberg rally.

46. In fact, one German worker's memoir from 1918 complained that he had been taught little else. His education, he contended, had equipped him only to "join a nomadic tribe of the ancient Hebraic sort." Alwin Ger, quoted in Mary Jo Maynes, *Taking the Hard Road: Life Course in French and German Workers' Autobiographies in the Era of Industrialization* (Chapel Hill and London: University of North Carolina Press, 1995), pp. 87–8.

47. In a 1936 sermon, for example, a German pastor in Stuttgart compared Genesis 3, where the serpent tempts Eve, to the fairy tale "Little Red Riding Hood." How different was the outcome, he stressed: on the one hand, "expulsion from paradise," on the other, "as generally in all German fairy tales, good triumphs." It was clear which form of teaching he considered closer to the nature of the *Volk*. See account of Pastor Schneider's sermon in report by Busse, Bielefeld, "Der Angriff auf die Grundlage unserer Kirche durch deutsch-christliche Lehre," March 1937, pp. 1–2, LKA Bielefeld 5,1/292,1.

48. For example, Luther denounced the Book of Esther as a favorite of Jews, "beautifully attuned to their bloodthirsty, vengeful, murderous yearning and hope." "On the Jews and Their Lies," trans. Martin H. Bertram, in *Luther's Works,* ed. Helmut T. Lehmann, vol. 47, *The Christian in Society,* ed. Franklin Sherman (Philadelphia: Fortress, 1971), pt. 4, p. 157. He said the Epistle of James "doesn't amount to much" and maintained "that some Jew wrote it who probably heard about Christian people but never encountered any." "Table Talk Recorded by Caspar Heydenreich, 1542–1543," no. 5443, summer or fall 1542, in *Luther's Works,* vol. 54, ed. and trans. Theodore G. Tappert (Philadelphia: Fortress, 1967), p. 424. Schleiermacher dismissed most of the Old Testament as nothing "but the husk or wrapping of its prophecy" and added that "whatever is most definitely Jewish has least value." Even the "utterances of the noble and purer Heathenism" might be as "near and accordant" to "Christian usage." Schleiermacher, *The Christian Faith,* ed. H. R. Mackintosh and J. S. Stewart (Philadelphia: Fortress, 1928, rpt. 1976), p. 62. Adolf von Harnack questioned retention of the Old Testament in the Protestant canon, characterizing it at times as archaic and outmoded. Important works include *Lehrbuch der Dogmengeschichte* (1885–1889); *Das Wesen des Christentums* (1899–1900), a series of lectures; and *Geschichte der altchristliche Literatur* (1893–1904).

49. See *Das Ringen der deutschen Christen um die Kirche,* no author, no. 5, *Deutsche Christen im Kampf—Schriften zur allgemeinen Unterrichtung,* ed. League for German Christianity (Weimar: Verlag Deutsche Christen, 1937), p. 4, LKA Bielefeld 5,1/292,1.

50. Pamphlet, "Das Alte Testament ein 'Judenbuch'?" no author, no date, responsible: Protestant Parish Service (Ev. Gemeindedienst) for Württemberg, Stuttgart, pp. 1–4.

51. Uriel Tal, "On Modern Lutheranism and the Jews," *Leo Baeck Yearbook* (1985), p. 204.

52. Rubenstein, *After Auschwitz,* pp. 3–13, and especially pp. 8–10.

53. As David Bankier put it, "Nazi antisemitism was successful . . . because large sectors of German society were predisposed to be antisemitic."

Bankier, *The Germans and the Final Solution: Public Opinion under Nazism* (Oxford and Cambridge, Mass: Blackwell, 1992), p. 155.

54. For example, a 1932 publication's outline of common criticisms against the Old Testament hinted at parallel stereotypes of Jews: it was a "Jewish book"; it was ethically a poor example for children—"Jacob was a cheat, Abraham a liar, David an adulterer." See Ernst Kalle, *Hat das Alte Testament noch Bedeutung für den Christen?* Der Kampf-Bund, no. 12, ed. Evang. Provinzialamt für Apologetik (Gütersloh: C. Bertelsmann, 1932), p. 3.

55. See, for example, Ian Kershaw, "The Persecution of the Jews and German Popular Opinion in the Third Reich," *Leo Baeck Yearbook* (1981), p. 284.

56. For a recent discussion of the Vatican and the Holocaust, see James Carroll, "The Silence," *The New Yorker,* 7 April 1997, pp. 59–62. There is of course a voluminous literature on the papacy and the Catholic Church during the war. See, for example, Gordon Zahn, *German Catholics and Hitler's Wars: A Study in Social Control* (New York: Sheed and Ward, 1962, rpt. University of Notre Dame Press, 1989); Guenter Lewy, *The Catholic Church and Nazi Germany* (New York: McGraw-Hill, 1964); Saul Friedländer, *Pius XII and the Third Reich* (New York: Knopf, 1966); and Michael Phayer, "The Catholic Resistance Circle in Berlin and German Catholic Bishops during the Holocaust," *Holocaust and Genocide Studies* 7, no. 2 (fall 1993): 224. Useful overviews of both the Protestant and Catholic Churches are John S. Conway, *The Nazi Persecution of the Churches, 1933–45* (London: Weidenfeld and Nicolson, 1968); and Klaus Scholder, *The Churches and the Third Reich,* 2 vols. (Philadelphia: Fortress, 1987).

57. On Wehrmacht chaplains, see Bergen, "Between God and Hitler: German Military Chaplains in the Third Reich" (paper presented at the Conference on Religion, Genocide, and Modernity, United States Holocaust Memorial Museum, May 1997).

58. Fein, *Accounting for Genocide: National Responses and Jewish Victimization during the Holocaust* (Chicago: University of Chicago Press, 1979), p. 67; see also chap. 4, "The Keepers of the Keys: Responses of Christian Churches to the Threat against the Jews," pp. 93–120.

59. See Yahil and Yaffa Eliach, introduction to Yaffa Eliach, *Hasidic Tales of the Holocaust* (New York: Vintage, 1988). Martin Gilbert also describes how the Germans used "Jewish festivals for particular savagery; these days had become known to the Jews as the 'Goebbels calendar.'" For specific examples on Purim and Passover, see Gilbert, *The Holocaust: A History of the Jews of Europe during the Second World War* (New York: Holt, Rinehart and Winston, 1985), pp. 297, 315.

60. See, for example, atrocities against Polish Jewish civilians outlined

in report of General Johannes Blaskowitz, commander, Eastern Division (Oberbefehlshaber Ost), Headquarters Castle Spala, 6 February 1940, Bundesarchiv-Militärarchiv Freiburg (hereafter cited as BA-MA Freiburg), RH 53-23. Some examples of German brutality directed at Jews who were easily distinguished by their appearance during the campaign against Poland appear in Alexander B. Rossino, "Destructive Impulses: German Soldiers and the Conquest of Poland," *Holocaust and Genocide Studies* 11, no. 3 (winter 1997): 351–64.

61. For examples of works on resistance that give little if any attention to Judaism as a religion, see Reuben Ainsztein, *Jewish Resistance in Nazi-Occupied Eastern Europe: With a Historical Survey of the Jew as Fighter and Soldier in the Diaspora* (New York: Barnes and Noble Books, 1975); Yuri Suhl, ed., *They Fought Back: The Story of the Jewish Resistance in Nazi Europe* (New York: Schocken, 1967); and Yisrael Gutman, *The Jews of Warsaw, 1939–1943: Ghetto, Underground, Revolt,* trans. Ina Friedman (Bloomington: Indiana University Press, 1982); and Gutman, *Fighters among the Ruins: The Story of Jewish Heroism during World War II* (Washington, D.C.: B'nai B'rith Books, 1988).

62. Eliach's book, *Hasidic Tales,* is not explicitly about resistance, but it includes many examples of resistance activities that were intimately linked to faith and tradition. Bauer links faith and resistance in *They Chose Life: Jewish Resistance in the Holocaust* (New York: American Jewish Committee, Institute of Human Relations, 1973). Bauer takes his title from the Hebrew Bible (Deuteronomy 30:19), and he includes subsections called "Roots of Jewish Strength," "What Makes for Survival," and "Many Meanings," in which he speculates about the impact of Jewish tradition on forms of resistance. He remarks that "Men may come to similar attitudes by different roads; while dissenting from religious Judaism, a Jew will often follow a path that is Jewish by historical tradition" (p. 57). The brevity of the work, however, means that Bauer cannot develop his insights in detail.

63. See, for example, Lucie Schachne, *Education towards Spiritual Resistance: The Jewish Landschulheim Herrlingen, 1933 to 1939,* trans. Martin M. Goldenberg (Frankfurt am Main: Dipa-Verlag, 1988).

64. Josef Bor, *The Terezin Requiem,* trans. Edith Pargeter (New York: Knopf, 1963).

65. Marianne May, one of the members of the chorus, described rehearsals of the *Requiem* as somehow invigorating. Working with a great conductor and singing great music, she felt she had found something that belonged to her. The intensity of the work contributed to some sense of community, and despite the physical weakness of everyone involved, helped keep body and soul together. In March 1995, I heard May talk about her experiences in a public lecture sponsored by the Terezin Project, in con-

junction with a performance of the Verdi *Requiem* by the Vermont Symphony Orchestra in Burlington, Vermont.

66. Quoted in Joza Karas, *Music in Terezin, 1941–1945* (New York: Beaufort Books, 1985), p. 135.

67. See Primo Levi, *Survival in Auschwitz,* trans. Stuart Wolf (New York: Simon and Schuster, 1993), pp. 129–30. "If I were God," writes Levi when describing a pious Jew in Auschwitz who prayed out of gratitude for being spared from a "selection," "I would spit" on his prayer. Levi, *Survival in Auschwitz,* p. 130. Levi's recollections of Jewish religious life are not all negative: he also remembers with admiration the spiritual and intellectual energy of one particular rabbi (p. 68). Elsewhere Levi gave poignant expression to despair as well: see, for example, *The Drowned and the Saved,* trans. Raymond Rosenthal (New York: Vintage, 1989), p. 69: "Like Rumkowski, we too are so dazzled by power and prestige as to forget our essential fragility. Willingly or not we come to terms with power, forgetting that we are all in the ghetto, that the ghetto is walled in, that outside the ghetto reign the lords of death, and that close by the train is waiting."

68. Isaacson, *Seed of Sarah: Memories of a Survivor* (Urbana: University of Illinois Press, 1990), see pp. 80–2, where Isaacson describes Sabbath services in Auschwitz-Birkenau.

69. Arendt, *Eichmann in Jerusalem: A Report on the Banality of Evil,* rev. ed. (New York: Viking, 1963).

70. Wiesel's remark made during his talk at Dartmouth University, in conjunction with Lessons and Legacies Conference on the Holocaust, 1995.

71. Emmanuel Levinas, "To Love the Torah More Than God," trans. Helen A. Stephenson and Richard I. Sugarman, with commentary by Richard I. Sugarman, *Judaism: A Quarterly Journal of Jewish Life and Thought* 28, no. 2 (spring 1979): 216–23.

Michael Phayer

The Holocaust in the Shadow of the Cold War
Moral Questions about Papal Policy

THE DISPOSITION OF THE CATHOLIC CHURCH TOWARD JEWS AND JUdaism did not change until the middle of the cold war at the time of the Second Vatican Council. After a protracted and difficult discussion the council passed the document known as *Nostra Aetate* that initiated a still ongoing process of Catholic-Jewish reconciliation. Why did the world have to wait until 1965 for this reconciliation to begin? Why could it not have begun immediately after World War II and the Holocaust? The answer is quite simple—in a word, Pope Pius XII.

A far more difficult question concerns the cold war context. After a two-thousand-year tradition of anti-Semitism, what difference could it possibly make whether that tradition was broken in 1945 or a mere twenty years later? If it can be argued that the Vatican's attitude toward the Holocaust, toward its survivors, and toward Israel in some way contributed to the cold war, the twenty-year delay takes on significance at least for the history of our turbulent century. An absence of moral integrity is given prominent play by contemporary historians who are attempting to uncover the reasons for the cold war.

Proceeding now to the substantive issues, there are several areas of concern to survivors of the Holocaust and to Jews everywhere with which the pope could have involved himself positively: the matter of Holocaust guilt, punishment of the guilty, indemnification and restitution for survivors, the question of Israeli statehood and the status of Jerusalem, and, lastly, the fundamental problem of Jewish-Christian relations. All of these issues developed immediately after the war and lingered on well into the cold war era.

It was Pope Pius's attitude about the Holocaust that allowed the

German Catholic church to embark on a triumphal path after the war by denying collective guilt for German crimes.[1] Pius's position on the matter contrasted with that of the Allies, who charged Germans with collective responsibility if not guilt.[2] Since Pius's own reputation was totally unspotted at the time, his pronouncements regarding the innocence of the German people at large had great impact, above all on the Germans themselves. By exonerating German Catholics as a group in a June 1945 radio address, and by calling them heroes and martyrs in August, Pius made it possible for the faithful to believe their claim of innocence or *Selbstfreispruch*.[3]

In April 1945 the Americans and British, who had been urging Pope Pius to speak out against genocide since 1942, tried to disabuse Pius of his ideas on German innocence by confronting him with photographs of the Nazi death camps.[4] The pictures indicated that not only the SS but also German "civilians in general found nothing reprehensible about such crimes" as had occurred there.[5] Pius would have none of it. Instead of asking for a statement of guilt, as did the World Council of Churches of the German Protestant church, Pius defended the integrity of the German church. Pius's inaccurate characterization of Catholics as "wholeheartedly" opposed to Hitler's regime demonstrated the pope's full acceptance of the German bishops' rejection of collective guilt in their Fulda statement of 1945.[6]

Jacques Maritain, France's postwar ambassador to the Vatican, tried to bring the pope around to the idea of collective responsibility, if not guilt, for atrocities. Maritain argued that in modern society individual freedom is tied to collective responsibility. From this it followed that even though many Germans were not themselves guilty of the crimes of the Gestapo and of the SS, all must answer for them because these organizations were prominent agents of the community. Collective responsibility rested as well on the shoulders of German Catholics, or, perhaps, especially on their shoulders. Who, Maritain asked, would engage in the process of repentance and renewal if believers did not?[7]

It appears that Pius explicitly rejected Maritain's ideas when he raised the bishops of Berlin, Cologne, and Münster to the cardinalate early in 1946 to indicate to the world his high esteem for the German Catholic Church. Pius told one of the new cardinals, Joseph Frings of Cologne, that "it is unjust to treat someone as guilty . . . only because he belongs to a certain organization."[8]

But what about the truly guilty, those who had been convicted of war crimes at Nuremberg and in the army courts of the zonal authorities? The saga of these criminals was to become one of the most conspicuous moral ambiguities of the cold war. In their 1945 Fulda statement German bishops had said bluntly that those who engaged in atrocities must be brought to justice and must pay for their crimes. No one pleaded for leniency for those who engaged personally in the Holocaust. Within months of this stand, however, Bishop Clemens August Graf von Galen—the "Lion of Münster" who had dared to challenge the Nazis on euthanasia—published a lengthy statement in which he baldly attacked the trials, saying that they were not about justice but about the defamation of the German people.[9]

Given the green light from Rome, where Galen published his attack on Allied justice, German bishops reversed themselves, questioning the validity of war crimes trials, and lobbying occupational authorities, especially General Lucius D. Clay, the first U.S. military governor in Germany, and John J. McCloy, the first high commissioner, for sentence reductions or outright amnesty for all convicted wartime criminals.[10] The most outspoken activist of the Catholic lobby, Auxiliary Bishop of Munich Johannes Neuhäusler, even pressed for leniency for notorious murderers such as Oswald Pohl and Otto Ohlendorf.[11]

The Vatican also interceded for war criminals. In 1948 Pope Pius urged General Clay to extend a blanket pardon to all war criminals who had received death sentences, which Clay refused to do, arguing that these people had been found guilty of specific, heinous crimes.[12] When the Vatican persisted in its efforts to secure clemency for German war criminals, Pius's American envoy to Germany, Bishop Aloysius Muench, wrote to Monsignor Giovanni Battista Montini, undersecretary of state and the future Pope Paul VI, warning him that Rome was on dangerously thin ice. His intervention saved the Vatican from becoming publicly associated with former Nazis, whose organization, the Association for Truth and Justice *(Bund für Wahrheit und Gerechtigkeit)*, also lobbied on behalf of German war crimes prisoners.[13]

About the church's efforts to secure leniency for Holocaust perpetrators there is no doubt. But did the Vatican also become involved in helping them escape to South America and elsewhere after the war? The eagerness of the Vatican to intervene across the board for convicted German war criminals suggests that we should not dismiss out of hand the tendentious work of Ernst Klee and the controversial account of coauthors John Loftus and Mark Aarons regarding Vatican efforts on behalf of criminals after the war.[14] The recently published books of these authors pick up where the more careful historian, Gitta Sereny, left off a decade earlier. Interviewing a number of clerical and nonclerical operatives in wartime Rome, Sereny found that Vatican money was indeed used to pay for the escape of war crimes fugitives.[15] While Sereny merely posed the question of whether the Vatican knew it was abetting the escape of war crimes fugitives, Klee and Loftus and Aarons look for a "smoking gun" in the highest, innermost circles of the Vatican. And, whereas Sereny related, without conjecturing about the closest advisers of the pope, that while the identities of notorious murderers like fugitives Franz Stangl and Adolf Eichmann were known to lower Vatican appointees (the Austrian bishop Alois C. Hudal), Loftus and Aarons are certain that the highest Vatican officials (Montini) knew the identity of the Croat genocide perpetrators such as the priest Krunoslav Draganović, and Ustaša leader Ante Pavelić.[16]

During the war Pope Pius and his top personnel, Monsignors Montini and Domenico Tardini, indeed knew a number of top Croatian government officials. In 1941 Pavelić had sought Vatican recognition of his pro-Nazi fascist government of Catholic Croatia. Croatian diplomatic emissaries to the Holy See were scolded by Tardini and Montini, who were aware of the Ustaša's atrocities against Jews and Orthodox Christians. Ante Pavelić had himself been received by the pope, an audience which the English ambassador to the Vatican warned would put the papacy's moral authority at risk.[17] Thinking diplomatically, Pius favored the establishment of a Catholic, anticommunist state in Eastern Europe, and never publicly protested the Ustaša's genocide or broke off (informal) relations with Croatia.

After the war Croat refugees from Yugoslavia, including a number of Ustaša members who were wanted for war crimes against Jews and Serbs, fled to cities in Western Europe and especially to Rome. There they lived off looted gold amounting to two hundred million Swiss Francs (about U.S.$857,265) that cannot be accounted for today and may have been deposited in the bank of Vatican City.[18] Ante Golik, the Vatican's liaison to the refugee Croats, set up shop in the monastery of San Girolamo where, according to Office of Secret Service reports, he provided the Holy See with intelligence reports on Marshal Josip Tito's communist movement in Yugoslavia, and used Vatican contacts to obtain passports so that wanted war criminals such as Ante Pavelić could flee to South American countries.

The Vatican's diplomatic response to Croatia's genocidal policies and its firsthand contact with Ustaša officials makes likely Loftus and Aarons's charge that the Holy See knew the identity of the Croatians it harbored after the war and for whom it provided false identity papers. British intelligence agents discovered that the Ustaša refugee Bishop Ivan Saric, one of Ante Pavelić's closest clerical supporters, was among the Ustaša Croats in Rome after the war.[19] In 1946 a Yugoslav diplomat asked the Vatican's Cardinal Eugene Tisserant how the pope could have given an audience to the murderer Pavelić, much less shaken his hand. Embarrassed, the cardinal changed the subject but assured the Yugoslav that "neither I nor the Vatican knows the whereabouts of Pavelić; if we did, we should denounce him to the Allied police."[20] One year later the United States intercepted a telegram en route from Argentina to Germany which said that the Italian liner *Andrea Grille* had arrived from Genoa five days previously with Ante Pavelić dressed as a priest as one of its passengers. The telegram reported further that Pavelić had been able to get his passport through the Dalmatian Ecclesiastical Institute, which supplied refugees with new identity papers and testimonials that were confirmed by the Vatican.[21]

The intercepted telegram would seem to compromise Cardinal Tisserant badly, but circumstances suggest otherwise. During the early months of World War II, just before the Holocaust, Tisserant had urged Pope Pius to write an encyclical on genocide. Pius declined. Tisserant had become disillusioned with Pius's conduct of diplomacy. In a letter to Cardinal Emmanuel-Célestin Suhard of Paris, which was seized by the Gestapo during the war, Tisserant voiced his feelings: "I fear that history will reproach the Holy See with having practiced a policy of selfish convenience and not much else."[22]

Not surprisingly, Tisserant was "left out of the loop" as far as the Vatican's conduct of diplomacy was concerned. Monsignors Tardini and Montini, both undersecretaries of state, dealt with Holocaust matters, and with the genocide perpetrated by Pavelić's Ustaša. Thus, when the Yugoslav diplomat came to Rome on the trail of the war criminal Pavelić, the Vatican forestalled him by arranging for him to interview the widely respected but uninformed Cardinal Tisserant.

Pope Pius saw his fears become reality in Eastern Europe after the war as Croatia was replaced by the reestablished Yugoslav state under the Communist Tito. The sensational trial conducted by the Tito government in 1946 of the Catholic, Croat nationalist, Archbishop Aloysius Stepinac, presaged the cold war. Whether or not the Vatican could, or did, recruit anyone—even war criminals like Pavelić—for the crusade against communism awaits final verification. What is clear, however, is that Pius was preoccupied with the Communist threat before, during, and after World War II.[23]

While the Vatican showed keen interest in getting the perpetrators of the Holocaust freed, it showed no interest in the question of restitution for the survivors of the Holocaust. Years after the remnant of German Jews returned to their native land, their property—houses, sideboards, silverware, and what have you—were still in other people's possession. Unwilling to leave this matter to German bureaucratic goodwill, General Clay made restitution the subject of Military Law No. 59 late in 1947.[24] Falling in step behind Clay, Commissioner McCloy supported Jewish demands and "repeatedly exerted strong and direct pressure on the German [state] governments . . . to speed up and complete the restitution program."[25]

German bishops recognized that restitution was a moral obligation, but they chose not to press the issue. In 1948 Gertrud Luckner, who founded the Freiburg circle in southwest Germany immediately after the war for Christian-Jewish reconciliation, successfully lobbied the bishops to tell the faithful in 1948 that as far as possible the injustice of the Holocaust had to be made good: "this means restitution."[26] Thereafter it pained Luckner and her philo-Semitic associates that they could not get a German bishop (other than Berlin's Konrad Preysing) to speak to the issue that would help reconcile church and synagogue.[27] Jews found restitution litigation increasingly difficult during the 1940s.[28] In the 1950s, when restitution questions made headlines nationally and secular authorities like Commissioner McCloy, West German federal Justice Minister H. Wilden, and Chancellor Konrad Adenauer insisted that restitution was a moral issue, church leaders remained mum.[29]

Pope Pius was no exception to the rule. The matter of restitution was never discussed by him with his envoy to occupied Germany. Bishop Muench, for his part, thought that "a lot of hardship and injustice comes about because of [restitution resulting from] denazification."[30] Proconsuls Clay and McCloy, pestered by pleas from German churchmen, Bishop Muench, and the Vatican on behalf of war criminals, never heard from them regarding the obligation to make restitution to survivors of the Holocaust.[31]

John Conway has pointed out that in the midst of the Holocaust the Vatican disapproved of Jews finding refuge from persecution by emigration to Palestine.[32] After the war Pius did not waver from this course. Told by an American rabbi that the survivors of the Holocaust wished to settle in Palestine, Pius said that he realized this, but preferred they find another homeland.[33] Thus, the Vatican's policy left stranded the quarter of a million Holocaust survivors, now displaced persons, who huddled in occupied Germany where they clamored for a Jewish homeland.[34] Even after Israeli statehood became a reality Pope Pius continued to be negative both diplomatically and theologically. Israel would jeopardize Christian "rights" to the holy places and would lead to too many conflicts in the land where Christ was born, lived, and was crucified, conflicts that might possibly damage church property or even the holy places themselves. James G. McDonald, special representative of the United States to the provisional government of Israel, reported in 1949 that the pontiff opposed Israeli control of the city of Jerusalem because he did not think the Jews would keep their promises regarding the religious rights of Christian churches.[35]

Pius became suspicious of a German Catholic group that was philo-Semitic and that favored Israeli statehood. In 1948 Gertrud Luckner and her Freiburg circle in southwest Germany joined with international Protestants in affirming that neither "theological considerations nor biblical teachings would justify a negative position among Christians toward the establishment of a Jewish state in Palestine."[36] Assuming a close connection between German anti-Semitism and the Holocaust, the Occupational Military Government— United States (OMGUS) promoted church-sponsored reconciliation between Christians and Jews within their zone. Gertrud Luckner, who had spent the last years of the war in the Ravensbrück concentration camp for trying to save Jews during the Holocaust, dedicated herself to the work of reconciliation after the war. Looking for these kinds of efforts, OMGUS embraced Luckner's newsletter, the *Freiburger Rundbrief.*

But the Vatican did not. Citing the danger of what the Holy See called "indifferentism" (the notion that one religion is as good as the next), Pius issued a *monitum* in 1948 regarding Luckner's philo-Semitic work and sent several of his closest advisers to investigate her circle in 1950. Under the Vatican's cloud of suspicion, Luckner found it difficult to win support of German Catholic leaders in her fight against anti-Semitism—even church-related anti-Semitism. Had the Holy See supported the work of Gertrud Luckner, German bishops would also have been more supportive of the Freiburg circle and of Jewish-Christian reconciliation. In this way the Holy See also indirectly interfered with the work in Germany of the religious affairs office of OMGUS.

The question posed at the outset—what difference did it make if the Vatican was twenty years late in adjusting its attitude toward Jews—now seems crass. Clearly, it made an enormous difference to survivors awaiting justice, restitution, and a homeland. Going now beyond the question of injury to survivors, we may ask what the wider, international effect of the Holy See's cold war policies may have been.

Looking back on a half century of German aggression that culminated in what came to be known as the Holocaust, world leaders resolved in 1945 to exorcise Germany's evil spirit. Pope Pius XII, an international religious authority, disagreed. The pontiff did not see Germany as differing significantly from other modern states. Pius viewed the war, and the crimes that were committed during it by a *number of belligerents,* as a product of modernity for which communism, fascism, and liberalism were all responsible.

In this way Pope Pius distributed responsibility for war crimes around generously but did not include Christianity. Today virtually everyone agrees that there is a greater or lesser connection between traditional Christian anti-Semitism and Nazi genocide.[37] Raul Hilberg's concordance of historical Christian and Nazi anti-Semitism makes the point explicitly. The Holocaust took place, historian Lucy Dawidowicz believed, because the two pillars of Western society, law and religion, were unable to protect human life. Not only did the Enlightenment's standards of tolerance and progress break down, but Christianity was also unable to answer the bell of common morality.[38]

Similarly, a Polish intellectual views the Holocaust as a "fundamental issue about contemporary culture [and] about Christianity."[39] Nowadays such views are more mainstream than fringe opinions. Humanists from many disciplines have joined with savants like Primo Levi and Terrence Des Pres in detecting in the Holocaust a deep, fundamental breakdown of Western civilization.[40]

Considered from this perspective, Pope Pius's postwar German policy, shrewd as it may have seemed in Western eyes at the onset of the cold war, invites speculation about alternative courses of action. Instead of becoming the world's first cold war warrior, would Pius have better served the interests of peace by choosing to deal with the Holocaust in terms of spiritual bankruptcy, anti-Semitism, and human rights?

Recent postmortem reflections on the cold war have suggested that when the Helsinki process (following the Helsinki Conference in 1975) replaced the moral ambiguity of cold war tactics, authoritarianism collapsed in Eastern Europe.[41] The moral ambiguities commonly cited in connection with the cold war are President Truman's 1947 exaggerations regarding communism in Greece and Turkey, the Central Intelligence Agency's postwar interference in the internal affairs of Italy and France, presidential candidate John Kennedy's "missile gap" rhetoric, and, in George F. Kennan's view, nuclear warfare itself.[42]

Put this way, we see that the discussion eclipses Germany. Cold war moral ambiguities relate exclusively to the East-West confrontation. Thus, the Marshall Plan would be included in the catalog of ambiguities, not because it erased the Nazi scar too quickly, but because it represented an effort by the United States to go well beyond mere national security by establishing a friendly international economic order.

We have seen, however, that proconsuls Clay and McCloy wanted to deal with the moral ambiguities of postwar Germany. These ambiguities related to the Holocaust: punishment for murder, restitution for stolen property, indemnity for broken lives of survivors, eradication of anti-Semitism. Precisely because these were moral issues, Clay and McCloy hoped to engage the churches—especially the Catholic Church, which they perceived to be free of Nazi contamination—in the reconstruction process.[43]

Jacques Maritain agreed with the American proconsuls. Immediately after the war, the French ambassador to the Holy See urged Pius to address the issue of anti-Semitism and human rights. Maritain sought to point out that the real danger for civilization was not in what might develop—the spread of communism—but in the present and continuing evil of anti-Semitism. Maritain wanted Pius "to awaken the consciousness of people regarding the horror of racism" by holding up the example of the "extermination of millions of Jews in gas chambers and their torture in death camps."[44] In vain, Maritain pointed out that Catholics were playing a part in the rise of postwar anti-Semitism in occupied Germany.[45] Even after the Kielce pogrom cost the lives of forty-one Polish Jews in July 1946, Pius XII kept his focus narrowly on the international danger of communism.

Shortly after the death of Pius XII in 1958, his more democratically minded successor summoned the Second Vatican Council. When a French survivor, Jules Isaac, visited Pope John XXIII and suggested that the council might take up Jewish-Christian relations, the new pope spontaneously accepted the idea. The 1965 conciliar document, *Nostra Aetate,* that resulted from Isaac's visit, revolutionized Catholic-Jewish relations by recanting the ancient Christian charge of deicide and recognizing Judaism as an ongoing, living religion.[46] In this manner the Catholic Church implicitly acknowledged its own anti-Semitic past and culpability for the Holocaust. The effect of the statement of the Second Vatican Council on Jews was to reopen the human rights issue for Catholics early on during the cold war.

This happened spectacularly in Poland. Reacting to the Vatican II view of Jews and Judaism, the antiestablishment minority movement Solidarity sparked a discussion about Poland's other minority, the Jews, and their historical relationship to the dominant Catholic majority.[47] When reactionary Poles began recirculating the *Protocols of the Elders of Zion* and other defaming literature, Solidarity protested, causing church authorities in Poland to condemn anti-Semitic publications. The discussion widened into a national debate when the French documentary film *Shoah* led Jerzy Turowicz, a well-known Catholic publicist, to criticize religious leaders. The Polish church, Turowicz asserted, having seen what anti-Semitism led to, should have conducted its own soul-searching look into the Holocaust.[48]

Ten years after the Second Vatican Council's statement affirming Judaism, human rights became a matter of international law. The Helsinki process guaranteed movements like Solidarity by allowing governments to protest the subversion of rights in other states.⁴⁹ The Vatican and Helsinki decisions complemented each other.⁵⁰ The Helsinki process moved authoritarian governments to accommodate themselves to human rights. Amazingly, it became possible for an American secretary of state to celebrate a Passover Seder in Moscow with Russian Jews, the refuseniks who demanded the right to emigrate.

In the end, then, liberal and moral values may have triggered the thaw of the cold war glacier as much as ICBMs and Star Wars. Preoccupied by the potential growth of communism rather than the reality of anti-Semitism, Pius XII ignored moral questions that related to the Holocaust in postwar zonal Germany. In 1948 Jacques Maritain resigned his ambassador post at the Vatican, decrying Pius's preoccupation with the political rather than the moral sphere.⁵¹ Maritain's perception was on the mark. Indeed, evidence mounts indicating that Pope Pius may have crossed over the boundary of moral ambiguity into the immoral by abetting the escape of World War II atrocity perpetrators, who, as fascists, would have opposed communism. It has always been an axiom of Catholic moral teaching that the end does not justify the means. Pope Pius XII lacked the moral vision that might have relaxed the tensions that produced the cold war.

NOTES

1. For an overview of the post-Holocaust German church, see my chapter "Die Katholische Kirche, der Vatikan und der Holocaust," in *Der Umgang mit dem Holocaust nach 1945, Europa-USA-Israel,* ed. Rolf Steininger (Vienna, 1994), pp. 137–46. For a specific discussion of the German church's postwar reaction to the Holocaust, see my article, "The Postwar German Catholic Debate over Holocaust Guilt," *Kirchliche Zeitgeschichte* 8, no. 2 (1995): 427–39.

2. Michael Ermarth, ed., *America and the Shaping of German Society, 1945–1955* (Providence [New Hampshire], 1993); introduction, p. 9. Pius also recognized the necessity of collective responsibility, and he admitted that "not a few even of those who call themselves Christians" were negligent. But Pius did not single out Germany and the murder of the Jews in this regard. See Reginald K. Walker, *Pius of Peace: A Study of the Pacific Work of His Holiness Pope Pius in the World War 1939–1945* (Dublin: M.H. McGill, 1946), p. 159.

3. Werner Blessing, "'Deutschland in Not, wir im Glauben . . .':

Kirche und Kirchenvolk in einer katholischen Region 1933–1949," in *Von Stalingrad zur Währungsreform,* ed. Martin Broszat et al. (Munich, 1988), pp. 68 ff. Vera Bücker, *Die Schulddiskussion im deutschen Katholizismus nach 1945* (Bochum, 1989), pp. 15–8.

4. Konrad Repgen, "Kardinal Frings im Rückblick—Zeitgeschichtliche Kontroverspunkte einer künftigen Biographie," *Historisches Jahrbuch* 100 (1980), p. 313.

5. Annual Report of Osborne for 1945, Rome, 22 February 1946, in the Public Record Office, London, FO 371/60 803; document reprinted in *Veröffentlichungen der Kommission für Zeitgeschichte,* Reihe A. (Mainz: M. Grünewald, 1995). 38, 904.

6. For my analysis of this statement, see Frank Buscher and Michael Phayer, "German Catholic Bishops and the Holocaust, 1940–1953," *German Studies Review* 11, no. 3 (October 1988): 163–85.

7. Le Centre d'Archives Maritain de Kolbsheim (hereafter cited as CAM), file ambassade I, Maritain to Montini (copy), Rome, 12 August 1946.

8. Dieter Froitzheim, ed., *Kardinal Frings* (Cologne, 1980), p. 263.

9. Graf von Galen, *Rechtsbewusstsein und Rechtsunsicherheit* (Rome, 1946). Galen's diatribe was printed only as a manuscript; there was no way that the OMGUS would have allowed its circulation in zonal Germany.

10. See Buscher and Phayer, pp. 473 ff., and Frank Buscher, *The U.S. War Crimes Trial Program in Germany, 1946–1955* (New York, 1989), pp. 93–7.

11. Ohlendorf was the *Gruppenführer* of a mobile killing squad and Pohl was in charge of death camp organization.

12. Jean E. Smith, *Lucius D. Clay: An American Life* (New York, 1990), pp. 301–2.

13. Catholic University of America Archives (hereafter cited as CUA) 37/133 #2, Muench to Giovanni Battista Montini, Kronberg, 2 February 1951. I am grateful to my brother, Richard Phayer, for translating this letter from the Italian.

14. Klee worked independently of Loftus and Aarons and also used different source material, but the authors agree that high Vatican officials were abetting known war criminals.

15. Gitta Sereny, *Into That Darkness* (New York, 1983), pp. 315 ff. One of the interviewees, Burkhardt Schneider, denied that Vatican money was used for this purpose.

16. John Loftus and Mark Aarons, *Unholy Trinity* (New York, 1992); see p. 25, for example, where Bishops Hudal and Montini are linked, and chap. 5, which deals with Croat fugitives: "It is virtually inconceivable that the key officials in the Vatican hierarchy were ignorant of Draganovic's

Nazi-smuggling network," p. 119. Ernst Klee, who specializes in ecclesiastical muckraking for the distinguished German weekly *Die Zeit,* is the only person to have gained access to Hudal's papers in Rome.

17. Léon Papeleux, *Les silences de Pie XII* (Brussels, 1980), 168.

18. U.S. National Archives, Washington, D.C. (hereafter cited as NA) RG 226, stack 190, row 9, compartment 22, shelf 05, box 29, folder 170, OSS report on Monsignor Ante Golik, alleged Ustaša subsidizer; 17 June 1946. See the report of historian of the State Department William Slany, *U.S. and Allied Wartime and Postwar Relations and Negotiations with Argentina, Portugal, Spain, Sweden, and Turkey on Looted Gold and German External Assets and U.S. Concerns about the Fate of the Wartime Ustasha Treasury* (Washington, D.C., 1998), pp. 141–56.

19. NA RG 84 (General Records, 1946:711.5–711.9) box 109, Office of the British Political Adviser to the Supreme Allied Commander, 30 October 1946.

20. NA RG 59, box 34, file marked 1947, interview between Vladimir Stakic and Cardinal Tisserant, 7 April 1946, Rome.

21. Ibid., folder marked "Political-General 1947," document titled "U.S. Civil Censorship Submission; Civil Censorship Division, USFET," 6 May 1947, from Antonio E. Vucetich, El Socorro, Argentina, to Olga Vucetich-Radnic, Foderreuthweg 5, Kempten, Allgäu, Bavaria.

22. Guenter Lewy, *The Catholic Church and Nazi Germany* (New York, 1964), pp. 306–7.

23. M. Shelah, "The Catholic Church in Croatia, the Vatican, and the Murder of the Croatian Jews," *Remembering for the Future,* vol. 1 (Oxford, 1988), p. 268.

24. Constantin Goschler, "The United States and *Wiedergutmachung* for Victims of Nazi Persecution: From Leadership to Disengagement," in *Holocaust and Shilumim: The Policy of Wiedergutmachung in the Early 1950s,* ed. Axel Frohn (Washington, D.C.: Oerman Historical Institute, 1991), p. 9.

25. Ibid., p. 25.

26. Rolf Rendtorff and Hans Hermann Henrix, eds., *Die Kirchen und das Judentum* (Paderborn, 1988), p. 239.

27. Institut für Zeitgeschichte (hereafter cited as IZG), Karl Thieme to Bishop Landersdorfer, Loerrach, Switzerland, 10 July 1950, IZG 163/49.

28. Ronald Webster, "Jewish Returnees to West Germany after 1945: Why They Returned and How They Fared," *YIVO* 21 (1993): 33–66.

29. See the comment by Berlin's famous Pastor Heinrich Grüber in the *Freiburger Rundbrief* 1, 4 (July 1949), p. 12, and Karl Thieme's letter to Bishop Landersdorfer, Loerrach, 7 July 1950, IZG 163/49. Two cases that

made national news over a considerable period of time were that of the fired Württemberg bureaucrat Otto Kuester, who was "overly" zealous in enforcing restitution regulations, and of the survivor Norbert Wollheim, whose case against slave labor employer I. G. Farben was successful; see the excellent account of this by Wolfgang Benz, *Zwischen Hitler und Adenauer* (Frankfurt, 1991), chap. 8.

30. CUA 37/30 #6, Muench to his mother, Kronberg, 28 October 1946.

31. Robert Hürtgen, "Untergang und Neubeginn, Köln in den Jahren 1942–1946," in *Kardinal Frings,* ed. Dieter Froitzheim (Cologne, 1980), p. 36.

32. John Conway, "Catholicism and the Jews," in *Judaism and Christianity under the Impact of National Socialism,* ed. Otto Dov Kulka and P. R. Mendes-Flohr (Jerusalem, 1987), pp. 448–9. Historian Stanford Shaw believes that Angello Roncalli, Pius's successor as Pope John XXIII, who served during the war and the Holocaust as the Vatican's apostolic delegate to Turkey, acted without Vatican orders, or possibly even against them, in pursuing rescue work that involved Jews escaping to Palestine: Stanford J. Shaw, *Turkey and the Holocaust* (New York, 1993), pp. 277 and 390 (and the footnote).

33. NA RG 59, box 28, Philip Bernstein to Gen. J. T. McNarney, 14 September 1946.

34. Ibid., Philip Bernstein to Gen. J. T. McNarney, 14 September 1946.

35. NA RG 59, Taylor papers, box 34, letter of 24 October 1949, from Tel Aviv from McDonald to AMVAT.

36. *Freiburger Rundbrief* 1, 1 (1948), p. 13.

37. In his keynote address at the Remembering for the Future II conference (Berlin, 13–17 March 1994), historian Yehuda Bauer insisted on a close, direct link between anti-Semitism and the Holocaust. For a discussion of other views, see Michael R. Marrus, "Reflections on the Historiography of the Holocaust," *Journal of Modern History* 66, no. 1 (March 1994): 92–116.

38. Alfred Gottschalk, "From the Kingdom of Night to the Kingdom of God: Jewish-Christian Relations and the Search for Religious Authenticity after the Holocaust," *Contemporary Jewry,* ed. Geoffrey Wigoder (Jerusalem: Institute of Contemporary Jewry, 1984), p. 238.

39. Andrzej Bryk, "Polish-Jewish Relations during the Holocaust: The Hidden Complex of the Polish Mind" (paper presented at the conference History and Culture of the Polish Jews, Jerusalem, 1988).

40. See, for example, Alan T. Davies, *Antisemitism and the Christian Mind* (New York, 1969), or G. M. Kren and L. Rappoport, *The Holocaust*

and the Crisis of Human Behavior (New York, 1980), Lucy Dawidowicz, *The European War against the Jews, 1933–1945* (New York, 1975), and, above all, Terrence Des Pres, *The Survivor* (New York, 1976). For a rich and wide sampling of humanist views of the Shoah, see the three-volume collection of essays resulting from the 1988 Oxford Holocaust conference, *Remembering for the Future* (Oxford, 1988).

41. See, for example, Don Oberdorfer, *The Turn: From the Cold War to the New Era* (New York, 1991), and John Lewis Gaddis, *The United States and the End of the Cold War* (New York, 1992).

42. Gaddis, 50 ff.

43. Armin Boyens, "Die Kirchenpolitik der amerikanischen Besatzungsmacht in Deutschland von 1944 bis 1946," in *Kirchen in der Nachkriegszeit,* ed. A. Boyens et al. (Göttingen, 1979), pp. 6–100.

44. CAM file ambassade I., Maritain to the Conference Internationale Extraordinaire pour Combattre l'Antisemitisme, Rome, 28 July 1947.

45. CAM file ambassade I., Letter of Maritain to Montini (copy), Rome, 12 July 1946.

46. The specific term "deicide" was unfortunately not rejected in the document, but Jews were clearly not held collectively guilty for the death of Christ, and the "curse" for having done so was renounced.

47. David Warszawski, "The Convent and Solidarity," *Tikkun,* 4, 6 (1990): 23–7.

48. Andrzej Bryk, "Polish Society Today and the Memory of the Holocaust," *Remembering for the Future,* supp. vol., pp. 55–66.

49. Gaddis, pp. 60–2.

50. Oberdorfer, p. 417.

51. In an unpublished white paper written at the time of his resignation, Maritain noted his impressions of Pius XII; see Cahiers Jacques Maritain, 4, L'Ambassade au Vatican (1945–1948) in CAM file ambassade I.

Robert A. Krieg

To *Nostra Aetate*
Martin Buber and Romano Guardini

THE SECOND VATICAN COUNCIL MADE A MAJOR BREAKTHROUGH IN Jewish-Christian relations when on 28 October 1965 it adopted *Nostra Aetate* ("in our day"), which is also known as the Declaration on the Relation of the Church to Non-Christian Religions. Along with expressing the church's desire to respect "what is true and holy" in other religions (no. 2), the council condemned "any discrimination against people or any harassment of them on the basis of their race, color, condition in life or religion" (no. 5). In particular, it declared that the church "deplores all hatreds, persecutions, displays of anti-Semitism leveled at any time or from any source against the Jews" (no. 4).[1]

Commentators have already described the remarkable genesis of *Nostra Aetate* during the Second Vatican Council (11 October 1962—8 December 1965). Because of the efforts of Jules Isaac, Pope John XXIII, Rabbi Abraham Heschel, Augustin Cardinal Bea, Monsignor John Oesterreicher, Pope Paul VI, and some German and U.S. bishops, the council generated a document that no one foresaw during the two years of conciliar preparations.[2] Also, research has revealed the declaration's origins in the decades prior to the council.[3] For example, the council's action was preceded by Pope Pius XI's encyclical *Mit brennender Sorge* (14 March 1937), his subsequent "hidden encyclical" condemning anti-Semitism, and Jules Isaac's superb contribution in 1947 to the International Conference of Christians and Jews at Seeligsberg, Switzerland.[4] Although much is now known about the background to *Nostra Aetate,* the deep-seated desire to sustain and strengthen the spirit of this extraordinary document continually prompts further studies of the history of Jewish-Christian relations.[5]

This essay reviews one interpersonal relationship that indirectly contributed to the Second Vatican Council's adoption of *Nostra Aetate,* namely, the professional friendship between Martin Buber and Romano Guardini. Martin Buber is well known; the outstanding Jewish philosopher of religion, born in Vienna in 1878, was a professor at the University of Frankfurt am Main (1924–1933) and at the Hebrew University in Jerusalem (1938–1951), and died in Jerusalem in 1965.[6] Romano Guardini was one of the most creative Catholic minds in the first half of the twentieth century. Born in Verona in 1885, he grew up in Mainz, served as a professor in Berlin, Tübingen, and Munich, where he died in 1968.[7] A review of the correspondence and contacts between these two religious thinkers clearly indicates, I propose, that Buber's efforts to communicate with Guardini during the 1920s led Guardini to change his stance on Jews, sadly after the Shoah. More specifically, because of the Jewish scholar's overtures to the Catholic theologian, Guardini eventually reached out to Martin Buber in Jerusalem after the war. A review of the scholarly association between these two outstanding religious leaders will lead in conclusion to a recognition of ways in which Jews and Christians can continue to improve their communications and mutual respect.

BUBER'S OUTREACH TO GUARDINI

Martin Buber and Romano Guardini came to know each other because Buber made the effort to engage Guardini in an exchange of ideas. The first contact between the two scholars occurred in 1918 or 1919 at Buber's initiative. After reading Guardini's *The Spirit of the Liturgy* (1918), Buber wrote to the young priest congratulating him on his use of phenomenology to illumine the dynamics of worship.[8] Guardini never publicly said how he felt about receiving Buber's letter; however, we can surmise that he appreciated Buber's gesture, for over the next four decades his thought developed in parallel to Buber's.[9]

The second contact also came at Buber's initiative. In the spring of 1922, Buber attended a lecture by Guardini in Bonn and stayed afterward to speak informally with him. Concerning this first meeting, Buber wrote to the Protestant theologian Friedrich Gogarten on 9 December 1922 that the Catholic scholar welcomed the opportunity to speak with the Jewish scholar, and yet in the following weeks (apparently in an exchange of letters) Guardini seemingly backed away from Buber. In Buber's words: "I have also met Guardini at the lecture which I heard. In our conversation he drew close to me, however subsequently withdrew to the distance of [an] assured sense of church."[10]

In the spring of 1923, Buber invited Guardini to a Jewish-Christian dialogue in Frankfurt am Main, and, although Guardini replied that he would attend, it is not clear that he in fact did so. Given his introverted personality and his habit of not attending conferences, Guardini's possible absence is not surprising. In any case, Guardini thanked Buber for the invitation and praised his book, *I-Thou* (1923). He wrote: "I have been reading your book for a long time. I am filled with respect, for it is well done. Perhaps I will come [to the conference in order] to tell you what I have questions about. However, these [questions] are entirely within my positive regard [for your work]."[11]

It is not known whether Guardini found an opportunity to discuss *I-Thou* with Buber. It is clear, however, that the Catholic theologian incorporated the Jewish scholar's insights concerning the relational character of personal existence into his theological anthropology and his understanding of divine revelation.[12] Indeed, Guardini cast much of his theology within the categories of dialogical personalism, which he learned in part from Buber.[13] For example, in *The World and the Person,* which originally appeared in 1939, Guardini developed the theme that a human being "does not exist as an enclosed block of reality or a self-sufficient figure evolving from within, but rather exists for that which he [or she] encounters from without."[14] Seventeen years earlier in *I-Thou,* Buber wrote: "In the beginning is the relation—as the category of being, as readiness, as a form that reaches out to be filled, as a model of the soul; the *a priori* of relation; *the innate you.*"[15] Further, in forming their respective ideas on the relational character of human life, both scholars judiciously drew on German phenomenology, especially the work of Martin Heidegger.[16]

Buber and Guardini continued to exchange correspondence into the late 1920s. In 1928 they agreed to hold a joint lecture, titled "Religion and Authority: Form and Freedom," at Stuttgart's Jüdisches Lehrhaus. For an unknown reason Guardini withdrew, and his friend Professor Herman Hefele of the University of Tübingen spoke in his place.[17] It remains unclear whether Buber and Guardini communicated with each other as the Weimar Republic ended and the Third Reich began. To be sure, they had increasingly less contact with each other during the mid-1930s. For the first five years of Hitler's tyranny, Buber labored to strengthen German Jews' spiritual and moral resources, and he moved to Jerusalem after the *Kristallnacht* (9–10 November 1938).[18] Guardini—who began teaching at the University of Berlin in 1923, thereby becoming the university's first Catholic theologian—voiced no support for Hitler's National Socialist government, although a few Catholic theologians publicly endorsed the Third Reich in the summer of 1933. In 1935, he published a sharp critique of Alfred Rosenberg's racist ideology and the neopagan German Faith Movement.[19] From this point on, Guardini was followed by Nazi agents, and, in early 1939, was dismissed from his professorship by the Reich because he taught a "worldview" incompatible with the Nazi *Weltanschauung*.[20]

GUARDINI'S OUTREACH TO BUBER

After the war, Guardini took a new stance toward Judaism in general and Martin Buber in particular. At the request of the German Bishops' Conference, he produced a new translation of the Hebrew Psalms, *Deutscher Psalter* (1950). Also, he wrote a book of meditations on the Psalms, titled *The Wisdom of the Psalms,* that appeared in German in 1963. One other expression of Guardini's new stance toward Judaism occurred during his last years. In his retirement, he began to rethink his theology in order to recognize the validity of the Jewish faith.[21] Guardini's new effort to appreciate Judaism manifested itself, in particular, in his relationship with Martin Buber. In 1952, Martin Buber and Romano Guardini renewed their scholarly friendship. But now, for the first time, the initiative came from Guardini, who from this time on found occasions to reach out to the Jewish scholar.

In the late 1940s and early 1950s, as the German people were rebuilding their society and participating in the Allies' program of denazification, there arose the question of Germans' "collective guilt."[22]

Asked to speak on this topic, Guardini gave a public lecture on 23 May 1952 at the University of Tübingen. In his paper, "Responsibility: Thoughts on the Jewish Question," he argued that Germans needed to seek reconciliation with Jews.[23] Why? Such an action was necessary not only to make amends to the Jewish people, but also so that the German people could overcome the evil that had eroded their personal character.[24]

Guardini explained that if Western civilization's most creative figures—"Planck and Helmholtz; Mommsen and the brothers Grimm; Goethe and Hölderlin; Mozart and J. S. Bach; Leibnitz and Pascal; Raphael and Erwin von Steinbach; Gottfried von Strassburg and Dante; Augustine and Plato, Aeschylus, Heraclitus, and Homer"—were brought to Auschwitz, they would be horrified and ask, "Where at the time was conscience? Where was honor? Indeed, where was—if we may understand the word to mean more than mere conceptual work—reason?" In response, it would have to be said: "Here something has come out of the dark underpinnings of human beings: the barbarian, the animal in the human being." Moreover, this sinister force gained strength through sophisticated human technology. As a result, "something has come about which until then had not yet occurred: the unity of the inhuman and the machine."[25] And, toward what end? The goal was the destruction of Jews and, hence, the violation of a sacred value within Western civilization: the dignity of the person. The Nazi program of extermination "fundamentally obliterates the basis of every ethical judgment, namely the person."[26] Since National Socialism called into question a primary conviction within Western civilization, it threatened the entire fabric of our society, in particular, our prized humanism. What then should Germans do after Auschwitz? First, they must honestly and openly admit what occurred. Further, instead of dwelling on their collective guilt, they must recognize their solidarity with and moral responsibility to the Jews. In following this course of action, Germans would, Guardini averred, once again act as persons. They would reclaim and strengthen the reality of personal existence that Adolf Hitler had deliberately set out to destroy.

In giving this lecture, Guardini took a relatively bold step in publicly challenging voices that either denied Germans' moral responsibility for the Nazi leaders' actions or urged silence regarding the Shoah. Politically speaking, this statement meant that Guardini concurred with Germany's Chancellor Konrad Adenauer, and, in concrete terms, that he supported the proposal that Germans should pay reparations to the Jewish people.[27] This proposal was eventually adopted as a national policy by the Federal Republic of Germany.

Shortly after delivering "Responsibility: Thoughts on the Jewish Question," Guardini sent a copy of it to Martin Buber in Jerusalem. In reply, Buber wrote to Guardini on 12 December 1952 that he was deeply moved by Guardini's lecture. He explained that "[w]hile reading it, I noticed that something had changed for me. It was again possible for me to speak publicly in Germany."[28] Indeed, from this point on—despite criticism from some Jewish quarters—Buber returned to Germany for visits, lectures, and awards.[29]

Guardini's new stance toward Martin Buber showed itself again in 1953. In the previous year, the German Book Association bestowed its prestigious Peace Prize upon Guardini—the prize which in 1951 it had given to Albert Schweitzer. Then, on 17 June 1953, the German Book Association announced its decision to award its Peace Prize to Martin Buber, which it then gave to him in a ceremony on 27 September.[30] Buber chose to receive this award, even though his decision drew an angry response from some Jews.[31] Romano Guardini deliberately joined Buber for the award ceremony in Frankfurt am Main's Church of Saint Paul.[32]

Immediately after the announcement in June 1953 that Buber was recipient of the Peace Prize, Guardini contacted Buber and invited him to give a lecture in Munich in October 1953. Declining the invitation, Buber explained in a letter to Guardini that he had a full schedule during the weeks after receiving the award, but he would gladly visit with Guardini in August when he would be staying in Munich for a short period.[33] This informal meeting occurred in Guardini's apartment on 9 August. Afterward, Guardini commented on the visit in his diary: "Martin Buber was here today for tea. He will [soon] receive the Peace Prize from the German Book Association, has spoken at different universities, and wishes to rest somewhat from now until the conferral of the Prize in Frankfurt. It was lovely to be together with him. He is wonderfully informed, wise and venerable."[34]

In these three sentences Guardini voiced his respect and affection for Buber and, as he did so, he spontaneously moved on to ask questions related to his own Christian belief. In his diary, he wrote: "What keeps someone in the [Christian] faith? What brings it about that someone, as in a breath, all at once no longer understands, so that everything is gone? From time to time an anxiety burdens me. . . . We are capable of understanding so little. . . ."³⁵

This entry suggests that Buber's Judaism and Buber himself challenged Guardini to consider anew the character of the Christian faith and its relationship to the Jewish faith. He had seemingly sensed that he and Buber shared a profound spiritual kinship, even though they professed formally distinct beliefs. At the very least, Buber's religious belief had called into question Guardini's implicit views of Judaism.

At the time, however, Guardini did not dwell on the questions that occurred to him in light of Buber's visit. In fact, in his diary, he immediately jumped to thoughts about moving to an apartment near the Nymphenburg. Nevertheless, Guardini did not forget his meeting with Buber and the questions that it raised in him. Beginning in June 1957, he set out to reread the Hebrew Bible, and by February 1958, he was making his way through the Second Book of Samuel. In his diary he wrote: "I am reading 2 Samuel in the translation by Buber. By means of it, everything attains a new forcefulness."³⁶ One cannot help but suspect that Guardini was rereading the scriptures in part because they were newly translated into German by Martin Buber and Franz Rosenzweig.³⁷ At the same time, he was likely reflecting anew about the common elements of Jewish and Christian beliefs and considering how to rework his theology so that it would explicitly acknowledge the validity of Judaism.

Throughout the late 1950s, Guardini and Buber remained in touch with each other. In the autumn of 1958, as Guardini was teaching a course on the philosophy of language, he received a request from Buber for a copy of his course's syllabus. Guardini immediately sent the Jewish philosopher this material along with a lengthy letter in which he clarified some aspects of his syllabus.³⁸

A decade after the Peace Prize of the German Book Association, a second distinction was awarded to both Buber and Guardini. In 1962 Prince Bernhard of the Netherlands conferred the Erasmus Prize upon Guardini for his work on behalf of Christian humanism.³⁹ And, in 1963 Prince Bernhard bestowed the Erasmus Prize upon Martin Buber for his work on behalf of Judaism and humanism.⁴⁰ (We get some sense of the importance of this award when we recall that the prince bestowed this honor also upon Austria's former president Adolf Schärf in 1958, the philosopher Karl Jaspers and the French statesman Robert Schuman in 1959, and the painters Marc Chagall and Oskar Kokoschka in 1960.[41])

Finally, it should be noted that Guardini showed his great respect for Martin Buber by making a substantial monetary gift to the State of Israel in 1963. On the occasion of the Jewish philosopher's eighty-fifth birthday, the Catholic theologian was among the German benefactors who donated funds so that the Martin Buber Forest could be planted in Israel's Kibbutz Hazorea. Moreover, although he rarely engaged in public projects, Guardini also assisted the fund-raising committee in locating donors.[42] Accompanying the gift to the State of Israel was a public statement that Guardini put in a telegram to Buber on 12 February 1963:

TREE DONATION TO ISRAEL IN HONOR OF MARTIN BUBER

Martin Buber reached his eighty-fifth birthday on February 8, 1963.

This fact makes a claim on our attention, for Buber is a man to whom we owe a debt of gratitude. In our day when material things have become overpowering, he has thought about the reality of the spirit. Against the danger which threatens us in the impersonality of machines and organizations, he has called to consciousness the significance of the person and personal relationships. In a time which experienced the absurd [sic] event of the persecution of the Jews, he has given us a new translation of the Hebrew Bible out of which the sound of the ancient revelation impacts us with fresh originality. He accomplished this difficult project by working initially with friend Franz Rosenzweig and then alone.

Martin Buber is a man of ideas and words. Academic custom usually requires that we honor such a person with a book of essays written by prominent scholars. However, those who join in this tribute are of the mind that it is better to honor this man by means of something living. We agree that in Israel where he now resides trees should be planted. And, not only one tree but a grove of trees should spring up.

Perhaps this idea may strike someone as a romantic one. If so, this person should remember that from the outset the tree has been the symbol of life and, to be sure, of life that perdures. A noble tree has always had the character of a memorial which abides through generations and awakens remembrances.

This is no artistically contrived gesture. Rather, the symbol of the tree belongs to that which arises out of the essence of things and is therefore always valued. Also, a tree attains an especially powerful presence when, as is the case here, it is planted in a land which is being made fruitful through hard work.

Thus all of those who have signed below wanted to honor Martin Buber by their donations [to the Martin Buber Forest].[43]

AN UNFINISHED ENDEAVOR

The change in Guardini's stance toward Buber, thanks to Buber's initiative, is remarkable in itself and also anticipated the transformation in attitude to which the Second Vatican Council has called all Christians. A glance at Guardini's prewar and postwar writings reveals that Guardini had begun to modify his view of Judaism in the 1950s so that it would become congruent with his lecture, "Responsibility: Thoughts on the Jewish Question," and also with his respect for Martin Buber. The unfinished character of Guardini's reconsideration of Judaism is evident in his books *The Lord* and *The Humanity of Christ*.

The Lord appeared in Germany in 1937 and immediately became a best-seller among German Catholics. Consisting of "meditations" upon the life and significance of Jesus of Nazareth, it presented Jesus as the one who was sent by God to bring about a new relationship between God and the human family; this Jesus is the true savior *(Heilbringer),* whose divine authority far surpasses the earthly authority of any human being, even of charismatic political leaders. In other words, the book communicated a covert criticism of Germany's *Führer,* Adolf Hitler—a criticism that was not lost upon German readers. Unfortunately, *The Lord* also expressed the view that God's revelation in Jesus had displaced God's covenant with Abraham and the people of Israel. In Guardini's words: "But the Jewish people did not believe. They did not change their hearts, so the kingdom did not come as it was to have come."[44] Further: "The failure of the Jewish people to accept Christ was the second Fall, the import of which can be fully grasped only in connection with the first."[45] And, when Christians see Jews, "[t]he whole heritage of sin with its harshness and distortion looms at us.... Their wisdom is both divine gift and fruit of long human experience; knowledge, cleverness, correctness. They examine, weigh, differentiate, doubt; and when the Promised One comes and prophecy is fulfilled, ... they cling to the past with its human traditions ... and their great hour passes them by."[46] Sadly, *The Lord* reiterated the distorted view of Judaism that had evolved in the church over many centuries and that fueled anti-Semitism. In particular, it sustained the misconceptions that God had revoked his covenant with the Jewish people and, by implication, that Christians need not defend the human dignity and civil rights of their Jewish neighbors.[47]

The Humanity of Christ appeared in German in 1958, hence approximately twenty years after *The Lord*. It shed light on the human qualities of Jesus while also insisting that he was an absolutely unique individual. Although this book was warmly received by its readers, it was overshadowed by the writings of a new generation of Catholic theologians such as Yves Congar and Karl Rahner. In any case, it is noteworthy that *The Humanity of Christ* did not state that God had withdrawn his covenant with the chosen people of Israel. Rather, it portrayed Jesus as a faithful Jew who "firmly upheld the Law and held scrupulously to the place which his Father had assigned him in history." According to Guardini, Jesus "claimed for himself the promises that had been made to David."[48] In other words, this book manifested a change in Guardini's thought about Judaism. The Catholic theologian had rejected the idea that Christianity had somehow displaced Judaism in God's eyes. At the same time, Guardini was apparently searching for a new way to understand the relationship between Judaism and Christianity. In this regard, *The Humanity of Christ* tried to convey some form of a fulfillment theory. In Guardini's words: "What the Jewish people should always have done, but actually did so seldom, i.e., ascend by faith above immediate, tangible nature to the realm of the mind and spirit so as to become what God desired them to be, had finally been accomplished in Christ."[49] Unfortunately, this statement gave a simplistic, negative assessment of Judaism. Nevertheless, it remained vague concerning the character of Jesus' realization of God's covenant with the Jewish people. This lack of clarity in *The Humanity of Christ,* joined with the deliberate absence of the view of displacement, indicates that Guardini was rethinking his ideas about Judaism and about the relationship between the Jewish and Christian faiths.[50]

In summary, Guardini had changed his thought about Judaism from 1937, when he published *The Lord,* to 1958, when *The Humanity of Christ* appeared. But he had not thought through his view of how Jesus had fulfilled God's promises to Israel by the time the later book went to press. This change in Guardini's thought should be primarily attributed to Martin Buber. It was Buber who time and again reached out to Guardini during the 1920s so that a scholarly friendship came to exist between the two men. In light of this "I-Thou" relationship, Guardini could not retain his inadequate understanding of Judaism, especially after the Shoah. Intellectual and moral integrity required that he revise his characterizations of Judaism and also his theoretical formulations of the relationship between Judaism and Christianity. Guardini was not alone among Christians in rethinking his view of Judaism. What happened to Guardini occurred as well among countless other Christians during the 1950s, thereby adding to the spiritual fermentation that produced Vatican II's wholly unexpected breakthrough in *Nostra Aetate.*

BEYOND *NOSTRA AETATE*

When the Second Vatican Council began on 11 October 1962, Martin Buber was eighty-four years old and Romano Guardini was seventy-eight years old, and when the council ended on 8 December 1965, Buber was dead, and Guardini was entering a period of illness that led to his death in 1968. Although both men followed the council's deliberations, neither of them was well enough to contribute directly to the council. Yet, they had already helped set the stage for the council's work on *Nostra Aetate.* The maturation of their personal ties foreshadowed the development of the relationship between Catholicism and Judaism that Vatican II affirmed and advanced. Today, Catholics are aware that, for historical, moral, and theological reasons, it is wrong to blame Jews for Jesus' death, and also that they must respect God's abiding covenant with the Jewish people. Moreover, they realize that they must continue to learn from Judaism, that they must endorse the existence of the State of Israel, and that they must safeguard the dignity and civil rights of Jews around the world.[51]

This review of the professional friendship between Buber and Guardini yields two thoughts on ways to improve Jewish-Christian relations. First, Jews and Christians must work as scholarly colleagues, inspired both by Buber's persistence in communicating with Guardini and also by Guardini's ability to change and act in a new way toward Buber. In their respective writings, both theologians crafted profound statements on the meaning of personal encounters. Each of them held that if our lives are to be journeys toward truth, then we must look for opportunities when we can deepen our "I-Thou" relationships with God and one another.[52] Yet, as we have seen, Buber and Guardini not only wrote about the character of personal encounter, but they also entered into a professional association that changed each of them. Thanks to Buber, Guardini came to think and act in new ways with regard to Buber, Judaism, and Christian faith. And, thanks to Guardini, Buber dared to renew his ties with intellectual and cultural organizations in Germany after the war. Buber and Guardini have taught us, therefore, that Jews and Christians must deliberately enter into an interreligious dialogue that will enrich both faiths. (This lesson is corroborated by the impact that Jews made upon the life and thought of Pope John XXIII and Pope John Paul II.[53])

Second, seeking guidance from their Jewish associates, Christians must revise their views of the relationship between Christian belief and Jewish belief. The inattentiveness of Guardini and other German scholars to the persecution of the Jews stemmed, in part, from the pervasive influence of the idea that God had revoked his covenant with Israel. In recent years, scholars have rightly begun to develop new theologies of Judaism and of the relationship between the Jewish and Christian faiths.[54] In this effort, Catholics are building on Vatican II's statement in *Nostra Aetate* that "the Jews remain very dear to God, for the sake of the patriarchs, since God does not take back the gifts he bestowed or the choice he made" (no. 4).

NOTES

An earlier version of this paper was presented at the conference of the Holocaust Education Foundation on 2 November 1966 at the University of Notre Dame. I am grateful to Professors Lawrence Baron, Susannah Heschel, Michael Phayer, and Michael Signer for their constructive criticisms of drafts of this paper. Also, I am indebted to Hanna Barbara Gerl-Falkowitz, Hans Mercker, and Arno Schilson for advising me on Romano Guardini's thoughts.

1. See Austin Flannery, ed., *Vatican Council II* (New York: Costello Publishing Company, 1996), pp. 569–74. On *Nostra Aetate,* see Pynchas Brener, Eugene Fisher, and Johannes Cardinal Willebrands in *Christian-Jewish Relations* 18 (1985), *passim.* Michael B. McGarry, *Christology after Auschwitz* (New York: Paulist Press, 1977), pp. 22–5.

2. See Otto Pesch, *Das Zweite Vatikanische Konzil* (Würzburg: Echter, 1993), pp. 292–303; Donald Nicholl, "Other Religions *(Nostra Aetate),*" in *Modern Catholicism,* ed. Adrian Hastings (New York: Oxford University Press, 1991), pp. 126–34; John M. Oesterreicher, "Declaration on the Relationship of the Church to Non-Christian Religions," in *Commentary on the Documents of Vatican II,* ed. Herbert Vorgrimler (New York: Herder and Herder, 1969), pp. 1–136. For other sources, see McGarry, *Christology after Auschwitz,* p. 23 n. 17.

3. See Donald J. Dietrich, *God and Humanity in Auschwitz* (New Brunswick, N.J.: Transaction, 1995); Frank M. Buscher and Michael Phayer, "German Catholic Bishops and the Holocaust, 1940–1952," *German Studies Review* 11 (October 1988): 463–85.

4. On *Mit brennender Sorge,* see Heinz Hürten, *Deutsche Katholiken 1918–1945* (Paderborn: Ferdinand Schöningh, 1992), pp. 370–9. On Pius XI's draft, see Georges Passelecq and Bernard Suchecky, *The Hidden Encyclical of Pius XI,* trans. Steven Randall (New York: Harcourt, Brace and Company, 1997); Donald J. Dietrich, "Catholic Theologians in Hitler's Reich," *Journal of Church and State* 29 (winter 1987): 19–45, see especially 32–33; Dietrich, *Catholic Citizens in the Third Reich* (New Brunswick, N.J.: Transaction, 1988). On the International Conference of 1947, see Geoffrey Wigoder, *Jewish-Christian Relations since the Second World War* (Manchester, England: Manchester University Press, 1988).

5. On Jewish-Christian relations, see Katherine T. Hargrove, ed., *Seeds of Reconciliation* (North Richland Hills: BIBAL Press, 1996); Hans Küng, *Judaism,* trans. John Bowden (New York: Crossroad, 1992); Eugene Fisher, A. James Rudin, and Marc H. Tanenbaum, eds., *Twenty Years of Jewish-Christian Relations* (New York: Paulist Press, 1986); John Pawlikowski, *Jesus and the Theology of Israel* (Wilmington, Del.: Michael Glazier, 1989); Pawlikowski, "Judentum und Christentum," *Theologische Realenzyklopädie* (1988) 17: 386–403; Leon Klenicki, ed., *Toward a Theological Encounter* (New York: Paulist Press, 1986).

6. See Maurice Friedman, *Martin Buber's Life and Work: The Early Years, 1878–1923* (New York: E. P. Dutton, 1981); Friedman, *Martin Buber's Life and Work: The Middle Years, 1923–1945* (New York: E. P. Dutton,

1983); Friedman, *Martin Buber's Life and Work: The Later Years, 1945–1965* (New York: E. P. Dutton, 1984); Christian Schütz, "Buber, Martin (1878–1965)," *Theologische Realenzyklopädie* (1981) 8: 253–8.

    7. See Robert A. Krieg, *Romano Guardini: A Precursor of Vatican II* (Notre Dame: University of Notre Dame Press, 1997); Krieg, ed., *Romano Guardini: Proclaiming the Sacred in a Modern World* (Chicago: Liturgy Training Publications, 1995); Hanna Barbara Gerl, *Romano Guardini 1885–1968* (Mainz: Matthias Grünewald, 1985).

    8. See Friedman, *Martin Buber's Life and Work: The Later Years,* p. 111.

    9. See Gerl, *Romano Guardini,* p. 134 n. 40; Anton Menke, "Das Gegenstands-Verständnis personaler Pädagogik-Systematik erörtert im Anschluß an Martin Buber und Romano Guardini als Beitrag zur Diskussion um den Begriff des 'Bildungsgutes'" (Univ. of Mainz: Doctoral Dissertation, 1964).

    10. This letter is quoted in Gerl, *Romano Guardini,* p. 133 n. 38. See also Haim Gordon and Jochanan Bloch, *Martin Buber: A Centenary Volume* (New York: KTAV Publishing House, 1984), p. 446; Martin Buber, *Briefwechsel,* vol. 2 (Heidelberg: L. Schneider, 1973), no. 114.

    11. See Gerl, *Romano Guardini,* pp. 133–4.

    12. See Donald J. Moore, "Martin Buber and Christian Thought," in *Martin Buber and the Human Sciences,* ed. Maurice Friedman (Albany: State University of New York Press, 1996), pp. 93–106, see especially 98. On Guardini's understanding of the human person, see Robert A. Krieg, "Romano Guardini's Theological Anthropology," *Theological Studies* 59 (1998): 405–25; Alfons Knoll, *Glaube und Kultur bei Romano Guardini* (Paderborn: Ferdinand Schöningh, 1993), pp. 338–73; Arno Schilson, *Perspektiven theologischer Erneuerung* (Düsseldorf: Patmos, 1986), pp. 158–96.

    13. Guardini also drew on the work of Ferdinand Ebner and Emil Brunner. See Bernhard Langemeyer, *Der dialogische Personalismus in der evangelischen und katholischen Theologie der Gegenwart* (Paderborn: Ferdinand Schöningh, 1963), especially pp. 247–64.

    14. Romano Guardini, *The World and the Person,* trans. Stella Lange (Chicago: Henry Regnery, 1965), p. viii.

    15. Martin Buber, *I-Thou,* trans. Walter Kaufmann (New York: Scribner's, 1970), p. 78.

    16. On Buber's use of Heidegger's thought, see Friedman, *Martin Buber's Life and Work: The Middle Years,* pp. 93, 274–77; Friedman, *Martin Buber's Life and Work: The Later Years,* pp. 51–52, 115–17, 138, 162–66. On Guardini's scholarly association with Heidegger, see Gerl, *Romano Guardini,* pp. 64, 87, 134, 144, 331, 359–60.

    17. See Gerl, *Romano Guardini,* p. 298, where she cites Martin Buber, *Briefwechsel aus sieben Jahrzehnten,* vol. 2, p. 326.

18. See Jerry D. Lawritson, "Martin Buber and the Shoah," in *Martin Buber and the Human Sciences,* pp. 295–309.

19. See Romano Guardini, "Der Heiland," *Die Schildgenossen* 14 (1935): 97–116. In 1946, Guardini expanded the essay into his book *Der Heilbringer in Mythos, Offenbarung und Politik* (Mainz: Matthias Grünewald, 1979).

20. For eyewitness accounts of life in Berlin for Guardini's students, see Heinz R. Kuhn, "Fires in the Night: Germany 1920–1950," and Regina Kuehn, "Romano Guardini in Berlin," in *Romano Guardini: Proclaiming the Sacred,* pp. 1–14, 87–91.

21. See Romano Guardini, *Theologische Briefe an einen Freund* (Paderborn: Ferdinand Schöningh, 1976), pp. 59–61.

22. Manfred Malzahn, *Germany 1945–1949: A Source Book* (New York: Routledge, 1991), pp. 90–2; Klaus Schatz, *Zwischen Säkularisation und Zweiten Vatikanum* (Frankfurt: Josef Knecht, 1986), pp. 287–8.

23. See Romano Guardini, *Verantwortung: Gedanken zur jüdischen Frage* (Munich: Kösel, 1952).

24. Six years earlier, on 4 November 1945, Guardini gave an address at the University of Munich in praise of Hans and Sophie Scholl and the others in the "White Rose." They had been executed by the SS on 22 February 1943 for "conspiracy to commit high treason" by writing and distributing literature in opposition to the Nazi state and the war. Guardini extolled them for accepting the "weight of personal existence." During the 1950s the University of Munich gave this text to all matriculating students. See Romano Guardini, *Die Waage des Daseins* (Tübingen: Rainer Wunderlich, 1946); reprinted in Carl Georg Heise et al., eds., *Deutsche Stimmen 1945–1946* (Hamburg: Maximilian-Gesellschaft, 1948); Hermann Vinke, *The Short Life of Sophie Scholl,* trans. Hedwig Pachter (New York: Harper and Row, 1984).

25. Guardini, *Verantwortung,* p. 17.

26. Ibid., p. 21.

27. See Kurt Hoffman, "Portrait of Father Guardini," *Commonweal* 60 (17 September 1954): 575–7.

28. See Friedman, *Martin Buber's Life and Work: The Later Years,* p. 111. This letter is available in Archiv no. 870 at the Romano Guardini Archives at the Katholische Akademie in Bayern, Munich. I am grateful to the archive's director, Hans Mercker, for making this letter and other documents available to me.

29. See Maurice Friedman, "Martin Buber's 'Narrow Ridge,'" in *Martin Buber and the Human Sciences,* pp. 3–25, see especially 11.

30. See Martin Buber, "Genuine Dialogue and the Possibilities of Peace," in Buber, *Pointing the Way,* ed. Maurice Friedman (New York: Harper and Brothers, 1957), pp. 232–9.

31. See Michael Keren, "Martin Buber's Impact on Political Dialogue in Israel," in *Martin Buber and the Human Sciences,* pp. 283–94, see especially 287.

32. See Gerl, *Romano Guardini,* p. 354; Friedman, *Martin Buber's Life and Work: The Later Years,* p. 118.

33. See Buber's letter (13 July 1953) to Guardini, Archiv no. 870, Romano Guardini Archives, Katholische Akademie in Bayern.

34. Romano Guardini, *Wahrheit des Denkens und Wahrheit des Tuns* (Paderborn: Ferdinand Schöningh, 1985), p. 50.

35. Ibid., p. 50.

36. Ibid., p. 108.

37. On the translation of the Hebrew Bible into German by Martin Buber and Franz Rosenzweig, see Klaus Reichert, "ZEIT IST'S: Die Bibelübersetzung von Franz Rosenzweig und Martin Buber im Kontext," in *Trigon 6,* ed. Guardini Stiftung (Berlin: Dreieck Verlag, 1997), pp. 163–90; Norbert Lohfink, "Begegnung mit Bubers Bibelübersetzung," *Stimmen der Zeit* 169 (1961–1962): 444–54.

38. Guardini's letter to Buber is dated 22 November 1958; see Archiv no. 871, Romano Guardini Archives, Katholische Akademie in Bayern.

39. See Romano Guardini, "Europa—Wirklichkeit und Aufgabe," in Guardini, *Sorge um den Menschen,* vol. 1 (Mainz: Matthias Grünewald, 1988), pp. 238–53.

40. See Martin Buber, "Believing Humanism," in Buber, *A Believing Humanism,* trans. with an introduction and commentary by Maurice Friedman (New York: Simon and Schuster, 1969), pp. 117–22.

41. On the Erasmus Prize *(Praemium Erasmianum),* see *Meyers Enzyklopädisches Lexikon* (1977) 19:193.

42. See Friedman, *Martin Buber's Life and Work: The Later Years,* p. 397; Nahum N. Glatzer and Paul Mendes-Flohr, eds., *The Letters of Martin Buber,* trans. Richard and Clara Winston and Harry Zahn (New York: Schocken, 1991), p. 657.

43. In the Romano Guardini Archives, the short telegram is located in Archiv no. 871 and the statement is located in Archiv no. 1309. Soon after writing this statement, Guardini wrote at greater length concerning the tree as a symbol of life; see Romano Guardini, "Die Bäume von Isola Vicentina" (12 October 1963) in Guardini, *Stationen und Rückblicke* (Würzburg: Werkbund Verlag, 1965), pp. 35–40.

44. Romano Guardini, *The Lord,* trans. Elinor Castendyk Briefs (Chicago: Henry Regnery, 1954), p. 40.

45. Ibid., p. 98.

46. Ibid., p. 268.

47. On the biblical witness to the permanence of God's covenant with

the Jewish people, see Norbert Lohfink, *The Covenant Never Revoked,* trans. John J. Scullion (New York: Paulist Press, 1991). It is unfortunate that, in recommending Guardini's *The Lord* to today's readers, Cardinal Joseph Ratzinger has not noted the book's limitations, including its inaccurate views of God's covenant with the Jewish people; see J. Ratzinger, "Guardini on Christ in Our Century," *Crisis* 14 (1996): 14–15.

48. Romano Guardini, *The Humanity of Christ,* trans. Ronald Walls (New York: Pantheon Books, 1964), p. 78; see also pp. 10–3.

49. Ibid., p. 79.

50. See Romano Guardini, *Jesus Christus: Meditations,* trans. Peter White (Chicago: Henry Regnery, 1957), pp. 20–21, 59–62, 93, 99.

51. For documentation, see Pope John Paul II, *Spiritual Pilgrimage: Texts on Jews and Judaism 1979–1995,* ed. Eugene J. Fisher and Leon Klenicki (New York: Crossroad, 1995); Fisher and Klenicki, *Catechism of the Catholic Church* (Liguori, Mo.: Liguori Publications, 1994), paragraphs 574–600 and 839–48; Helga Croner, ed., *Stepping Stones to Further Jewish-Christian Relations* (New York: Stimulus Books, 1977); Helga Croner, *More Stepping Stones to Jewish-Christian Relations* (New York: Stimulus Books, 1985). An invaluable resource is the journal *SIDIC (Service International de Documentation Judéo-Chrétienne).* In light of the advances in Jewish-Christian relations, many Jews and Christians were rightly disappointed with the document "We Remember: A Reflection on the Shoah," which the Vatican's Commission for Religious Relations with the Jews issued on 16 March 1998; see *The Pope Speaks* 43 (July/August 1998): 243–50.

52. See Buber, *I-Thou,* pp. 77, 83; Guardini, *The World and the Person,* pp. 126–9, 141–3.

53. See Carl Bernstein and Marco Politi, *His Holiness* (New York: Doubleday, 1996), pp. 30–2; Pesch, *Das Zweite Vatikanische Konzil,* pp. 292–3; Pinchas E. Lapide, *The Last Three Popes and the Jews* (London: Souvenir Press, 1967).

54. These Catholic scholars in North America include Gregory Baum, Mary Boys, Eugene Fisher, Monika Hellwig, John Oesterreicher, and John Pawlikowski. Two recent Christian efforts to find a common access to the world religions are John Macquarrie, *Mediators between Human and Divine* (New York: Continuum, 1996); Karl Josef Kuschel, *Abraham: A Sign of Hope for Jews, Christians, and Muslims,* trans. John Bowden (New York: Continuum, 1995).

III. L·E·G·A·L·I·T·Y

Ruth Bettina Birn

War Crimes Prosecutions
An Exercise in Justice? A Lesson in History?

INTRODUCTION

THE SHEER ENORMITY OF THE CRIMES COMMITTED BY NAZI GERMANY demanded atonement. While the war was still continuing, information about the Nazi crimes came slowly to the attention of the Western world. The necessity of dealing with these crimes was apparent to all political forces involved and was confirmed in a number of agreements between the Allies; starting with the Declaration of St. James in 1941, followed by the Moscow Declaration in 1942. In both, the Allies made clear their intention to see justice done. Thus, the decision to try at least the main culprits of the Nazi genocide in an international court was a logical and natural next step.[1]

The International Military Tribunal at Nuremberg tried only twenty-two accused, representing the higher levels of the Nazi government. The military prosecutions following the IMT at Nuremberg selected groups of perpetrators that were chosen from the most criminally involved of the Nazi state and party authorities. It fell to the national courts in Germany and the rest of Europe to try the majority of Nazi cases.

National prosecutions of Nazi crimes took place in a variety of settings. The European members of the Allies conducted their own prosecutions, outside and apart from Nuremberg. In countries liberated from Axis occupation, occupiers and indigenous collaborators were brought to justice. The question of collaborators, in particular, was a hotly contested legal and political issue. Finally, in the perpetrator countries, prosecuting Nazi crimes was an act of self-cleansing, a manifestation of new and changed political values, as represented by the new political forces in power who, in part, were former victims of the Nazis.

Critics have argued that the results in Nazi trials in West Germany are highly unsatisfactory and were influenced by continuing identification with Nazi ideology or German nationalism by the German judiciary.[2] Through a comparison with Dutch trials, with a judiciary consisting of immaculate antifascists, Christian Rueters, the Dutch jurist and editor of a series of verdicts in Nazi cases, cast doubt on this argument. He found that the results in Germany and Holland are very similar and concluded that the cause is the nature and function of criminal law.[3] As the history of Nazi prosecutions has demonstrated, without changing the courts' structures and rules to account for these exceptional problems, a fraction of the offences and offenders will be prosecuted, while politicians will nonetheless be able to disassociate themselves from their responsibility.

A closer analysis of Nazi trials reveals how commonly held beliefs and political views, based on perceptions of history, influenced court decisions beyond the easily discernable bad intentions to lead to bad results.[4] There are two sides to this process. Not only does history impact court findings, the perception of historical facts can be changed by court cases. Nuremberg has already proven this as the mass of documents presented as evidence has dominated historiography for some time.[5] In the following discussion, the suitability of judicial procedures for dealing with state-sponsored crimes will be considered in the context of the influence and shifting of historical images. The discussion examines three different geographic settings: the Soviet Union, Germany, and North America.[6]

THE SOVIET UNION

The first prosecution for crimes committed by the Nazis took place in Krasnodar, Russia, in the summer of 1943.[7] Soviet authorities prosecuted non-German auxiliaries of the *Einsatzkommando 10a*. A trial in Charkov followed in the fall of 1943. While the extent to which the Nazi elites were troubled by the general announcements by the Allies is not as clear, the Soviet prosecutions had an impact on the top level of the SS. After the Charkov trial, the feeling that the day of reckoning might be close began to spread. When HSSPF Heinrich Schmauser, in whose district Auschwitz was located and who was locally the highest person responsible in the SS and police hierarchy for the death factory, disappeared one day in early 1945 and was rumored to have fallen into the hands of the Red Army, SS leaders exchanged gloomy predictions that Schmauser would soon appear in a "Soviet show trial."[8]

Very early in the war, the Soviet Union established "extraordinary commissions" to record the crimes committed by the Axis powers during the occupation of Soviet territory. These extraordinary commissions had the monumental task of recording statements of crimes, identifying what had been plundered and pillaged, counting the dead in mass graves, and generally recording the details of what the Nazis had done. Hard on the heels of the German retreat from Soviet territory, these reports offer a timely account of the nature and scope of the Nazi crimes committed in all regions of Nazi-occupied Soviet territory. The structure of the commissions' reports suggests that their investigations were established to produce presentable evidence. For example, protocols were taken in a painstakingly formal way; doctors and forensic specialists were present at excavations of mass graves and identified in the protocols by name and capacity. The stress on recording material losses suggests that a potential claim for reparation was one of the primary reasons behind the establishment of the commissions. While the work of the commissions was directed centrally from Moscow, the evidence recorded by these commissions offers an impressive grassroots-level reading.[9]

The Soviet Union dealt with the issue of war crimes and war losses and put structures in place to address the issue long before the other Allied nations. The efforts were guided by two motives: first, to expose the crimes committed by the Nazis to the world and punish the perpetrators, and second, to support the legitimacy of Soviet power and of communist ideology. Juxtaposed with the evil "fascist" deeds, Soviet rule was good and just and, in addition, anyone who had not supported Soviet power had collaborated with the enemy and acted out of the most despicable motives.[10]

The propagandistic and symbolic functions of Soviet Nazi trials are clearly demonstrated in three major trials that were held immediately after the war in Riga, Minsk, and Kiev. Each trial covered one of the major theaters of war and occupation, and the defendants, who were Germans and varied widely in rank, appear to have been selected to represent the various parts of the German occupation apparatus:

army, Gestapo, police, camp personnel, agriculture administration. In Riga, the highest-ranking defendant was the HSSPF Friedrich Jeckeln. In Kiev, the most prominent representative of the SS and police was the commander of the order police, Paul Scheer.[11] Some defendants are so low in rank that one can only assume they were selected to represent a certain aspect of Nazi occupation or because an admission was expected from them. Soviet authorities filmed the trials and later made documentaries of each trial. In the documentary of the Minsk trial, footage of the defendants' testimony is interspersed with footage showing the misery and hunger of the local population, corpses, burning villages, and so on. These images are in stark contrast to the footage showing the peaceful landscapes and the smiling faces of the Soviet peoples before the Nazi invasion.[12] The "showcase" character of these trials is further supported by public hangings of those condemned to death, also liberally documented on film, in photographs, and in newspapers, all depicting the final triumph of the "Soviet people" over the fascist aggressors.[13]

Were these trials "show trials," in the sense of stage-managing falsehood? Were all the confessions and frank statements obtained under torture? A comparison of the dates and times of statements recorded in these three trials suggests that the timing was carefully coordinated by Moscow. However, as Manfred Messerschmidt, in his analysis of the Minsk trial,[14] demonstrates, the defendants were given more recourse to legal means than a comparable German military court would have allowed, and their defense counsel were certainly given a wide latitude in presenting arguments on behalf of their clients. Not all accused were sentenced to death; some were acquitted. Furthermore, a review of Jeckeln's statements, every page of which he signed, confirms that he did not accept only what his interrogators put in front of him. Parts smacking of communist phraseology are crossed out. In his testimony, Jeckeln did not flinch from admitting his responsibility for the mass murder of Jews in the Baltic countries; facts that are corroborated from sources outside the Soviet sphere of influence. Moreover, his stance was in keeping with his character and his communications with Himmler just prior to the end of the war.[15] In Riga, Minsk, or Kiev immediately after the war, avoidance or denial would not work; those charged had been part of the Nazi apparatus, their wartime roles known, and the destruction they had caused visible. No one could hide behind twenty years of collective amnesia or forty years of distance; no one could deny the facts. The statements of Paul Scheer show that in this situation, given the shock and humiliation caused by the defeat, a certain soul-searching took place and in its form of expression recorded in the statements could not have been the result of KGB pressure. Scheer clearly tries to come to grips with his own role and the politics of the regime that he had been serving. Again, the way he expressed himself is almost identical to the self-reflections of SS leaders in American custody.[16]

A large number of other trials against Germans were held in the Soviet Union. Many defendants were given only summary trials, which from the Soviet perspective was dictated in part by the urgent need for forced labor to assist in the rebuilding of the country.[17] Then in 1955/56, after German Chancellor Adenauer visited Moscow and negotiated the release of the remaining German POWs, war criminals who had been sentenced by Soviet courts for their crimes were released together with ordinary German soldiers. Thus, the Soviets did precisely what they accused the Western countries of: drawing a final line at a politically convenient time.[18]

The two closely intertwined motives of punishment of crimes and legitimization of Soviet power, apparent in the trials of Germans, are also present in subsequent proceedings against Soviet citizens, who were indicted and sentenced for "betrayal of the motherland," basically high treason.[19] While this was logical within the framework of communist ideology, it was clearly unacceptable with respect to the Baltic countries that had been delivered into Stalin's hands only through his pact with Hitler. It was likewise resented in the Western Ukraine with its historically strong nationalistic tendencies. Particularly in the first few years after the war, the allegation of collaboration or betrayal of the motherland was abused by the Soviet regime to suppress any political opposition to Soviet authority.[20]

Were, then, Soviet war crimes trials just a means to suppress anti-Bolshevists? This overly simplistic view held by many North Americans is unfounded. The KGB did not habitually throw together sham cases based on a few preprepared witness statements. As a rule, particularly after the first few years when the suppression of national resistance was over, the KGB did conduct thorough investigations. Many witnesses stated that they had nothing to say, which was accepted and was as carefully recorded as everything else. Of course, there is no doubt that the KGB used means to obtain confessions that would be considered unlawful or unacceptable by current Western standards. But does that mean they were necessarily false? When one matches these statements with information from Western sources, such as survivor statements and documents, the facts stated in the majority of them are borne out.[21]

GERMANY

A discussion of German prosecutions over a period of fifty years requires a differentiation between phases, reflecting structural and political conditions. In 1952 when the Allies finally withdrew from the programs for identifying Nazi perpetrators, investigations and prosecutions could be initiated only by victims making complaints with the police. This limited investigations to crimes committed in concentration camps and ghettos where there was a longer period of confrontation between victim and perpetrator. As a result a large proportion of Nazi crimes were excluded, in particular those committed by mobile killing units, like the *Einsatzkommandos,* or by police battalions during antipartisan warfare.

In the immediate postwar phase, many survivors tried to locate torturers and murderers in postwar Germany.[22] Sometimes authorities were informed after perpetrators bragged about their deeds. In one case someone had shown to acquaintances photos of executions of Jews and the stolen valuables of murdered Jews kept in his apartment.[23] More systematic efforts were started; for example, the Council of Liberated Jews in the American Zone collected statements in DP camps identifying perpetrators and filed complaints with German authorities. The work was complicated because many victims were still traumatized by their experiences and were incapable of confronting the past so soon, there was a very haphazard knowledge of the facts, and the conditions of life in postwar Germany were chaotic. Public transportation frequently did not function, thus preventing witnesses from attending court to testify, which resulted in acquittals.[24]

In 1958 fundamental changes occurred as a result of a civil proceeding in Ulm. Bernhard Fischer-Schweder, the former head of the police department of Memel (now Klaipeda, Lithuania), had sued the government for readmission into the public service. Like others, he felt safe from prosecution, given the cold war and political mood in Germany during the 1950s. A newspaper report about the case caused witnesses to come forward and identify Fischer-Schweder as a major figure in the Holocaust in Lithuania. During the course of the investigation it became apparent to the government that, contrary to popular belief, only the tip of the iceberg of Nazi crimes had become visible in German courts.[25]

As a consequence, the Central Agency for the Investigation of National-Socialist Crimes was established in 1958 in Ludwigsburg, Germany, to investigate Nazi crimes in a systematic way. The Central Agency collected witness statements, and evaluated original historical documents and materials found in German and Western archives. It also obtained assistance from Soviet authorities during investigations. In the 1980s, when access to the UN war crimes files was obtained, a number of new investigations resulted. The Central Agency built up a substantial collection of information on individuals, units, and geographical localities. It is the most important tool for investigating Nazi war crimes.

The overall achievements of German courts in prosecuting Nazi war crimes are not impressive. By 1982, 88,587 investigations resulted in 6,465 convictions, including 158 life sentences.[26] The conduct of the participants during many trials is equally unimpressive, and the reasons given for the verdicts are even less so. Some results are entirely scandalous. The majority of contemporary writers on the subject (particularly forceful is Jörg Friedrich) argue that the results were a by-product of a continuous identification with Nazi and nationalistic views.[27] The existence of overt or subconscious pro-Nazi leanings cannot be denied. Did this attitude influence judicial decision making? A study of the law applicable to Nazi war crimes cases suggests that the German judicial system may have reinforced commonly held beliefs and permitted psychological defense strategies.

EVIDENCE *(WAHRHEITSFINDUNG)*

It is rare for a Nazi war crimes prosecutor to find specific historical documentary evidence. The Nazis attempted to destroy the most condemning documentation before the war was over. Thus, a prosecution relies mainly on witness testimony to prove the specifics of the crime. Police and prosecutors were not able to obtain full confessions from many of the perpetrators interrogated immediately after the war. The reasons for their lack of openness vary. Confessions were the exception, the sum of the lies enormous.[28] Lies by perpetrators and nonperpetrators alike mark the basic difference between investigations of Nazi crimes and other investigations. Perpetrators lied to avoid prosecution. Typical lies include only observing (as opposed to participating in) the persecution of Jews in Poland or being unaware of the ghetto-clearing actions because of illness or absence at the time. Nonperpetrators, who had no fear of prosecution, lied just as much. Their continuing identification with National Socialism may be one reason.

The interrogations of the former members of a police unit who had guarded Jewish transport trains from a border-station until they reached Auschwitz offer a good example. While the rank and file of the unit did not have to fear prosecution at that time, their statements differ widely. Upon entering Auschwitz-Birkenau by train, some said the fate awaiting the Jews was clear. "Flames, four to five meters high were shooting out of square chimneys. Once we arrived at the ramp, we could see what was going on here." Others stated that "it has never been announced to us, what would happen to the Jews," and some did not even admit to reaching Auschwitz. Those admitting reality often described the images of the people crowded into cattle cars. Many claimed to have given them water contrary to orders. Those denying knowledge reveal through their use of derogatory language in describing the victims that they were in favor of the Nazi policies to persecute Jews.[29]

Phrases suggesting deeply seated Nazi convictions or Nazi-period stereotypes are commonplace in perpetrators' statements. Some examples are the "Jewish conspiracy" with the perpetrators as victims, the struggle between "good and evil" with the perpetrators representing "good." Accepting the Nazi master race theory, Nazi perpetrators professed their innocence, claiming to be "decent people" with "decent predispositions" entirely incapable of any evil. The wives of SS perpetrators were frequent users of the latter line of argument. Their statements are often devoid of self-criticism and full of self-pity for having had to endure such a hard fate in postwar years.[30]

Even bystanders often did not admit seeing criminal acts, albeit for different motives. German women who worked as secretaries or clerks in German-occupied Poland or the Soviet Union had no fear of prosecution. Rather than give unvarnished accounts of their observations and experiences, they stated that they never saw anything because as women, they were interested in men and amusement, not "politics." "Politics" meant observing the Jewish population murdered and deported, often walking over corpses on the way to work. This denial becomes understandable considering everyday life for the German occupiers in the East. For individuals who had all the advantages of the "master race" in psychological terms (shooing Poles or Russians from the sidewalk) and material terms (having their clothes made by tailors in the ghettos, spending weekends on SS estates, having access to special foods), these memories remained important, and the crimes were removed from the picture.[31]

Group denial strategies also exist, particularly among those remaining in close contact after the war. Prevalent among ethnic Germans from Poland or Russia is a collective memory of the war events that is false. Ethnic Germans were often organized into SS and police units immediately after the German invasion, subsequently participating in mass-killing actions. Statements by ethnic Germans reveal old hatreds when excusing their crimes, often expressed as "self-defense" against the Poles. Strong anti-Polish or anti-Semitic sentiments are pronounced in statements taken even as late as the 1960s. Nonperpetrators from these communities also deny knowledge of the crimes. It is often the outsider in the community during the war years who will recall the events. Group pressure through continuous close contact during and after the war, reinforced by the experience of having been displaced at the end of the war, has prevented these groups from coming to terms with their past.[32]

THE DEFENSE OF SUPERIOR ORDERS

According to German law, members of the army or police units can advance the defense of superior orders. In Nazi trials, this defense developed its own dynamic. Numerous defendants claimed that they would have been shot if they refused an order. They also claimed the SS and police courts had ordered persons refusing an execution order to be shot or sent to a concentration camp. The Central Agency carefully reviewed every claim and was unable to authenticate any of them. Not surprisingly, section 47 of the German Military Criminal Code prevents it. Moreover, it has been shown that SS and police courts were not equipped to make somebody disappear. In the overwhelming majority of cases, German courts rejected the defense of superior orders as not being substantiated by fact. The historical facts reveal that the SS leadership had no desire to punish those refusing killing orders.[33] They were evaluated as not "tough" enough to be an SS leader and were transferred to a different position, ending all career aspirations. Himmler's statement that whoever was "too soft" simply had to say so was described by one defendant as a "vicious trick" because no "SS leader would have made such an exhibition of himself" and ruined his future in the SS.[34]

The persistent use of the defense of superior orders was but one facet of the collective German strategy of exoneration. The perpetrator became the tool, a mere cog in the wheel. He had to obey orders and, for this reason, he too was a victim. In addition, "order and obedience" are basic facts of war. Using this notion, all Nazi crimes were described in the larger context of war in an attempt to remove the specific criminality of the perpetrators. In the same vein, Nazi apologists routinely referred to sentenced Nazi criminals as "German POWs in Allied custody," argued that war crimes were committed by both sides, and used the suffering of the German population caused by Allied bombing to attempt to equalize criminality. It is not surprising that it took historiography so long to describe appropriately the participation of the German army in war crimes and why this has caused such a hostile reaction in parts of the German population.[35]

THE WILL TO COMMIT A DEED *(TÄTERWILLE)*

German law recognizes a difference in culpability between a perpetrator, who willfully commits the crime, and an accessory. Subjective intention is the essential requirement to indict for murder. The decision that led to this distinction was a case unconnected with Nazi crimes. But when dealing with Nazi crimes, many German decisions reflect an almost standardized formula of the "perpetrators," the unholy trinity of Hitler, Himmler, Heydrich, and the "accessories," the defendants. Considering the number of victims and the severity of the crimes, this permitted rather mild sentences. "Ten minutes in jail per corpse" is a succinct description. The courts had other possible approaches open to them. Indeed, the Federal Court *(Bundesgerichtshof)* allows other ways of dealing with crimes of the nature of Nazi crimes.[36]

It is striking how closely this legal formulation mirrors the notion of the *Führerstaat* (state under a leader), with Hitler on top of the pyramid and the followers below. This notion relieves the conscience of the individual follower. The SS leadership used this psychological strategy during wartime. Proclaiming that the leaders bore total responsibility for all orders given, the SS leadership unburdened the followers of responsibility and permitted them to see themselves as tools. In Germany, the frequency with which the legal concept of *Täterwille* has been applied in Nazi trials likely corresponds to the level of acceptance of the notion of the *Führerstaat*.

CONCENTRATION CAMP TRIALS

Given the enormity of the crimes committed during the Holocaust, it is questionable whether justice was done. Compared to the number of people involved in the death camp machinery, the number prosecuted, convicted, and sentenced is but a small percentage. There is another dimension, however: that is, the impact of Nazi trials on the Germans' public perception of the past. This is best illustrated by comparing three concentration camp trials that took place within roughly ten years of each other.

In 1955 public interest in Nazi prosecutions was at its lowest ebb and the German collective defense strategies were at their strongest. In the wake of the release of German POWs from Soviet camps in 1955, it became known that the last transport included personnel of the Sachsenhausen camp. Returning to his home village, one created quite a stir among the inhabitants. Initially, the prosecutor's office in charge was rather hesitant, but in the following weeks and months, a veritable deluge of statements from former inmates of Sachsenhausen was obtained. Witnesses came from all strata of postwar German society: leaders of trade unions, Communists, church leaders, social democrats. The dean of a faculty of the University of Cologne pressed charges for the murder of his predecessor. A member of the family of the president of the Federal Republic, Theodor Heuss, had been killed in the camp. The number of victims was so large and so representative of all parts of German society that formerly successful defense strategies like "only Communists and criminals had been in concentration camps" could not work. The former inmates were united in their solidarity, first established in the camp. A former camp elder, Harry Naujocks, was not ostracized for being a Communist, although such ostracism was normal at this time, but was shown respect by everybody. Germans learned that every German could have been thrown into a concentration camp, not only certain groups at the fringe of society.

In scrupulous detail the prosecution established that an enormous number of criminal acts were committed by the two defendants, Gustav Sorge and Wilheim Schubert, as part of their daily routine. There was no room for the defense of "acting under superior orders." The court, counsel for the defense included, had no doubt about the moral repugnancy of these crimes. In one case, a witness reported that the defendant Schubert had ill-treated a blind inmate, who died as a result. Schubert asked, "Do you really believe that I could ill-treat a blind person?" to which the presiding judge answered, "Yes, I do believe it, and everybody in this courtroom believes it as well."[37]

The biggest impact on public opinion in Germany was as a result of the Auschwitz trial. It was heard in Frankfurt am Main from 1964 to 1965. The trial received extensive media coverage. A large number of Jewish and non-Jewish witnesses from all countries testified. Many talked in public about their experiences, and all confronted their former torturers for the first time since the war. The twenty-two defendants represented all levels of German society. This fact eliminated the possible exculpatory argument that the perpetrators had been sadists and primitive brutes. The defendants were representative of German society, and German society recognized that a neighbor could have been a perpetrator.

Auschwitz was at the core of the Nazi crimes and has rightfully become a symbol for them. In sober detail the prosecution proved the existence of well-organized, conveyor-belt-like machinery of mass murder by gassing. This evidence came from the victims. The defendants did not dispute the essential facts. The majority of defendants denied only allegations of excessive personal conduct. These "seemingly unobtrusive good citizens" tried to minimize allegations showing how far beyond normal human behavior they had gone. One defendant, Wilhelm Boger, is reported to have met a new child inmate holding an apple. Boger grabbed the child by the feet and smashed his head, then picked up the dead child's apple and started to eat it.[38]

In the end the Nazi attempt to murder the Jewish population of Europe was established as a fact.

Helping to increase public awareness and change public opinion during this period were the substantial number of publications, including reports of the proceedings, personal memoirs, works of art, and so on that dealt with Auschwitz and the trial. In respect of historiography, the four expert opinions commissioned by the court were later published and remain among the most authoritative and important texts on the SS and police apparatus.[39]

A decade later, public opinion had definitely changed. Between 1975 and 1981 when the Majdanek trial took place in Düsseldorf, confronting historical realities and proving facts was no longer in the forefront. The main facts about Nazi crimes were accepted by a majority in Germany. The focus shifted to recognizing the moral and political consequences of the Nazi past, to teaching the past appropriately, and to passing on a legacy. The media coverage was extensive, but no longer was restricted to reporting events in court. There were public discussions. A movie was made. Educational institutions took a greater interest. Groups of high school students went to watch the trial proceedings. There was open discussion in the classroom and students wrote on the subject. This change in approach and attitude was a manifestation of generational change since the end of the war.[40]

NORTH AMERICA

North American soldiers witnessed Nazi crimes, mainly when concentration camps were liberated. Their observations were confined to Western Europe. They did not witness the horrors of German rule in the East. For North Americans, the war was an event that occurred far away in geographical and emotional terms. In the early 1950s when the International Tribunal and subsequent military tribunals were disbanded, Canada and the United States believed that their contribution to prosecuting war criminals was over.

When the war in the East was being lost, local collaborators retreated from Soviet territory with the Germans. The Germans wanted to protect them against retaliation and wanted to have local elites ready when they retook the territory. In this way many Ukrainian, Russian, Baltic, and other collaborators came to live in wartime

Germany. Prior to May 1945, it was not possible to live in Germany without Nazi permission, which generally was given only for slave laborers or collaborators. At the end of the war, the Allies found millions of non-Germans in the country. These "displaced persons" became the concern of international organizations. The effectiveness of the international relocation program was influenced by a political conflict that developed between West and East. The communist countries insisted that all former citizens be repatriated. The Soviet Union also supported the punishment of Nazi collaborators for the crimes committed during Nazi occupation of Soviet territories. Having become suspicious of Soviet aims, Western countries changed the repatriation policy in favor of immigration programs. Although not eligible for these programs, collaborators and Nazi sympathizers through deception and misinformation used them to avoid repatriation to the East and to immigrate to Canada, Australia, the United States, and other Western countries.[41]

Soon after the war ended, allegations surfaced that Nazi perpetrators and collaborators had escaped and started new lives overseas. Perpetrators were identified on ships taking displaced persons to their new host country. Former victims discovered former torturers had also been given refuge. When the police were informed, generally no action was taken. There are a variety of political, moral, and legal reasons for Western countries not taking action against war criminals living on their territory. In the United States and Canada, criminal law is based primarily on the principle of territoriality: that is, a person can be prosecuted only for an offense committed on its territory. Prosecution for crimes committed abroad before the person came to North America was impossible. While extradition of Nazi war criminals was a possibility, during the cold war, no Western country would extradite to the Soviet Union for prosecution.

In the late 1970s and early 1980s, extensive media and lobby campaigns by public interest groups pressured governments in Great Britain, Australia, and Canada to establish commissions of inquiry to investigate Nazi war criminals and to reconsider extradition to the Soviet Union. Commissions of inquiry substantiated that Nazi war criminals had immigrated to these countries in such numbers that action could no longer be avoided. War crimes investigation units were created to investigate and criminal laws were amended to permit prosecution of Nazi war crimes in those jurisdictions.[42]

Supported by cold war notions in North America and by the right-wing opinions of some Western scholars of Soviet history, the political views and the collective rearrangement of the past by Nazi collaborators and perpetrators had found a sympathetic ground in their host countries and influenced the perception of historical events during the war. The majority of North Americans did not have a true picture of what German occupation in the East was really like. To this day it reflects Hollywood images, not history. This facilitated the promotion of false historical perspectives by certain émigré communities.[43] Notions of Soviet misinformation campaigns, KGB forgeries, and so on, still loom large. The final report produced by the Special Investigations Unit of Australia is instructive in regard to how effectively public opinion had been influenced by the émigré view of history. The report points out how public opinion was against taking seriously and investigating allegations coming from the Soviet Union, and enumerates the various related problems the SIU encountered once war crimes investigations commenced.[44]

In Canada, similar problems have been encountered. In the case of Mihail Pawlowski, who was accused of having participated in the killings of several hundred Jews as a member of the auxiliary police in Byelorussia, the prosecution was discontinued because the trial judge would not order a commission to take evidence from key witnesses living in Byelorussia. Among his reasons was the notion that no truth could be found in the (then still existing) Soviet Union. The ruling also illustrates judicial acceptance of standard exculpatory arguments of Nazi collaborators, such as no one volunteered, they were pressed into service by the Germans.[45] The German police forces in the occupied East suffered from a severe manpower shortage and had a massive enlistment of non-German auxiliary police. The Germans needed willing collaborators, and they found them. They were in no position to force a body of auxiliaries that outnumbered them by a ratio of 1:10 to 1:50 to collaborate. Following the discontinuance in the Pawlowski case, an article appeared in the *Law Times*[46] praising the defense lawyer for his victory over the Soviet propaganda machine against the innocent anticommunist immigrant. A number of American court decisions reflect similarly preconceived notions of KGB forgeries and defamation campaigns, as well as an acceptance of a highly distorted view of history.[47]

A more striking example of the impact of preconceived but erroneous notions of history is found in the Imre Finta decision of the Supreme Court of Canada. Indeed, much of the majority decision in Finta is unsupported by historical fact. The majority decision illustrates how wide a gap exists between the realities of 1944 in Hungary and the Canadian understanding of them. The best illustration is the majority's revisionist-style description of the Holocaust.[48] Equally disturbing is the finding that Finta had a defense by reason of his belief (never proven, as Finta did not testify) that the deportation of the Jewish inhabitants of his hometown in Hungary was lawful. The Court's reasoning was that Nazi propaganda suggesting that the Jews were against Nazi war goals could have led Finta to believe in the lawfulness of his actions. The Court's circular reasoning—if a state produces anti-Semitic propaganda, then directs its police forces to destroy the Jewish population, the agents of the genocide become immune from conviction, whether or not they are aware of or believe in the propaganda—effectively put an end to Canada's efforts at prosecuting war criminals in the criminal courts.[49]

In North America, the common understanding about the Nazis and the Nazi period in Europe has been influenced greatly by former Nazi collaborators themselves. The substantial numbers of former Nazi supporters influenced the picture of history, and their distortions have become common understanding. This might have impacted the course of justice. Comparing three Nazi war crimes trials that were held during the same period in the early 1990s—Ivan Poljukovich in Australia, Imre Finta in Canada, and Josef Schwamberger in Germany[50]—reveals that the evidence against all three defendants was equally compelling, but the results are strikingly different. Finta and Poljukovich were acquitted, Schwamberger was convicted and received a life sentence. The acquittals were the result of jury verdicts, while Schwamberger was convicted by a court of three judges. This introduces the additional question of suitability of the common law system, particularly whether juries are appropriate triers of fact in genocide cases involving highly emotional issues and facts unconnected with the juror's life experience.

THE ROAD AHEAD

Concerns about a state's ability to prosecute and punish war criminals survive the prosecution of Nazi crimes. Political criminals continue to find safe haven in countries like the United States, Australia, and Canada. Questions about whether existing domestic law can deal adequately with serious violations of international law continue to be asked nationally and internationally. It is universally accepted that a system not equal to this challenge presents a serious and legitimate problem.

International jurisdiction over serious violations of international criminal law was assumed for the crimes committed in the former Yugoslavia and Rwanda. After more than fifty years of discussion by international criminal law experts, the international community has recently agreed to the establishment of a permanent international court to try serious violations of international criminal law. That is not to say that there is unqualified support; serious doubt about the effectiveness of the international tribunal model exists. In Rwanda, for example, the mere numbers of people detained for participating in genocide makes prosecution of all before an international tribunal impossible. On the other hand, questions arise as to the ability or willingness of the national courts in Rwanda and the former Yugoslavia to deal with the problem.

Some critics see the establishment of these criminal tribunals as an attempt by the United Nations to save itself from declaring bankruptcy because of its obvious inability to broker a political solution or peace in Yugoslavia. More cynical critics argue that the United Nations international tribunals are not really established to promote international justice, but are a sinecure for international bureaucrats.[51] These critics point to the fact that the United Nations appointed twelve judges, including three appellate judges with substantial tax-free salaries, before it appointed a chief prosecutor or established a prosecutor's office to investigate the allegations. They also highlight that only one potential defendant was in custody in Germany at the time, and he had been identified by volunteers of a German human rights organization.

Notwithstanding the cynicism, it is hoped that the United Nations' tribunals will stand above national political concerns and successfully enforce the international rules regarding serious violations of international criminal law. As the legacy of Nuremberg has shown, the international court model is complicated by the accommodation of different legal systems and philosophies, resulting in fundamental issues of jurisdiction, evidence, application of international criminal law, retroactivity, and so on. Although Nuremberg is often used as a model for dealing with state-sponsored crimes, it is far from settled as to whether the international or national model is preferable. Istvan Deak reopened this debate a few years ago by advocating the superiority of national jurisdiction based on the argument that the German courts subsequently convicted and sentenced accused who had been acquitted by the International Military Tribunal.[52] Although Deak's argument caused quite a controversy, the importance of trials in a national setting is indisputable. With the recent international agreement for an international criminal tribunal to try serious violations of international law, it is certain that the debate will continue.

Perhaps the greatest lesson from the fifty years of prosecuting Nazi crimes is that historical truth about them has been established. While the surviving documentary evidence leaves important gaps, trial records and witness statements have helped to more than adequately fill many of them. In fact, the first comprehensive history of the death camps of the *Aktion Reinhardt* was written using witness statements and trial records from the prosecutions of the personnel of these camps.[53]

While trial records reflect only a partial image of the past and can be influenced by defense strategies and by their own point and time in history, they provide a unique perspective to the historian, the one and only occasion when survivors, victims, and perpetrators talk about the same events. The testimonies of the many perpetrators often admit to the historical truth about the Holocaust and deny only their specific involvement. The evidence from the former Soviet Union, despite its propagandistic slant, is still very useful, but must be carefully checked against evidence from other sources. The factual information presented during Soviet trials is a valuable starting point and has often been borne out by independent investigations conducted fifty years later. However, one should neither accept these reports unquestioningly, as some suggest,[54] nor reject them altogether.[55]

Because the media in the Soviet Union was state controlled and the Western free press was given only limited and controlled access, it is very difficult to say how the population really reacted to war crimes trials. Trial observers' horror recorded in the Soviet press has every appearance of having been orchestrated; however, as a rule, such reactions seem to correspond to the collective memory of the population. The memory of the atrocities committed by the Germans was quite vivid. Private correspondence of the time confirms the enormity of the atrocities and the extent of the suffering.

The full facts of the Holocaust have been proven in international and German courts, and in domestic courts of many countries. Although revisionist denial of the Holocaust is now seen as denial of reality,[56] there is nonetheless a continuing challenge for historians to educate society about the Holocaust, as expert witnesses in court, as scholars, as public speakers, and so on. Despite all that has been accomplished to date, there is still work to be done to counter the false images of history, as the section on North America has illustrated.

One final example on recent events in the Baltic states. Arturs Silgailis, the second-in-command of the Waffen-SS in Latvia, described the Nazi occupation in Latvia as problematic only if one was a Jew, a Gypsy, or mentally handicapped.[57] Living in Canada after the war, he became a prominent spokesman in Latvian circles and for the group attempting to whitewash the image of the Waffen-SS. Not surprisingly, these groups also reject allegations of local collaboration in Nazi war crimes in Latvia and other Baltic states as Soviet propaganda. Yet, on the other hand, the collective memory of past sufferings under the Soviet regime has justified the commencement of judicial proceedings against former Soviet functionaries for crimes that in part took place before the German invasion of the Baltic states.[58] The standard excuses of age and passage of time used by ethnic groups in Western countries as the basis for not pursuing Nazi crimes have not been raised.

The challenge of ensuring that justice is consistent with historical truth is complicated by the false images of history painted by the perpetrators and their sympathizers. These false images of history must be corrected. The truth of the past must be established and reported. The lessons learned from Nazi war crimes prosecutions can serve as beacons for the international community as it deals with more recent genocides. Let us hope these lessons will be heeded and justice will be done.

NOTES

1. The literature on the Nuremberg trials is massive. For an overview on the developments leading to Nuremberg and on alternative plans, see Telford Taylor, *The Anatomy of the Nuremberg Trial: A Personal Memoir*

(New York, 1992). An overview of the literature is in Norman Tutorow, ed., *War Crimes, War Criminals, and War Crimes Trials: An Annotated Bibliography and Source Book* (New York, 1986).

2. Succinctly expressed by Jörg Friedrich, *Die kalte Amnestie: NS-Täter in der Bundesrepublik* (Frankfurt, 1984). With respect to Austria, see Helmut Butterweck, "Österreich und seine NS-Prozesse nach 1945: Politischer Opportunismus warf Mörder und Mitläufer in einen Topf," in *Tabu und Geschichte,* ed. P. Bettelheim and R. Streibel (Vienna, 1994).

3. Christian Frederik Rueters, "Die strafrechtliche Ahndung von Staatsverbrechen, begangen durch Militär und Polizei," in *Licht in den Schatten der Vergangenheit: Zur Enttabuisierung der Nürnberger Kriegsverbrecherprozesse,* ed. Jörg Friedrich and Jörg Wollenberg (Frankfurt am Main, 1987), pp. 67–82.

4. Henry Rousso has studied this problem in respect to France. He retraces the complex web of political interests, redefinition of history and the legal consequences in postwar France and describes the process in psychoanalytical terms as a mental disease of society. Henry Rousso, *The Vichy Syndrome: History and Memory in France since 1944* (Cambridge, Mass., 1991). The question of how memory and history influence judicial findings in general terms for countries other than Germany has only recently been addressed.

5. The "Nuremberg documents" were for quite some time accessible only to research teams working for the prosecutions. This explains, to a certain extent, the outstanding impact of this document collection on historiography.

6. The level of detail in which these three countries, singly or collectively, can be discussed is quite uneven. This is due for one to the length of time in which prosecutions have taken place: in Germany, fifty years; in Austria, only six years. Second, while the German trial records have been accessible to many scholars, resulting in a number of works, war crimes trial records in the former Soviet Union have only recently become open and mainly to members of other war crimes units. While the information used here is admittedly sketchy, this author has been among those fortunate enough to have had access to records on a large scale, and the results of this work might be of interest.

7. Krasnodar Trial, Archives of Ministry of Security, Moscow, case 700.

8. Chef der Sicherheitspolizei to RFSS, 10 March 1945; v. Herff to Martin, 9 March 1945, Berlin Document Center, Schmauser file.

9. On the central level, the reports by the commissions are kept in Moscow in the State Archives, fond 7021. The reports pertaining to each former Soviet Republic are kept in the Central Archives of the Republic (the

former October Revolution Archives) and, following the same logic, in each oblast archive. On the grassroots level, the questionnaires distributed by the commissions and other interesting details on the reinstallment of Soviet powers and their handling of the consequences of German occupation can be found in local archives (rayon archives, or local archives in the Baltic states). This author had occasion to gain an impression of what the material contains when surveying all local archives in Lithuania. The questionnaires about material losses, for instance, go into details like the number of chickens lost by each individual family. One can also find information on matters such as the return of Holocaust victims to their former residence and ensuing attempts to regain possession of their property.

10. Publications "unmasking" Nazi criminals and collaborators and accusing the West of protecting them use a typical terminology by which, by implication, the opposite positions are defined. It is: "Barbarians," "Hitlerite butchers," "Nationalist turncoats," "reactionary organizations and forces, supported by imperialist bourgeois-nationalist circles in the West," versus "the heroic Soviet people," and "the invincible banner of Socialism." See, as some among many: *History Teaches a Lesson* (Kiev, 1989); *Lesson from History* (Prague, 1962); Michael Hanusiak, *Lest We Forget* (Toronto, 1976); Valery Styrkul, *We Accuse* (Kiev, 1984).

11. *Military Court Riga v. Friedrich Jeckeln et al.*, Zentrale Stelle Ludwigsburg (hereafter cited as ZStL), UdSSR 245Ae; Minsk Trial, Film and Photo Archive, Dscherschinsk, Byelorussia; Manfred Messerschmidt, "Der Minsker Prozess 1946, Gedanken zu einem sowjetischen Kriegsverbrechertribunal," in *Vernichtungskrieg: Verbrechen der Wehrmacht 1941–44*, ed. H. Heer and K. Naumann (Hamburg, 1995); *Kiev Trial v. Paul Albert Scheer et al.*, reviewed at procuratura Kiev 1990, original in Archive of Ministry of Security, Moscow. The HSSPF in Minsk, Curt von Gottberg, committed suicide by the end of the war. Hans-Adolf Prützmann, HSSPF for the Ukraine, committed suicide in British custody in the summer of 1945, which might have been a response to his anticipated extradition.

12. Film on Minsk Trial in Film and Photo Archive in Dscherschinsk, Byelorussia.

13. In Kiev, for instance, in the Photo Department of the State Archive.

14. See Minsk Messerschmidt trial, passim.

15. ZStL UdSSr 243 Ae; on Jeckeln see Ruth Bettina Birn, *Die Höheren SS- und Polizeiführer: Himmlers Vertreter im Reich und in den besetzten Gebieten* (Düsseldorf, 1986), pp. 391 ff. Ezergailis refutes Soviet propaganda use of Jeckeln's statements, but does not deal with the substance of his testimony. Andrew Ezergailis, *The Holocaust in Latvia 1941–44* (Historical Institute of Latvia, 1996), pp. 1ff.

16. Witness statements by Paul Albert Scheer, 15, 18, 20, 21, 24, 29 December 1945, Kiev Trial. Scheer is quite accurate as to chains of command, spheres of competence, and so on. He does not admit to every accusation, but denies involvement or responsibility on a number of points in keeping with historical facts. Of particular interest is a handwritten report, "Meine politische Verurteilung der Strafmassnalmen der faschistischen Politiküberhaupt," 25 December 1945. While the title reflects Soviet terminology, parts of the statements are typical for immediate postwar reactions of SS and police leaders. For instance, on Hitler: "Schliesslich hat er dann ein bequemes Ende, den Selbstmord gewählt und sich dadurch den Folgen seiner Politik und der Verantwortung entzogen. Schliesslich hat er das deutsche Volk seinem Schicksal überlassen," which corresponds almost verbatim to the statements by other SS leaders commenting on Hitler's and Himmler's suicides. See Birn, *HSSPF,* passim.

17. See the following reports on work in progress: Stefan Karner, "GUPVI: The Soviet Main Administration for Prisoners of War and Internees during World War II," and Stefan Karner and Barbara Marx, "World War II Prisoners in the Soviet Economy," both in *Bulletin du Comité International de l'Histoire de la Deuxième Guerre Mondial, 1945: Consequences and Sequels of the Second World War* (Montreal, 2 September 1995).

18. Defendants from trials conducted in the Soviet zone of occupation in Germany and Austria were released, as described in the following text on the Sachsenhausen trial.

19. In latter years, while the allegation of "betrayal of the motherland" is still maintained, the allegations refer also to other criminal offenses.

20. Following the breakup of the Soviet Union, many convictions were reviewed and set aside by the authorities of the new independent states of which the people who were convicted and sentenced were now citizens. This process, too, had political motivations; though, as a rule, people who had been sentenced for criminal acts were not rehabilitated and only politically motivated convictions were set aside. Given the practice of the Soviet authorities immediately after the war, however, the possibility exists that real war criminals who had been convicted for the wrong reasons are now rehabilitated for the right reasons but with wrong results.

21. The former German Democratic Republic (GDR) provides an interesting parallel. The inner workings of Nazi war crimes prosecutions can now be studied in full detail. All investigations of Nazi crimes were done by the Stasi (the GDR equivalent to the KGB) and were used as a propaganda tool to embarrass the West. In a recent article Alfred Streim has described how GDR prosecutions were stage-managed to occur at the same time as major trials in the West. Through careful manipulation of courts, press coverage, and access of the public to the trials, the GDR ensured a smooth pro-

cess and made timely media statements that it took Nazi prosecutions seriously, in contrast to West Germany, which was bogged down by an open legal system that included obstructive defense counsel, sensationalist media, and so on. Whether the true motive behind these prosecutions was to serve justice is doubtful, because the allegations, while fully investigated, were not brought to court until it was politically convenient. After unification, German prosecutors identified a number of Stasi files on Nazi criminals living in the former GDR and opened several investigations. See Alfred Streim, "Saubere Wehrmacht? Die Verfolgung von Kriegs- und NS-Verbrechern in der Bundesrepublik und der DDR,D" in *Vernichtungskrieg,* pp. 569 ff. passim. See Ina Eschebach, "SS Aufseherinnen des ehemaligen Frauenkonzentrationslagers Ravensbrück in den Akten der DDR-Justiz"; Henry Leide, "Die Nichtverfolgung von NS-Straftätern durch das Ministerium für Staatssicherheit der ehemaligen DDR," both papers read at the German Studies Association Twentieth Annual Conference in Seattle, 12 October 1996. Based on literature and studies of political scientists, the GDR's antifascist appearance aided its consolidation and legitimization of the communist regime. See Irma Hanke, *Alltag und Politik: Zur politischen Kultur der DDR* (Opladen, 1987); Lutz Niethammer, *Die volkseigene Erfahrung: Eine Archäologie des Lebens in der Industrieprovinz der DDR* (Berlin, 1991), pp. 248 ff.; Sigrid Meuschel, *Legitimation und Parteiherrschaft in der DDR: Zum Paradox von Stabilität und Revolution in der DDR 1945–1989* (Frankfurt, 1992), pp. 29 ff.

22. For instance, witness statement J.H., who went all over Germany with the hope to find one of the murderers, ZStL 207 AR-Z 18/58.

23. Statement R. Sch., ZStL 213 AR-Z 294/60, Bd. 21.

24. The files of the "Council" can be found in Yad Vashem, Jerusalem, file M I.

25. See Adalbert Rückerl, *Die Strafverfolgung von NS-Verbrechen 1945–1978: Eine Dokumentation* (Heidelberg, 1979), pp. 49 ff.; Reinhard Henkys, *Geschichte und Gericht der nationalsozialistischen Gewaltverbrechen,* ed. D. Goldschmidt (Stuttgart, Berlin, 1964).

26. Adalbert Rückerl, "Staatsanwaltschaftliche Ermittlungen der NS-Verbrechen," in *Vergangenheitsbewältigung durch Strafverfahren,* ed. P. Steinbach and J. Weber (Munich, 1984), pp. 71–83.

27. See examples cited by Henkys, pp. 236 ff. passim; in respect to serving sentences, Ulrich-Dieter Oppitz, *Strafverfahren und Strafvollzug bei NS-Gewaltverbrechen* (Ulm, 1976); Friedrich, *Die kalte Amnestie.*

28. See statement A.K., ZStL 207 AR-Z 51/58, "Ich will endlich fertig werden, wieder zur inneren Ruhe kommen"; W.G., ZStL 213 AR 1900/60, Bd. 7, "Lange Jahre war ich nicht fachig, ein Kind schreien zu hören."

29. Statements H.G., E.G., G.E., K.S., P.B., E.E., H.R., A.H., L.K.,

M.L., G.L., O.P., F.R., G.W., H.W., F.Z., G.E., H.G., M.W., F.B., H.Sch., ZStL 502 AR-Z 60/58.

30. Defendant T., ZStL 207 AR-Z 367-59, for whom the "world conspiracy" was now "Israeli"; Defendants L. and K., ZStL 502 AR-Z 60/58; F.G., ZStL 502 AR-Z 60/58; Mrs. K., ZStL 207 AR-Z 18/58; Mrs. Z., wife of the former SS and police leader in Minsk, ZStL 202 AR-Z 538/59; Mrs. H., wife of a former concentration camp guard, ZStL SA 70.

31. Two examples from many: Witness I.W., ZStL 203 AR-Z 113/60; Witness Mrs. W., ZStL 203 AR-Z 161/67.

32. Report 22 December1960, witnesses W. Sch., C.T., R.Z., H.P., E.N., P.Z., L. Z.-G., ZStL 203 AR-Z 113/60; Pater N.P., ZStL 213 AR-Z 294/60. One big problem, which was particularly severe in proceedings against police, was the networks created by former members of the order police (many of whom were still in police functions in the Federal Republic), which made prosecutions impossible. This "network of comrades" helped to design lines of defense in readiness for interrogation, found the "right" type of lawyer, and even put pressure on those who did not want to conform to the defense agreed upon. Many trials are proof of the effectiveness of these strategies.

33. One exception is a verdict by the courts in *Freiburg v. Policebatallion 332, Justiz und NS-Verbrechen,* Bd. 19, pp. 413ff.

34. W.M., ZStL 207 AR-Z 18/58.

35. The major work on the defense of "acting under binding orders" is Herbert Jäger, *Verbrechen unter totalitärer Herrschaft: Studien zur nationalsozialistischen Gewaltkriminalität* (Frankfurt am Main, 1982).

36. Henkys, *Geschichte und Gericht,* passim; Jürgen Baumann, "Die strafrechtliche Problematik der nationalsozialistischen Gewaltverbrechen," in Henkys, passim.

37. *KZ-Verbrechen vor deutschen Gerichten,* vol. 1, ed. Hendrik George von Dam and Ralph Giordano (Frankfurt am Main, 1962), pp. 151–510; ZStL SA 70; LG Bonn 8Ks 2/59.

38. Bernd Naumann, *Auschwitz: Bericht über die Strafsache gegen Mulka und andere vor dem Schwurgericht Frankfurt a.M.* (Frankfurt am Main, 1968), pp. 126ff.; LG Frankfurt am Main 4 Ks 1/67. Richard Böckh, formerly a driver in Auschwitz, is one of those giving truthful statements about the crimes committed in Auschwitz, ZStL 402 AR-Z 37/58, SB 39, 85 u. 3. The Auschwitz trial, not as it is sometimes argued, the Eichmann trial, had the biggest impact on public opinion in Germany.

39. *Anatomie des SS-Staates,* 2 vols., ed. H. Buchheim et al. (Munich, 1967). The literature on Auschwitz using the trials is extensive; see for instance the works by Hermann Langbein; in respect of works of art see Peter Weiss, *Die Ermittlung: Oratorium in 11 Gesängen* (Reinbek, 1979).

40. Heiner Lichtenstein, *Majdanek—Reportage eines Prozesses* (Frankfurt am Main, 1979); Ingrid Müller-Münch, *Die Frauen von Majdanek: Vom zerstörten Leben der Opfer und der Mörderinnen* (Reinbek, 1982).

41. Louise Holborn, *The International Refugee Organisation: Its History and Work 1946–52* (Oxford, 1956); Wolfgang Jacobmeyer, *Vom Zwangsarbeiter zum heimatlosen Ausländer* (Göttingen, 1985).

42. *Report of the Investigations of War Criminals in Australia,* Attorney-General's Department, Canberra, 1993; *Commission of Inquiry on War Criminals Report Part I: Public* by the Honorable Jules Deschenes, Commissioner, Ottawa, 1986; Alan Ryan Jr., *Quiet Neighbors: Prosecuting Nazi War Criminals in America* (New York, 1984); Mark Aarons, *Sanctuary: Nazi Fugitives in Australia* (Melbourne, 1989); David Matas, *Justice Delayed: Nazi War Criminals in Canada* (Toronto, 1987); David Cesareani, *Justice Delayed: How Britain Became a Refuge for Nazi War Criminals* (London, 1992).

43. A recently published and highly acclaimed novel can serve as an example for this. Anne Michaels, in her novel *Fugitive Pieces* (Toronto, 1996), describes the life of Jewish survivors under Nazi occupation and afterward in Canada. While her picture of Nazi occupation is aggravatingly wrong mainly for the historian, it becomes problematic when she introduces the sinister figure of the perpetrator, who also has made it to Canada. The description of the perpetrator is clearly fed by Hollywood wartime movies, but bears no resemblance to the prototype of the actual perpetrators who migrated to Canada. The same phenomenon is found in allegations from the public against suspected "war criminals," which are based upon German accents and German shepherd dogs and a propensity to orderliness—all of which are sadly beside the point.

44. *Investigations of War Criminals in Australia,* passim; Konrad Kwiet, "Am Ende war dann doch alles umsonst: Anmerkungen zur späten Verfolgung von NS-Kriegsverbrechern in Australiend," in *Universalgeschichte und Nationalgeschichte,* ed. G. Hübinger, J. Osterhammel, and E. Pelzer (Freiburg, 1994).

45. *Regina v. Michael Pawlowski,* Ontario Court of Justice (General Division), Court file no. 293 SCO, judgment by Justice Chadwick dated 21 June 1991. Judgment of Justice Chadwick on the local auxiliary police: "They were all pressed into service in the local police force by the Germans under threat of execution of their parents or family," p. 29.

46. George F. Takach, "War Crimes: A Defendant's Nightmare, A Lawyer's Dream: The Strange Story of How Our Legal System Triumphed over KGB Scheming and the Dark Arts of International Politics," *National* (Canadian Bar Association) 3, no. 4 (May 1994); *Regina v. Michael Pawlowski.*

47. For instance: *United States of America v. Elmars Sprogis,* United States District Court, Eastern District of New York, CV-82-1804, 18 May 1984; *United States of America v. Elmars Sprogis,* United States Court of Appeals, Second Circuit, decided 31 May 1985. Of particular interest is the minority vote: *United States v. Edgars Laipenieks,* United States Court of Appeals, Ninth Circuit, No. 83-7711.

48. From the majority judgment, *R. v. Finta* (1994) 28 Criminal Reports (4th) 265: "The implementation of the 'final solution' by the German government meant that Jews were deprived of all means of earning an income, of their property, and eventually were deported to camps in Eastern Europe, where they provided forced labor for the German war effort. In these dreadful camps many were put to death" (at p. 280). See by comparison the minority judgment at p. 347: "Once there, these Jews faced either immediate extermination or forced labor followed by eventual extermination. . . . There can be no doubt that this process . . . was an integral part of what the Nazis themselves dubbed the 'final solution' to the 'Jewish problem,' namely the systematic slaughter of every last European Jew."

49. See *R. v. Finta* at pp. 323-5.

50. On Ivan Timofeyevich Poljukovich: *Investigations of War Criminals in Australia,* pp. 55-8; Randolph L. Braham, "Canada and the perpetrators of the Holocaust: The Case of *Regina v. Finta*" in *Holocaust and Genocide Studies* 9 (winter 1995): 293-317; *R. v. Finta,* Supreme Court of Canada, judgment 24 March 1994. Schwamberger was tried by the LG Stuttgart; he received a life sentence in May 1992. The only publication on the Schwamberger case—by two lawyers, who are associated with the Simon Wiesenthal Center—does not reflect on such fundamental legal issues, but surprisingly manages to introduce anti-German diatribes into the account; Martin Mendelsohn and Aaron Freiwald, *The Last Nazi: Josef Schwamberger and the Nazi Past* (New York, 1994).

51. Recently, Madame Justice Arbour of the Ontario Court of Appeal has been appointed chief prosecutor of the UN tribunals. Justice Arbour's war-crimes-related experience was her participation as one of the panel of judges that heard the Finta appeal in the Ontario Court of Appeal and in writing the majority decision upholding the acquittal. This acquittal is based on reasons that legal scholars have suggested would have led to the acquittal of many of the Nazis convicted in Nuremberg.

52. Istvan Deak, "Misjudgement at Nuremberg," *New York Review of Books,* 7 October 1993, pp. 46-52. Professor Deak's article has led to a lively debate in letters to the editor.

53. Adalbert Rückerl, *NS-Vernichtungslager im Spiegel deutscher Strafprozesse* (Munich, 1977).

54. For instance, Johannes Heer in *Vernichtungskreig,* passim. In par-

ticular, photos must be used with great caution; reliability of their documentation varies. A comparison of photo collections of various formerly Soviet archives show that pictures, in particular impressive ones, have been circulated widely, so that it can be difficult to authenticate their point of origin and what they depict. This problem is not reflected in *Vernichtungskrieg,* though throughout the book photos are used extensively.

55. Ezergailis in *Holocaust in Latvia,* passim, is entirely negative on the "extraordinary commission" reports, but more balanced in Andrew Ezergailis, "War Crimes Evidence from Soviet Latvia" (paper presented at the Eleventh Conference of Baltic Studies, 9 June 1988).

56. While it is easy to cast doubts on the veracity of statements taken by the KGB, for instance, it is much more complicated to explain why, in the setting of a German court, defendants would tell lies, in particular lies to their own disadvantage. This did not stop certain revisionists from doing exactly so; one of the most hair-raising was concocted in connection with the Auschwitz trial in Frankfurt. The argument runs as follows: the German judiciary had joined in a conspiracy to produce the "Auschwitz lie"; only the last commander of Auschwitz, Richard Baer (who died in detention, awaiting trial) had been upright enough to withstand pressure, and therefore he had been murdered in custody, with active corroboration of the "Jewish" head prosecutor of the state of Hesse, Fritz Bauer. Fanciful yarns like this, which attempt to turn the respectable courthouse in Frankfurt into a den of torturers, are so far outside common sense that they only serve to stress that there is no reason for any sensible person to deny the Holocaust. Wilhelm Stäglich, *Der Auschwitz-Mythos* (Tübingen, 1979); Hans Laternser, *Die andere Seite im Auschwitz-Prozess, 1963–65* (Stuttgart, 1966).

57. Testimony by Arturs Silgailis in immigration hearing in the case of Vilis A. Hazners, New York Southern District Court, file A 10303 336, p. 1251. Silgailis—cross, "Q: You testified before that you considered the Nazi the lesser of two evils? A: Oh, yes. Up till now, you see. You can't compare the communism with National Socialism. It is maybe, you see, I will say what was who suffer, you see that was the Jews and there was gypsies and maybe the mentally ill, you see, that is another. But how we were treated, you see, compared with the one year of Latvian occupation is quite different. You see, you must understand the Latvian people. . . ."

58. Alfred Noviks, the former Latvian KGB chief, age 87, was charged with genocide, among other charges for the deportations from Latvia prior to German occupation, *Baltic Independent,* Tallin, Estonia, vol. 5. 30 June–6 July 1995. Noviks was convicted and died in prison at age 88. A similar case was indicted in Estonia where the defendant was 85 years old, *Globe and Mail* (Toronto), 20 June 1996.

Randolph L. Braham

The National Trials Relating to the Holocaust in Hungary
An Overview

BACKGROUND

IT IS GENERALLY RECOGNIZED THAT THE HOLOCAUST IN HUNGARY, THE last major chapter in the Nazis' war against the Jews, was unique—a chapter replete with paradoxes and controversies. While the Jewish communities throughout the rest of German-dominated Europe were being systematically destroyed, the Jews of Hungary—although subjected to severe discriminatory measures and occasional physical abuse—continued to enjoy the protection of the conservative-aristocratic government until the German occupation on 19 March 1944. After the occupation, however, it was this highly assimilated patriotic Jewish community that was subjected to the most ruthless destruction program of the war. The occupation enabled the German and Hungarian Nazis, each previously eager but unable to act alone, to unite their forces in carrying out the Final Solution at lightning speed. What took years to implement in other parts of Europe, took only a few months in Hungary! By 9 July all of Hungary, with the notable exception of Budapest, had become *Judenrein*.[1] The destruction of the Hungarian Jews took place on the eve of Allied victory, when the secrets of Auschwitz were already widely known.[2] Except for a few die-hard Nazis who continued to believe Hitler's promises about new wonder weapons, even the perpetrators realized the defeat of the Axis was inevitable. The imminent military defeat notwithstanding—or precisely because of it—the perpetrators became even more committed to winning at least the genocidal war against the Jews. They won this phase of the war in Hungary because the quisling government of Döme Sztójay, installed with the blessing of Regent Miklós Horthy a few days after the German occupation, placed the instruments of state power—the police, the gendarmerie, and the civil service—at their disposal. While not always enthusiastic, the policemen, gendarmes, and civil servants operating at the various levels of government carried out the Final Solution—the isolation, expropriation, ghettoization, concentration, and deportation of the Jews—with a routine and an efficiency that impressed even the Eichmann-*Sonderkommando.* The latter, numbering less than 100 SS-men, clearly could not have carried out the program without the wholehearted cooperation of the Hungarians.[3]

As the Soviet forces advanced westward toward Hungary, many thousands of the perpetrators fled in the same direction, together with countless other fascists. Many among them managed to escape altogether; others were captured by the British or the Americans in occupied Austria and Germany. Quite a few of the latter managed to hide their criminal background and ended up in various parts of the free world, especially Argentina, Australia, Britain, Canada, and the United States, where they lived out their lives—or continue to live—undetected, having capitalized on their credentials as reliable anticommunists during the cold war.[4] The major Hungarian war criminals who had played a leadership role in the various pro-Nazi governments and political parties and had been actively involved in the planning and implementation of the anti-Jewish measures could not hide their background. Once they became the target of special investigative efforts, those among the Hungarian governmental and political figures in Allied hands were easily unmasked. The same happened to a number of top German officials with whom they had collaborated during the occupation.

The postwar Hungarian government requested that the Western Allies arrest and extradite 483 Hungarians and 38 Germans suspected as war criminals. The Hungarian demands for the extradition of these criminals, especially those of German nationality, caused considerable friction between the Hungarian and American authorities.[5] The tensions were eased when 390 of the Hungarian suspects were returned and the Americans consented to the extradition of three top SS officials who had been active during the occupation to serve as witnesses in the major Hungarian war crimes trials. These were *SS-Brigadeführer* Edmund Veesenmayer, Hitler's plenipotentary; *SS-Obergruppenführer* Otto Winkelmann, the higher SS and police leader; and *SS-Standartenführer* Kurt Becher, Heinrich Himmler's "economic" representative.[6]

The major Hungarian war criminals were rounded up and first interrogated by a team headed by Martin Himler, a Hungarian-American who headed the Hungarian Section of the Office of Strategic Services in Salzburg, Austria. Most of these were returned to Hungary in October 1945, escorted by Lieutenant George Granville, an American Air Force officer of Hungarian background. Among these were practically all the leading figures of the Sztójay and Szálasi governments. Upon their return to Budapest, they were handed over to Major General Gábor Péter, the head of the political police (*Politikai Rendészeti Osztály*).[7]

Of the three Germans extradited by the Western Allies to serve as prosecution witnesses only Veesenmayer was eventually tried (see below). Many other German and Austrian nationals who had been involved in the Hungarian chapter of the Nazis' Final Solution, however, were tried elsewhere. Among the most important of these trials were those held in Germany, Austria, Czechoslovakia, and Israel. A number of Hungarian nationals, in turn, were tried outside Hungary: locations included Romania, Yugoslavia, the United States, and Canada. Some, like those who were tried in Yugoslavia, were extradited by the Hungarian government; others, many of whom had originally been tried in absentia in Hungary, were placed on trial abroad after being unmasked.

HUNGARY

By far the most important trials relating to the destruction of Hungarian Jewry were those held in Hungary. Many of the accused, especially people suspected of having been active in the roundup, ghettoization, and deportation of the Jews, were tried in the appropriate county's people's tribunal. The major war criminals, those who had served in top government positions and collaborated with the SS and other German agencies in the planning and implementation of the Final Solution, were tried in Budapest.

The courts involved in the trials operated in accordance with the provisions of Article 14 of the Armistice Agreement of 20 January 1945, under which Hungary undertook to cooperate in the apprehension and trial of persons accused of war crimes and crimes against humanity. In compliance with these provisions, the Provisional National Government adopted Decree No. 81/1945.M.E. (25 January 1945), establishing a system of "people's courts." These were envisioned to function until a duly elected legislature could set up a permanent court system.[8] Under the decree, two types of courts were established: (1) people's tribunals *(népbíróságok),* lower trial courts that functioned in most county seats, with each court presided over by a professional judge acting in conjunction with five lay judges or "people's assessors."[9] (2) The National Council of People's Tribunals (*A Népbíróságok Országos Tanácsa*—NOT), which heard appeals from the people's tribunals. NOT was headed by a professional judge appointed by the minister of justice and operated through several appellate councils, each consisting of five professional judges working in conjunction with lay deputies representing the coalition parties.[10]

The trials of the major war criminals began shortly after their extradition by the Western Allies. Even before their return to Budapest, however, "revolutionary courts" tried and convicted a number of Hungarian officers and guards who had committed horrendous crimes against labor servicemen (*munkaszolgálatosok*), especially in the Ukraine and Serbia.[11]

The series of trials involving the major war criminals began in Budapest on 29 October 1945. The first to be tried was former Prime Minister László Bárdossy. During his eleven-month tenure as premier (April 1941–March 1942), Hungary participated in the invasion of Yugoslavia, declared war on the Soviet Union and the United States, and became firmly committed to the Third Reich. It was also during his premiership that Hungary adopted the third major anti-Jewish law (clearly based on the Nazis' Nuremberg Law of 1935), exacerbated the Jewish labor service system, rounded up and deported close to eighteen thousand "alien" Jews (most of whom were slaughtered near Kamenets-Podolsky in late August 1941), and witnessed the massacre of close to a thousand Jews (along with three thousand Serbs) by Hungarian army and genadarmerie units in the Bácska area in January–February 1942.[12] Convicted on 3 November, Bárdossy was executed by a firing squad on 10 January 1946, following his unsuccessful appeal to NOT.[13]

Bárdossy's trial was followed by that of former Prime Minister Béla Imrédy. He was accused of crimes associated with his involvement in pro-Reich and anti-Jewish activities during his brief tenure as premier (May 1938–February 1939) and especially in connection with his services in the quisling government of Döme Sztójay. Originally an Anglophile, Imrédy was indicted, among other things, for his responsibility in the enactment of the major anti-Jewish laws of 1938 and 1939, and in preparing the ground for the close cooperation with the Third Reich. During the German occupation, he served as minister without portfolio in charge of economic coordination. Convicted on 23 November 1945, Imrédy was executed on 28 February 1946.[14]

Of greatest interest in connection with the destruction of Hungarian Jewry in 1944 was the trial of the three top officials of the Sztójay government in charge of handling the so-called Jewish Question, Minister of the Interior Andor Jaross, and his two state secretaries, László Baky and László Endre. The "deportation trio," as they were commonly referred to, went on trial on 18 December 1945. By the time the trial ended on 4 January 1946, Hungary and the world at large had heard the gruesome details on the planning and implementation of the Final Solution. In addition to responsibility for the destruction of the Jews, the three war criminals were also accused of plotting and cooperating with the SS to the detriment of Hungary's national interests. They were sentenced to death on 2 January 1946: Baky and Endre were hanged on 29 March, and Jaross was shot by a firing squad on 14 April.[15]

Another major trial that aroused great interest was that of Ferenc Szálasi, the leader of the Nazi-type Arrow Cross Party (*Nyilaskeresztes Párt*) and head of the government that was established with German assistance following the anti-Horthy coup of 15 October 1944. He and several leading figures of his regime were charged with crimes against the Jews, especially those of Budapest, and with political and military-related activities that virtually ruined Hungary during their six-month rule.[16] A major point of the indictment was their collusion with the SS in preventing the regent from extricating Hungary from the war. The trial also provided details about the evolution of the various right-radical Arrow Cross (*Nyilas*) movements and parties and about the reign of terror that characterized the Szálasi era.

The last major Hungarian trial of interest in connection with the Holocaust was that of Döme Sztójay, the former Hungarian minister in Berlin, who had been appointed prime minister after the German occupation. It was during his tenure that the Jews of Hungary, except those of Budapest, were liquidated. Sztójay's chief codefendants in the trial that began on 14 March 1946 were members of his government, including Antal Kunder, Jenö Rátz, Lajos Reményi-Schneller, and Lajos Szász. Accused of sacrificing the interests of the nation by collaborating with the Third Reich, the accused were found guilty on 22 March. Kunder was condemned to life imprisonment; the others were condemned to death and executed shortly thereafter.[17]

Concurrently with these mass trials, the people's courts held individual trials of several persons who had played important roles in the destruction of Hungarian Jewry. Among these were Lieutenant Colonel László Ferenczy, the gendarmerie officer in charge of the ghettoization and deportation program, and Péter Hain and László Koltay, the leaders of the state security police. All three were found guilty and executed in early spring 1946. Their trials were succeeded by those of a relatively large number of officials who had played a "secondary" role in Hungary's political life during the Nazi era.[18]

As in several other countries during the immediate postwar period, the Hungarian authorities also considered indicting the top leaders of the Budapest Jewish Council and of the Zionist-dominated Relief and Rescue Committee "for collaboration with the enemy." Working at top speed on the preparation of war crimes trial cases, the Political and Police Division of the Hungarian State Police of Budapest in fact collected a number of depositions and other evidence toward this end in 1945–1946.[19]

A similar plan was under way in Transylvania, where there was considerable bitterness, especially in Kolozsvár (Cluj), against the local wartime Jewish leaders. However, only one member of the Budapest Jewish Council was actually tried. Identified by several of his council colleagues as an informer in the service of the Hungarian Nazis, Rabbi Béla Berend of Szigetvár was convicted by a people's tribunal in Budapest and condemned to ten years' imprisonment in 1946. A year later, however, NOT reversed the lower court decision and Rabbi Berend was allowed to leave Hungary for the United States.[20] The three lawyer members of the Budapest Jewish Council—Ernö Boda, Ernö Petö, and Károly Wilhelm—were summoned to account for their activities on the council by the Budapest Bar or Chamber of Lawyers *(Ügyvédi Kamara),* but were eventually exonerated.[21] The controversial role played by the traditional and Zionist leaders of Hungary during the war in general and the German occupation in particular was revealed during the 1953–1955 Grünwald-Kasztner trial in Israel (see below).

The Hungarian people's tribunals continued their activities for several years, handling progressively fewer and less important cases. By 1 March 1948, criminal proceedings had been initiated against 39,514 persons, and 31,472 cases had been disposed of. Of these, 5,954 were dismissed and 9,245 ended with not guilty verdicts. Of the 16,273 convictions, 8,041 resulted in imprisonment of less than one year and 6,110 in terms between one and five years. Only 41 individuals were condemned to life terms at forced labor. In the country as a whole, 322 individuals were condemned to death; however, only 146 of these sentences were carried out, while the rest were commuted to life imprisonment.[22] There is no way to determine how many of the convicted criminals were released or had their sentences commuted under the various amnesty programs of the communist regime. György Berend, the former deputy president of NOT, summed up the record of the Hungarian people's tribunals as follows:

> If one takes into account how many leaders in respectable positions, how many warmongers and agitators against the people, and how many thousands of forced labor company murderer guards and *Nyilas* mass murderers were produced during the 25 years before the liberation, the above statistics elicit serious doubts even in the most ardent opponents of the people's tribunals.[23]

In addition to Hungary, Hungarian nationals accused of involvement in the destruction of Jews—and of crimes against Romanians and Serbs—were also tried in Romania and Yugoslavia. Their trials took place soon after the war and involved crimes committed in Hungarian-occupied Northern Transylvania and the Bácska, respectively.

ROMANIA

In connection with the tragedy of Hungarian Jewry, two trials were held in 1946 in Cluj (Kolozsvár), the capital of Transylvania, in people's tribunals set up under the provisions of Decree-Law No. 312 of the Ministry of Justice, dated 21 April 1945. The structure and organization of these tribunals were basically the same as those of Hungary. In the first of the mass trials, sixty-three individuals were accused of crimes against Romanians and some Jews during the occupation of Northern Transylvania by Hungarian troops in September 1940.[24] The destruction of the Jews of Northern Transylvania was the subject of the second mass trial, involving 185 individuals. Among these were the government, military, police, and gendarmerie officers and officials of the counties and of the cities that had been involved in the implementation of the Final Solution in the province. The sentences handed down by the court were stiff—twenty were condemned to death and many more to life imprisonment. Many of the accused, however, were tried in absentia. They represented the group that received the harshest penalties. Among them was Colonel Tibor Paksy-Kiss, the gendarmerie officer in charge of the ghettoization in the province. Of these only a few were eventually tried, mostly in Hungary. None of those condemned to death were executed.[25] Moreover, many of the criminals in custody were freed shortly after Romania's transformation into a Soviet-style people's democracy early in 1948. These were deemed "socially rehabilitated and politically reeducated"; among them were a number of fascists who had been condemned to life imprisonment for crimes against Jews.[26]

YUGOSLAVIA

In accordance with the provisions of Article 14 of the Armistice Agreement, the Hungarian authorities extradited to Yugoslavia several top-ranking Hungarian officers charged with complicity in the massacre of thousands of Serbs and Jews in the Bácska (Bácka), the area occupied by Hungary from 1941 to 1944.[27] The accused, including General Ferenc Szombathelyi, the former chief of the General Staff; General Ferenc Feketehalmy-Czeydner, the commander of the Fifth Army Corps; Major General József Grassy; and Captain Márton Zöldi, were first tried in Hungary.[28] The trial of the latter two, who were also accused of active involvement in the Final Solution in 1944, began on 8 January 1946. They were condemned to death by hanging four days later. The Hungarian trial of Generals Feketehalmy-Czeydner and Szombathelyi began on 21 March and 28 March, respectively. They too were found guilty by the court. All four were then handed over to the Yugoslavs, who retried them together with several Hungarian county and city officials active in the

Bácska area during the occupation era. The trial began on 24 October 1946 in Ujvidék (Novi Sad), the site of the greatest massacre. All of them were condemned to death six days later. They were executed early in November.[29]

The destruction of Hungarian Jewry was also the subject of several major war crimes trials that were held in the Federal Republic of Germany (West Germany), Austria, Czechoslovakia, Poland, and Israel. These involved top-ranking Nazi officials associated with the German Foreign Office and the Reich Security Main Office (*Reichssicherheitshauptamt*—RSHA), especially the Eichmann-*Sonderkommando*.

WEST GERMANY

Trials by Non-German Courts

Prior to the emergence of the Federal Republic of Germany as a sovereign entity, the crimes committed against the Jews of Hungary were the subject of the International Military Tribunal at Nuremberg, the twelve cases tried before the U.S. Military Tribunals, and the trials conducted by the British in their zone of occupation. At Nuremberg, the tragedy that befell Hungarian Jewry was dealt with primarily in the cases involving RSHA chief Ernst Kaltenbrunner and Foreign Minister Joachim von Ribbentrop. The Americans brought up the case of Hungarian Jewry in connection with the cases involving Oswald Pohl, the Flick, I. G. Farben, and Krupp combines, and the so-called Ministries cases. The British dealt with it primarily in the case involving Josef Kramer and forty-four other defendants associated with the Auschwitz, Natzweiler, and Bergen-Belsen camps. The two other occupation powers, France and the USSR, also held a few war-crimes-related military trials that dealt peripherally with the wartime plight of Hungarian Jewry.[30]

By far the most important trial relating to Hungarian Jewry was that of Edmund Veesenmayer, the former plenipotentiary of the Third Reich in occupied Hungary. As a leading defendant in the Ministries Case (1948), Veesenmayer was convicted on several counts of the indictment and condemned in April 1949 to twenty years' imprisonment.[31] In pursuit of U.S. postwar policy objectives in

Germany, John J. McCloy, the U.S. high commissioner for Germany, commuted Veesenmayer's sentence in January 1951 to ten years. He was freed a year later on the recommendation of a special U.S. clemency board.[32]

German Trials

The reconstituted German courts held a number of trials that dealt specifically with the tragedy of Hungarian Jewry. By far the most important of these was that of *SS-Obersturmbannführer* Herman Alois Krumey and *SS-Hauptsturmführer* Otto Hunsche, two leading figures of the Eichmann-*Sonderkommando* in Hungary. Though they played a crucial role in Hungary,[33] they lived in Germany undisturbed for fifteen years after the war. They were tried and convicted shortly after their arrest in 1960, only to be freed by an appellate court. They were retried in 1964–1965 in Frankfurt am Main: Hunsche was acquitted, Krumey was sentenced to five years at hard labor (3 February 1965). On the prosecutor's appeal, the Appellate Court at Karlsruhe nullified the Frankfurt court's decision in 1968 and ordered a new trial. This time Krumey was condemned to life imprisonment and Hunsche was sentenced to twelve years (29 August 1969). Their conviction was upheld on 17 January 1973.[34]

In the Auschwitz trial (December 1964–August 1965), the catastrophe of Hungarian Jewry was discussed especially in connection with the case against Victor Capesius, the Transylvanian pharmacist who had served as Josef Mengele's assistant on the selection ramp in Auschwitz. He was condemned to nine years' imprisonment but was freed shortly afterward, following the Karlsruhe higher court's order that the years Capesius spent in internment after the war be counted as part of his sentence.[35]

The West German authorities launched criminal proceedings against three other high-ranking officials of the Third Reich who had played an important role in the destruction of Hungarian Jewry: Horst Wagner and Eberhard von Thadden, the two leading officials of the Inland II Section of the German Foreign Office, and Albert Theodor Ganzenmüller, the state secretary in charge of the railways in the Reich Ministry of Transport. None of them served any time in prison. Thadden was killed in a car accident (8 November 1964); Wagner, whose trial actually began on 29 May 1972, but was suspended and periodically postponed because of illness, died in Hamburg on 13 March 1977.³⁶ Ganzenmüller, who was indicted for, among other things, providing the railroad cars used in the deportation of the Jews, went on trial on 3 May 1973. The trial was first delayed because of his lawyer's involvement in another prolonged case, then indefinitely postponed on medical grounds. Like many of his Nazi colleagues, Ganzenmüller also escaped punishment.³⁷ Among the several top-ranking Nazi officials who had served in Hungary during the occupation but were never brought to trial were *SS-Obergruppenführer* Otto Winkelmann and *SS-Standartenführer* Kurt Becher.³⁸

AUSTRIA

Two of the major war crimes trials held in Vienna related directly to the Holocaust in Hungary. The first one was that of *SS-Hauptsturmführer* Siegfried Seidl, the former commander of the Theresienstadt concentration camp and a leading member of the Eichmann-*Sonderkommando*. In Hungary, Seidl had served as an expert adviser in the roundup and deportation of several large Jewish communities, including those of Eger, Marosvásárhely, Mátészalka, Nyíregyháza, and Székesfehérvár. Found guilty as charged, Seidl was executed in Vienna on 4 October 1946.

The second trial involved *SS-Hauptsturmführer* Franz Novak, the *Sonderkommando*'s transportation expert and liaison with the Reich Ministry of Transport. After living unmolested for fifteen years, he was the subject of several trials. In his first trial (November 1964), Novak was condemned to eight years. On appeal, the Appellate Court *(Oberlandesgericht)* of Vienna nullified the judgment and ordered a new trial. After the second trial, held in September 1966, the court ordered Novak's release a month later because the jury was deadlocked over the issue of "superior orders." After the Appellate Court nullified the acquittal in February 1968, Novak was placed on trial once again on 20 December 1969. Convicted on one count, he was sentenced to nine years' imprisonment. This time, though, the Appellate Court concurred with the appeal by the defense and ordered still another trial, scheduled for August 1971. This fourth trial was held in March 1972 and the jury adopted the position of its predecessor in the first trial. Novak was condemned to seven years in prison on 13 April 1972.[39]

Also of interest in connection with the destruction of Hungarian Jewry was the trial in Vienna early in 1972 of Walter Dejaco and Fritz Karl Ertl, the SS officers and architects who designed and built the Auschwitz gas chambers and cremation furnaces. Both defendants were acquitted and released from custody on 10 March, the jury having concluded that they had acted under military orders and were ignorant of the use to which the death ovens would be put![40]

OTHER COUNTRIES

Trials of interest to Hungarian Jewry were also held in Poland, Czechoslovakia, and Israel. In Poland, the liquidation of Hungarian Jewry was a subject in the trial of Rudolf Franz Ferdinand Höss, the former commandant of Auschwitz. He was condemned to death by a Warsaw tribunal on 29 March 1947, and executed in Auschwitz a few days later.

In Czechoslovakia, the Bratislava trial of *SS-Hauptsturmführer* Dieter Wisliceny, a leading member of the Eichmann-*Sonderkommando* in Hungary, was of special interest. Wisliceny played a determining role in the roundup and ghettoization of the Jews, applying expertise he had acquired in the liquidation of the Jewish communities of Slovakia and Greece. Convicted on 27 February 1948, Wisliceny was hanged in Bratislava on 4 May.[41]

In Israel, many details of the Holocaust in Hungary—and the tragic fate of European Jewry as a whole—came to light during the trial of Adolf Eichmann, the former head of Section IV.B.4. of the RSHA. Captured by Israeli agents in Argentina in May 1960, Eichmann was tried in Jerusalem in 1961. He was hanged in Ramla on 31 May 1962.[42]

The catastrophe of Hungarian Jewry was also at the core of one of the most controversial trials ever held in Israel. It involved Rezsö (Rudolf) Kasztner, the former de facto head of the Budapest Relief and Rescue Committee—the *Vaadah*. The trial, which started out as a libel suit brought by Kasztner against Malkiel Grünwald, a *Mizrahi* Zionist who had accused him of collaboration, began on 1 January 1954. Intertwined with domestic political and governmental issues, the trial ended with the conviction of Kasztner. In a three-hundred-page opinion dated 22 June 1955, Judge Benjamin Halevi of the Jerusalem District Court concluded that "Kasztner sold his soul to the devil." The judgment of the lower court was reversed by a 3:2 decision of the Supreme Court on 15–17 January 1958, clearing Kasztner of the stigma of "collaboration." However, by that time Kasztner was dead: on 4 March 1947, he had been shot by zealots in Tel Aviv.[43]

The United States and Canada

A few Hungarian nationals were also the subject of judicial proceedings in the United States and Canada. These North American democracies became more sensitive to issues relating to the Holocaust only after the easing of the cold war in the era of detente. They became increasingly responsive to allegations that they were harboring thousands of individuals who had been actively involved in the Final Solution. Many among these suspected war criminals lived undisturbed for decades, hiding behind the cloak of anonymity. Others, enjoying the support of sundry ultraconservative elements, prospered openly as frontline champions of anticommunism.

The United States was the first to act, largely as a result of the legislative initiative of Congresswoman Elizabeth Holtzman (D-NY). In 1979, it brought about the establishment of the Office of Special Investigations (OSI) within the framework of the Department of Justice. Relying exclusively on civil proceedings (the United States lacks jurisdiction to bring criminal prosecutions against individuals whose crimes were committed outside the country against non-American citizens), the OSI achieved considerable progress in identifying and taking legal action against Nazi perpetrators residing in the United States. By April 1996, it had succeeded in stripping fifty-three such persons of U.S. citizenship and removing forty-five from the United States.

Among these were two former Hungarian nationals: József Szendi, a former gendarme who was involved in the deportation of "alien" Jews in 1941 and participated in the Hungarian anti-Jewish campaign in 1944, and Ferenc Koréh, the former "responsible editor" of *A Székely Nép* (The Székely People), an anti-Semitic daily published in Sepsiszentgyörgy in Northern Transylvania. Koréh was also associated with other anti-Jewish and anti-Allied periodicals and served in the Hungarian Propaganda Office during the Holocaust. After coming to the United States in 1958, Szendi lived and worked as a janitor in Cookeville, Tennessee, until his retirement in the 1970s. It was Szendi's personal vanity that led to his unmasking: he had revealed part of his background in a book published in Hungary shortly after the collapse of the communist system.[44] The OSI initiated denaturalization proceedings against him on 9 September 1992, and on 18 June 1993 the U.S. District Court in Cookeville revoked his citizenship. Under an agreement that was not totally unfavorable to him, Szendi "voluntarily" left the United States a few days later and went back to Hungary.

Ferenc Koréh, 86 years of age in 1996, had come to the United States in the early 1950s and worked for several decades after his arrival as a Hungarian specialist for Radio Free Europe. The OSI began denaturalization proceedings against him in the early 1980s, but for some internal reason the case was left dormant until the early 1990s. After lengthy legal wranglings, a Federal District Court in Newark, New Jersey, awarded summary judgment to the U.S. Government in June 1994 after finding, among other things, that Koréh's admitted service as responsible editor of the *Székely Nép* constituted "advocacy and assistance in persecution" and "membership and participation in a movement hostile to the United States." The court's order revoking Koréh's citizenship was upheld by the Third Circuit Court of Appeals in Philadelphia on 14 July 1995. On 19 April 1996, the U.S. Justice Department initiated deportation proceedings against Koréh, who at the time of this writing tries to remain with his family in Englewood, New Jersey, on grounds of advanced age and illness.

The pitfalls of the criminal approach followed by Canada almost forty years after the war were revealed in the ill-fated Finta case (October 1989–May 1990). The trial involved Imre Finta, a Hungarian gendarmerie captain who was charged with, among other things, the confinement, imprisonment, and robbery of 8,617 Jews who had been concentrated in the brickyard ghetto of Szeged, one of the largest provincial cities of Hungary, in 1944. As the head of a special gendarmerie investigative unit, Finta was in charge of gendarmes who, often working in plain clothes, interrogated and tortured Jews for the "recovery" of their hidden wealth. He and his gendarmes were also actively involved in the 25–28 June 1944 deportation of the Jews from Szeged.[45]

The trial of Finta was initiated by the Canadian Department of Justice following the recommendations of a special commission headed by Justice Jules Deschenes. According to the commission's report, which was submitted to the Canadian Parliament on 12 March 1987, only 20 of the 882 investigated cases included prima facie evidence of war crimes warranting urgent legal action. Shortly after the criminal code was amended to make possible the prosecution of these cases, the attorney general of Canada gave his consent to the indictment of Finta on 18 August 1988, presumably considering his case as the prosecution's strongest. But this trial, in the Supreme Court of Ontario in Toronto, turned out to be an unfortunate test case in the criminal pursuit of suspected war criminals. Although the Canadian Department of Justice made a tremendous effort and invested relatively large sums of money in the collection of documentary evidence, the roundup of witnesses, and the recruitment of a variety of experts, the prosecution could not, more than forty years after the commission of the crime, satisfy the judiciary requirements of a Western-type criminal court. The jury reached a verdict of not guilty only one day after it was charged on 24 May 1990—an outcome that was upheld by the Court of Appeal for Ontario (29 April 1992) and the Supreme Court of Canada (24 March 1994).[46]

A CRITICAL ASSESSMENT

The civil and criminal trials conducted in the United States and Canada once again brought to the fore the many still controversial issues concerning the wartime and postwar positions of the Allies on the Nazi-era plight of the Jews. Although fully aware of the details of the Nazis' Final Solution and of the anti-Jewish measures that preceded it, the Allies consistently rejected any active involvement in rescuing of Jews as incompatible with their war aims and strategies.[47] They asserted, not without justification, that their objective—the speediest possible defeat of the Third Reich—was the best possible hope for the Jews as well. Driven by political and strategic considerations, the Allies even refused for a long time to acknowledge publicly, and condemn, the Nazis' pernicious campaign against the Jews. It was not until 17 December 1942 that the Allies issued a declaration acknowledging that the Nazis were engaged in a genocidal campaign against the Jews. Condemning "the bestial policy of cold-blooded extermination," the Allies prudently balanced their inaction on rescue by a declaration of warning against the perpetrators: "[The Allies] reaffirm their solemn resolution to insure that those responsible for these crimes shall not escape retribution, and to press on with the necessary practical measures to this end."[48] The effectiveness of the warning was undercut by its implication that nothing would be done before final victory and by its failure to provide for some immediate threat of retaliation against the Nazis and their accomplices.

The Allies' lamentable record of wartime rescue was largely matched by their postwar record of retributive justice. With the division of the world into two spheres of influence and the emerging cold war, the Allies effectively reneged on their wartime commitments as they began to reshape their national priorities in accord with their swiftly changing national interests. The Western Allies, eager to develop the areas under their control along democratic, anticommunist lines, became increasingly reluctant to proceed with the prosecution of those actively involved in the Final Solution, including Germans, Austrians, and East European fascist refugees under their jurisdiction. In the new anticommunist climate, they also became progressively more lenient toward those already convicted. As a result of amnesties and arbitrary actions on the part of the occupation authorities, and later of the governments of the reestablished sovereign states, many convicted Nazis had their sentences reduced or were actually freed without going to prison. Moreover, many Nazis and their sundry collaborators involved in anti-Jewish crimes managed to escape prosecution altogether and lived out their lives in various parts of the free world.

The record of the Soviet Union is almost as bleak as that of the Western Allies. Eager to reconstruct their devastated country and develop their own version of communism in East Central Europe, the Soviets also refused to prosecute an unknown number of Nazis deemed useful to their interests. They were particularly lenient toward Nazis with expertise in the sciences, technology, and police security. Moreover, in their eagerness to bring about the transformation of the conquered states into full-fledged people's democracies, the Soviets encouraged the respective communist parties to strengthen their ranks by admitting rank-and-file fascists and Nazi collaborators. Retribution for wartime crimes against Jews was subordinated to the needs of postwar political realities in both spheres of influence.

The belated attempt at retributive justice in the Western world[49] coincided with the drive for the "reevaluation" of cases involving war crimes and crimes against humanity in the former Soviet bloc nations. Within a short time after the dissolution of the communist system in 1989, the people's tribunals became the subject of heated political debates. More frequent as well as more pointed questions were raised about their legitimacy and the "political" nature of their judgments. Many individuals, especially nationalists on the Right side of the new political spectrum, have argued that the people's courts, lacking constitutional legitimacy, were, in fact, only political instruments of vengeance in the hands of Jews seeking revenge for their alleged wartime suffering. In most of these newly democratic states, well-organized xenophobic nationalist groups have been increasingly active since 1989 in seeking the rehabilitation of their particular wartime pro-Nazi leaders.

The reevaluation process and the debate over the legitimacy of the people's tribunals seem to have surfaced with particular vehemence in Hungary, as compared to the other former Soviet bloc nations. This is due primarily to the relatively large number of survivors, especially among labor servicemen and the Jews of Budapest, and the disproportionate role some of them played in the immediate postwar security forces. The critique of the people's tribunals' work has become intertwined with an anti-Semitic interpretation of the work in the courts of some of the liberated Jews. Even moderate Christians had distinctly negative views of the disproportionate and highly visible involvement of Jews in Hungary's court and security systems, since no Jews had been permitted to play any role in them during the pre-1945 era. As early as 1948, István Bibó, one of the most respected scholars and statesmen of postwar Hungary, was convinced that one of the primary reasons for the resurfacing of anti-Semitism in post-Holocaust Hungary was the Jews' disproportionate representation in the political police and their identification with the Soviet-imposed communist system.[50] In his view, the presence of a relatively large number of Jews in the people's courts and the security forces gave the impression that Jews were now passing judgment on Hungarians in retaliation for the judgment they had been subjected to in the past. The ends of justice, Bibó argued, would have perhaps been better served if the Jews had voluntarily abstained from being involved in the court and security systems. He was, however, quick to recognize that imposing such an abstention would itself again involve a fascist-type distinction, based on religion, between groups of Hungarian nationals.

There is no doubt that, under the impact of the murder of close to six hundred thousand Jews, a number of survivors, especially among the former labor servicemen, entered the security forces for vengeance. It is also certain, however, that many other survivors joined these forces, the people's courts, and the leftist movements, in pursuit of justice and the creation of a new, genuinely social democratic Hungary. The argument over their presence in these organs of state power is tainted by anti-Semitism. Rightist extremists, chauvinistic nationalists, and those who distort or actually deny the Holocaust have endeavored, especially after the collapse of the communist system in 1989, to identify the evils of the Soviet era with the power the Jews allegedly wielded in the instruments of state power.[51] As Shlomo Avineri, a highly respected Israeli political scientist, observed, the reason Jews became rather visible in the political police forces of the emerging communist regimes was simple:

> After 1945 the main task of the political police in those countries was to trace fascist collaborators and bring them to trial, and to prevent the resurgence of fascist and near-fascist movements. Who but Jews could be trusted not to have been involved in such movements and not to have brothers and cousins and uncles and nephews who were involved? And who but Jewish people had an unquestioned motivation to bring Nazi collaborators and fascists and antisemites to trial? That this would become a pact of the Stalinist devil became clear to many of these people only much later.[52]

And indeed much of the criticism of the people's courts is a reflection of the legitimate critique of the abuses of the Stalinist era. Clearly, the postwar Hungarian trials did not uphold the guiding principles of judicial procedures in criminal cases in well-established democratic societies. But given the governmental vacuum of the immediate postwar era and the fascist character of the Hungarian judiciary system during the Sztójay and Szálasi periods, there was no viable alternative to the establishment of a temporary court system based on the provisions of the Armistice Agreement. As to the accusation that the people's courts lacked constitutional legitimacy and historical continuity, no rational person could expect that the Hungarian courts, which had been dominated by the Arrow Cross before the Soviet forces took over, could have done justice in cases involving war crimes and crimes against humanity.

In retrospect it is clear that the people's courts pursued not only the punishment of those accused of active collaboration with the Third Reich and involvement in the Final Solution, but also longer-range political objectives. With the political strings increasingly in the hands of Soviet-backed communists, the people's courts were also exploited, among other things, to bring about the gradual liquidation of the counterrevolutionary regime that had ruled Hungary since 1919, reeducate the masses along new political-ideological lines, and prepare the ground for the establishment of an antifascist, pro-Soviet people's democratic system. It is fair to assume that not all those who were associated with the security forces and the people's courts during the immediate postwar years were privy to these objectives of the so-called Moscovite leaders of the Hungarian Communist Party and their Soviet mentors.

Shortly after the systemic change of 1989, legal measures were started to redress the judicial-political injustices of the past. On 11 January 1994, the Constitutional Court *(Alkotmánybíróság)* of the new democratic republic of Hungary found most provisions of Law VII/1945 (which incorporated Decree No. 81/1945.M.E.) unconstitutional on the grounds that they provided punishment for acts that were not deemed criminal at the time of their commission. It left standing, however, Paragraph 5 of Article 11 and Paragraph 2 of Article 13, which relate to war crimes identified as punishable under both international law and Hungary's criminal code (Law No. IV of 1978).[53]

The ruling of the court resulted in the nullification of many of the decisions of the people's tribunals. As a consequence, an indeterminate number of fascists who had actively participated in various phases of the Final Solution, including police and gendarmerie officers and officials of the Sztójay and Szálasi governments, had their sentences reversed. Feeling officially vindicated, a number of them even received compensation for their suffering "at the hands of the communists." Some, though aged, were actually emboldened to resume their ultrarightist, neofascist political activities. Providing ammunition for the small but vocal group of "historical revisionists," they are in the forefront of distorting, denigrating, and denying the Holocaust. The elusiveness of retributive justice has once again been matched by the durability of anti-Semitism.

NOTES

1. At the time of the German occupation, the Jewish population of Hungary was 825,000, including the approximately 100,000 converts or Christians identified as Jews under the Nazi laws. According to the census of 1941, the Jews represented 4.94 percent of the total population. The Jewish losses during World War II came close to 600,000. See Randolph L. Braham, *The Politics of Genocide: The Holocaust in Hungary* (New York: Rosenthal Institute for Holocaust Studies of the City University of New York, 1994), pp. 1296–1301 (hereafter cited as Braham, *Politics*).

2. See ibid., chap. 23. See also Martin Gilbert, *Auschwitz and the Allies* (New York: Holt, Rinehart and Winston, 1982), and Walter Laqueur, *The Terrible Secret* (Boston: Little, Brown, 1980).

3. For details on the destruction of Hungarian Jewry, see Braham, *Politics,* passim.

4. On Hungarian Nazis and ultrarightists who had escaped to the West, see refs. 2335–41 in Randolph L. Braham, comp. and ed., *The Hungarian Jewish Catastrophe: A Selected and Annotated Bibliography* (New York: Institute for Holocaust Studies of the City University of New York, 1984) (hereafter cited as Braham, *Bibliography*).

5. On the extradition issue, see Jenö Lévai, "The War Crimes Trials Relating to Hungary," in *Hungarian Jewish Studies,* vol. 2, ed. Randolph L. Braham (New York: World Federation of Hungarian Jews, 1969), pp. 263–5 (hereafter cited as Lévai).

6. On these Nazis' activities in Hungary, see Braham, *Politics,* passim.

7. On the Hungarian suspected war criminals, see Martin Himler, *Igy néztek ki a magyar nemzet sírásói* (This is what the gravediggers of the Hungarian nation looked like) (New York: St. Marks Printing, 1958).

8. The decree went into effect on 5 February 1945. Amended several times, it was formally enacted into law by the Provisional National Assembly on 14 September 1945 as Law No. VII of 1945. For text see *1945 évi országos törvénytár* (National code of laws for 1945) (Budapest: Athenaeum, 1945), pp. 33–52.

9. The presiding judges and their deputies were appointed by the minister of justice. The lay judges represented the five anti-Nazi political parties constituting the Hungarian National Independence Front *(Magyar Nemzeti Függetlenségi Front):* the Democratic Bourgeois Party *(Demokrati-*

kus Polgári Párt), the Independent Smallholders' Party *(Független Kisgazdapárt)*, the Hungarian Communist Party *(Magyar Kommunista Párt)*, the National Peasant Party *(Nemzeti Parasztpárt)*, and the Social Democratic Party *(Szociáldemokrata Párt)*.

10. The people's courts, including NOT and the prosecution offices, were supplanted on 1 January 1952 by new organs of justice established under Law No. III of 1951 of the new pro-Soviet people's democratic regime. For some details, see Braham, *Politics,* pp. 1317–23. See also Lévai, pp. 255–63.

11. The wartime system of labor service in Hungary was unique in Nazi-dominated Europe. For details, see Braham, *Politics,* pp. 284–380. See also his *The Hungarian Labor Service System: 1939–1945* (Boulder: East European Quarterly, 1977).

12. For details, see Braham, *Politics,* pp. 198–209.

13. *A Bárdossy per: A vád, a vallomások és az itélet* (The Bárdossy trial: The indictment, the testimonies, and the verdict), ed. Ferenc Abrahám and Endre Kussinszky (Budapest: Híradó Könyvtár, 1945), and *Bárdossy László a népbíróság elött* (László Bárdossy before the people's tribunal), with notes and introduction by Pál Fritz (Budapest: Maecenas, 1991). See also Elek Karsai, *Itél a nép* (The people judge) (Budapest: Kossuth, 1977), pp. 17–71.

14. On the trial, see *Az Imrédy per: A vád, a vallomások és az itélet* (The Imrédy trial: The indictment, the testimonies, and the verdict), ed. Ferenc Abrahám and Endre Kussinszky (Budapest: Hiradó Könyvtár, 1945). See also Karsai, *Itél a nép,* pp. 72–119.

15. For the transcript of the trial with comments and notes, see *Az Endre-Baky-Jaross per* (The Endre-Baky-Jaross trial), eds. László Karsai and Judit Molnár (Budapest: Cserépfalvi, 1994). See also Karsai, *Itél a nép,* pp. 185–215. For details on their role in the Holocaust of Hungarian Jewry, see Braham, *Politics,* passim.

16. The Szálasi trial began on 5 February 1946. Along with leading members of his government, including Károly Beregfy, Sándor Csia, József Gera, Gábor Kemény, Jenö Szöllösi, and Gábor Vajna, Szálasi was convicted and condemned to death on 1 March. They were all executed later that month. Two of Szálasi's cabinet members, László Budinszky and Count Fidél Pálffy, were tried in December 1945, and executed early in March 1946. For some details, see *A Szálasi per* (The Szálasi trial), ed. Elek Karsai and László Karsai (Budapest: Reform, 1988). For details on the Szálasi era in Hungary, see Braham, *Politics.*

17. For some excerpts from the trial, see Karsai, *Itél a nép,* pp. 140–84. For details on the anti-Jewish measures enacted during the Sztójay era, see Braham, *Politics.*

18. Ibid., pp. 1321–2.

19. See, for example, the 19 July 1946 statement by Mrs. László Szántó, née Gabriella Kertész, incriminating Joel Brand and Rezsö Kasztner. This, and several other similar depositions, may be found in file NB.2600/1946, relating to the trial of Rabbi Béla Berend, a member of the Budapest Jewish Council. See "RG-52 Randolph Braham Collection" in the archives of the U.S. Holocaust Memorial Museum in Washington, D.C.

20. For details on this controversial case and its aftermath, see Braham, *Politics,* pp. 480–9.

21. Ibid., p. 905.

22. Lévai, p. 277. For sources relating to the war crimes trials held in Hungary, see refs. 2022–2315 in Braham, *Bibliography.*

23. Lévai, p. 278. See also György Berend, *A népbíróskodás* (People's justice) (Szeged: György Berend, 1948).

24. Hungary acquired Northern Transylvania from Romania under the so-called Vienna Award of 30 August 1940, imposed by the Axis Powers. For details, see Braham, *Politics,* pp. 167–76.

25. For the records of these and other war crimes trials held in Cluj and elsewhere in Romania, see RG-25.004M in the archives of the U.S. Holocaust Memorial Museum, Washington, D.C.

26. These criminals were freed under the provisions of Decree No. 72 of 23 March 1950. For text see *Buletinul Oficial* (Official gazette), 23 March 1950. For the English translation of the judgment and details about the proceedings, see Randolph L. Braham, *Genocide and Retribution: The Holocaust in Hungarian-Ruled Northern Transylvania* (Boston: Kluwer-Nijhoff, 1983).

27. Hungary occupied the Bácska (also known as the Délvidék) area in April 1941, following the defeat of Yugoslavia by the Germans. See Braham, *Politics,* pp. 181–5. On the massacres, see ibid., pp. 214–22.

28. Feketehalmy-Czeydner, Grassy, and Zöldi were originally tried in Budapest in 1943 during the administration of Prime Minister Miklós Kállay. Inasmuch as Hungary was an ally of the Third Reich, the trial of high-ranking officers for murdering Jews and Serbs was an act of great political courage. The defendants were condemned to imprisonment ranging from eleven to fifteen years, but they fled the country and found refuge in Vienna as guests of the Gestapo. They returned to Hungary with the German occupation forces in March 1944 and played an active role in the liquidation of Hungarian Jewry. For details, see ibid., pp. 218–22.

29. Ibid., pp. 1324–5. See also Lévai, pp. 288–9.

30. The French courts were primarily concerned with crimes committed in concentration and forced labor camps. Of the Soviet trials, by far the most important from the Hungarian Jewish point of view was that of Friedrich Jeckeln, the higher SS and police leader, *Ostland,* who was com-

mander of the forces that slaughtered over 23,000 Hungarian and Ukrainian Jews near Kamenets-Podolsky in late August 1941. Jeckeln was executed in 1946. For sources relating to the French and Soviet trials, consult Jacob Robinson and Philip Friedman, comps., *Guide to Jewish History under Nazi Impact* (New York: YIVO Institute for Jewish Research, 1960), pp. 190–209 and 209–10, respectively.

31. For the transcript of the trial, see "Ministries Case" (court 4, case 11), transcript pp. 2702–50, 3617–59, 7143–58, 13062–460, 26156–189. U.S. National Archives, Washington, D.C. See also *Trials of War Criminals before the Nuernberg Military Tribunals under Control Council Law No. 10* (Washington, D.C.: Government Printing Office, 1949–1953) vol. 14, pp. 825–31, 646–60, 812–17, 858–59. See also refs. 2005–10 in Braham, *Bibliography*.

32. On the composition of the clemency board, see Raul Hilberg, *The Destruction of the European Jews* (Chicago: Quadrangle, 1961), pp. 684–715.

33. See Braham, *Politics*, passim.

34. On these trials, see refs. 2000–2 in Braham, *Bibliography*.

35. On Capesius and others involved in the destruction of Hungarian Jews, see Bernd Naumann, *Auschwitz: A Report on the Proceedings against Robert Karl Ludwig Mulka and Others before the Court at Frankfurt* (New York: Praeger, 1966).

36. On Wagner's and Thadden's activities in connection with the Holocaust in Hungary, see Braham, *Politics*, passim.

37. For some additional details on the trials held in West Germany, see ibid., pp. 1325–8. See also Lévai, pp. 285–8.

38. On their activities during the German occupation of Hungary, see Braham, *Politics*, passim. Winkelmann died in Bordersholm on 24 September 1977. Becher died in Bremen in early August 1995. See also refs. 1943–5 and 2011–6 in Braham, *Bibliography*.

39. Braham, *Politics*, pp. 1328–9. See also ref. 2003 in Braham, *Bibliography*.

40. *New York Times*, 11 March 1972.

41. For Wisliceny's statement concerning his and the *Sonderkommando*'s role in Hungary, see doc. 440 in Randolph L. Braham, comp., *The Destruction of Hungarian Jewry: A Documentary Account* (New York: World Federation of Hungarian Jews, 1963). See also ref. 2017 in Braham, *Bibliography*.

42. For references to all aspects of Eichmann's activities and to his pursuit, capture, and trial, see *The Eichmann Case: A Source Book* (New York: World Federation of Hungarian Jews, 1969). See also refs. 1946–95 in Braham, *Bibliography*.

43. On all aspects of the Kasztner case, see Braham, *Politics,* pp. 1088–112. See also refs. 1911–35 in Braham, *Bibliography.*

44. Szendi's book, titled *Csendörsors: Hernádnémetitöl Floridáig* (Gendarme's fate: From Hernádnémeti to Florida), was published in 1990 by the Miskolc branch of the Hungarian Democratic Forum Party, postcommunist Hungary's dominant party at the time.

45. Finta escaped from Hungary in January 1945. He was first tried in absentia in Szeged early in 1948, and sentenced to a minimum of five years of forced labor (Szeged, People's Court, Case No. 221/1947/10). He was eventually captured by the Americans, who kept him in a POW camp for eighteen months without learning of his background. He emigrated to Canada in 1951, settled in Toronto, and lived as a restaurateur virtually until his indictment for war crimes.

46. On many ramifications of the case, see Randolph L. Braham, "Canada and the Perpetrators of the Holocaust: The Case of Regina v. Finta," *Holocaust and Genocide Studies* 9, no. 3 (winter 1995): 293–317. For the Hungarian-language version, see "Kanada és a Holocaust bünelkövetöi: A Regina kontra Finta büntetöper," *Századok* (Centuries) (Budapest) 129, no. 6 (1995): 1331–54.

47. For details about the Allies' awareness of the Final Solution, see references in note 2.

48. "German Policy of Extermination of the Jewish Race," *Department of State Bulletin* 7, no. 182 (19 December 1942): 1009.

49. In addition to the United States and Canada, Australia and Great Britain also began to deal with suspected Nazi war criminals in their midst in the early 1990s. In their test cases, they followed the strategy of criminal judicial procedure that had already been used in Canada's Finta case, and ended up with the same negative result.

50. See his "Zsidókérdés Magyarországon 1948-után" (The Jewish Question in Hungary after 1948), *Válasz* (Response) (Budapest), no. 8 (October–November 1948): 778–877.

51. This is a standard theme of the several Right-radical parties that emerged after 1989 and their press organs.

52. See his "The Return to History and Its Consequences for the Jewish Communities in Eastern Europe," in *The Danger of Antisemitism in Central and Eastern Europe in the Wake of 1989–1990,* ed. Yehuda Bauer (Jerusalem: Hebrew University of Jerusalem, 1991), p. 98.

53. For the text of the decision, including its justification, see "A 2/1994.(I.14)AB határozat" (Decision No. 2/1994.(1.14)AB), *Az Alkotmánybíróság határozatai* (Decisions of the Constitutional Court) (Budapest), no. 1 (1994): 9–20.

Piotr Wróbel

Hitler's Helpers?
The Judenräte *Controversy*

THE PROBLEM OF THE JEWISH COUNCILS, *DIE JUDENRÄTE*, IS ONE OF THE most important, difficult, explosive, and, at the same time, most neglected segments of Holocaust studies. While every year thousands of new books on the Holocaust appear, the entire list of English-language works on the *Judenräte* consists of about thirty titles, including only one major book, Isaiah Trunk's *Judenrat*, already twenty-five years old, not comprehensive enough, and incomplete in terms of primary sources.[1]

Of course, every synthesis of the Holocaust discusses the Jewish Councils. Yet, most of these discussions are relatively short and frequently very controversial—so controversial, in fact, that their authors have been accused of slander, ignorance, and even anti-Semitism.[2] The works of Hannah Arendt, especially her 1944 essay "The Jew as Pariah: A Hidden Tradition," and the famous 1963 *Eichmann in Jerusalem,* implied that the victims of the Final Solution were partially responsible for their own fate—thereby causing outrage among survivors.[3] Léon Poliakov wrote about the Jewish Councils in his 1954 *Harvest of Hate: The Nazi Program for the Destruction of the Jews of Europe:*

> An indelible shame would seem to stick to these organs of collaboration. Their members enjoyed certain prerogatives and were the lords of the ghetto; they may be compared with the Quislings and the Lavals. . . . Historically, the Jewish councils were inevitable. Different judgments may be passed depending on the specific case, on the motives of these men, and on the manner in which they exercised their functions. One judgment, however, is certain: many outright scoundrels insinuated themselves into the councils.[4]

Where Poliakov views *Judenrat* members as scoundrels, Raul Hilberg in *The Destruction of the European Jews,* published in 1961, considers the *Judenräte* as a part of the Nazi bureaucracy. Gerald Reitlinger's 1953 *Final Solution* gives a more complex evaluation of the Jewish Councils. Most scholarly and popular works of the 1950s and 1960s condemned the *Judenräte*. Later, additional research and public debate started a "gradual loosening of the more general and stigmatizing approach" to the study of the Jewish Councils.[5]

Subsequently, Holocaust scholars began to consider various stages of *Judenräte* activities, personal changes in their makeup, their different characters in various German-occupied countries, and other elements of their behavior and history. Yet, still no generally accepted and balanced synthesis of the *Judenräte* exists. Isaiah Trunk concluded his research with the following statement: "[W]hen all factors are considered, Jewish participation or nonparticipation in the deportations had no substantial influence—one way or the other—on the final outcome of the Holocaust in Eastern Europe."[6] Yehuda Bauer wrote in 1977 that "The *Judenräte* as a whole were groups of Jewish men who tried to act for the good of the community over which they were appointed according to the best of their understanding and under impossible conditions."[7] Most scholars who have published since the mid-1970s appear to share this conviction, or disregard the problem of *Judenräte* responsibility entirely. Neither of these approaches is fully satisfactory for those who seek to understand the role of the *Judenräte* in the history of the Holocaust.

Nazi occupation and crimes created such extreme situations and challenges to the human mind that "in many cases the criteria of traditional morality had ceased to be applicable."[8] During World War II a widespread belief appeared that new criteria, new approaches, and a new methodology were necessary to evaluate and punish those guilty of, or responsible for, war crimes. After the war, a series of trials took place, among them the trials of former members of various *Judenräte*, Jewish policemen, and Kapos in the German camps. Can these trials be helpful in our search for a proper evaluation of the *Judenräte*? Usually, courts of law collect large numbers of documents to support both prosecution and defense. The trials were frequently organized with the intention of preparing historical testimony,[9] and their transcripts are sometimes among the best historical sources. Judges, prosecutors, and lawyers, such as Jacob Robinson, Gideon

Hausner, Michael A. Musmanno, or Yehuda Bauer, were also frequently active as historians.[10] So let us examine how these trials have contributed to the historical evaluation of the *Judenräte*.

In Holland after the war, the new Jewish leadership decided to organize a court of honor to try council members and collaborators. Yet, from the court's inception the organizers faced many serious difficulties. The majority of the survivors had been connected, in some way, with the *Joodse Raad*. Several of the judges of the Jewish Court of Honor resigned during its proceedings. An effort to establish a court of appeal also failed. Eventually, the court tried members of the *Joodse Raad* and condemned them for their acceptance of membership on the council, for publishing the *Joodse Weekblad*, which publicized Nazi propaganda, for participation in the selection and transportation of the Jews to the Nazi extermination camps, and on several other counts. Yet, the court assumed that the *Joodse Raad* members did not know that they were sending their coreligionists to death. The court of honor's sentence decreed that the presidents of the *Joodse Raad*, Abraham Asscher and David Cohen, could not hold any office for the remainder of their lives. At the same time as the Jewish Court of Honor was trying Cohen and Asscher, they were arrested by the Dutch state authorities. The Dutch prosecuting attorney stated that "Cohen and Asscher, as Jews, collaborated with the enemy, and shall not see the light of freedom." Eventually, the Dutch minister of justice decided to drop the case, adding that "this should not be construed as a rehabilitation of the party in question."[11]

Several courts of honor were established in the Jewish displaced persons and survivors camps in Germany and Italy between 1945 and 1948. The judges of the courts were mostly survivors themselves. They also did not know how to evaluate the role and activities of the Jewish Councils, the Jewish policemen, and the Kapos, and did not take a firm position on this. Nobody was sentenced for merely being a member of a council in the various Jewish ghetto administrations. Jewish postwar centers in Europe gathered only individual survivors of various ghettos and camps; it was impossible to find numerous witnesses, as many had been killed by the Nazis or died in the camps. Moreover, the accusation of a single person was not enough to open an investigation.[12]

The courts of honor established in Germany and Italy tried mostly former Kapos and Jewish policemen. Punishment tended to be lenient. Those found guilty of collaboration with the German police and Gestapo, and those who helped organize the deportations to the death camps, were forbidden to hold any position in Jewish institutions, denied material assistance from Jewish organizations, or, in some cases, excommunicated.[13] The verdicts were announced in the Jewish press. Isaiah Trunk studied the documentation of 42 trials against former ghetto policemen and Kapos held by the courts of honor in Germany and Italy. Only 27 cases resulted in sentences. The rest were discontinued for various reasons. In 9 of the 27 cases resulting in sentences, the convicted were later rehabilitated. In 13 cases, the defendants were declared traitors to the Jewish people, forbidden to hold any positions in Jewish public life, or excluded from the community. Some were denied rehabilitation with no punishment. During the trials in Italy and Germany, the courts of honor realized that sometimes the same person was a member of a prewar Jewish council, a wartime *Judenrat,* and a postwar self-government of a displaced persons or survivors camp.[14]

In 1950, the Knesset accepted the Nazis and Nazi Collaborators (Punishment) Law and, between 1951 and 1964, a number of former Jewish policemen and Kapos—but no council members—were tried. The Israeli courts were also rather lenient. They often accepted as a mitigating factor that a defendant's life was in danger if he refused to carry out the orders of the German authorities. In some cases, when ghetto policemen were sentenced to several years in jail or to death, the Supreme Court quashed the sentences, citing extenuating circumstances as the reason.[15] An Israeli court accepted the explanation that the stern attitude of an accused toward those in her charge had saved them from much worse treatment by the Germans, thus clearing even a cruel Auschwitz Kapo of guilt.[16] The Supreme Court declared that membership in, and the activities of, the Jewish Councils and their institutions during the war constituted a historical problem—not a legal one. Judge Moshe Landau, a member of the Supreme Court, stated: "We should not interpret the basis of the individual crime, as formulated in the Nazis and Nazi Collaborators (Punishment) Law, by a yardstick of moral behavior of which only a few were capable. . . . Every one cares for himself and his family, and the prohibitions of criminal law, including the Nazis and Nazi Collaborators (Punishment) Law, were not written for heroes, extraordinary individuals, but for simple mortals with their simple weaknesses."[17] In addition, it appears that the Israelis were not really interested in the trials of the Nazi collaborators, and only the Kasztner case provoked a stir.[18] The postwar courts of honor in Western Europe and the Israeli trials are relatively well known. Less well known is the case of the so-called people's courts (*Sądy Społeczne*) in Poland. Popularly, the name was used in the plural although, in fact, there was only one central institution, which should be called the People's Court. The Warsaw Archives of the Jewish Historical Institute in Poland (Archiwum Żydowskiego Instytutu Historycznego w Polsce) contains a large collection of the documents of the Central Committee of the Jews in Poland (Centralny Komitet Żydów w Polsce—CKZP) The collection includes a section (No. 313) comprising the documents of the People's Court.[19]

In 1945, the Central Committee of the Jews in Poland decided to reckon with the past, to settle the painful issue of Jewish collaboration with the Nazis, and to settle accounts with *Judenrat* members, Jewish policemen, and other employees of the Nazi-sponsored wartime Jewish self-government. They were asked by special announcements in the press, published by the Central Committee of the Jews, to submit rehabilitation applications. Former policemen were supposed to apply before 15 January 1946 (or before 15 March 1947 if they lived abroad). Former members of the *Judenräte* and employees of their administration were asked to apply before 1 October 1947. Although officially an application for rehabilitation was considered a citizen's obligation, pressure was frequently put on individuals to go through the rehabilitation process. In several cases the rehabilitation applications were rejected without a trial. In one case, a refusal to apply for rehabilitation was recognized as an offense, and Z. Wolfowicz, a former policeman in the Warsaw ghetto, was publicly reprimanded.[20]

The People's Court was established in the fall of 1946. A protocol of its organizational meeting is dated 28 September 1946.[21] The main office of the court was located in Warsaw, at Sienna Street 60. There was a *Sekretariat Koła Rzeczników Oskarzenia* (Secretariat of the Persecution Spokesmen's Circle) in Cracow, at Długa Street 38. Most trials took place in Warsaw and Cracow, but there were also "field sessions" (*sesje wyjazdowe*) in Lodz and smaller Polish towns. Most trials took place in 1949. Altogether, between 1946 and 1950, there were about 160 trials of former members of the Jewish Councils, their officers, Jewish policemen, and Kapos from over forty camps and ghettos, mostly from Warsaw, Lodz, Cracow, Międzyrzec Podlaski, Częstochowa, and Lublin. The prosecution was usually represented by Marian Lasota, Marek Stok, and Ludwik Gutmacher. The list of judges includes over thirty names, but the court was most frequently presided over by Anatol Truskier, Stanisław Temczyn, or Leon Lew. Róża Koniecpolska usually served as the secretary of the court.[22]

According to its statute, the court could pass only relatively mild sentences: exclusion from the Jewish community for a period of one to three years; withholding somebody's electoral rights in a Jewish community; and public reproach. In only fifteen cases were sentences passed. Fourteen cases have no concluding document of any kind. In thirty-nine cases, investigations were stopped and material was given to a historical commission, because it was impossible to locate a defendant. Sixty-three cases were closed for various reasons: no clear evidence of guilt, the death of a defendant, or, in fifteen cases, rehabilitation. Sixteen cases included elements of civil and inheritance law and were beyond the competencies of the court. Twelve cases were transmitted to the regular Polish law courts.[23]

It appears that the major Jewish collaborators who managed to survive left Poland very soon after the war, or changed their identities, and the People's Court tried only a small fraction of them. Juliusz Ajzenberg, a policemen from Częstochowa, who participated in roundups in the ghetto, was sentenced to a reprimand.[24] Szapsi Rotholc, a former policeman in the Warsaw ghetto and a professional boxer, exceptionally brutal toward the ghetto population, was denied membership in the Jewish community in Warsaw for two years and lost his right to participate in community elections for three years, and his case was published in the press. Two years later the sentence was commuted.[25] The case of Julian Gejcherman, aka Feliks Dobrowolski, an employee of the infamous "13" office[26] in the Warsaw ghetto, was suspended because the defendant disappeared and it was difficult to find witnesses to testify against him.[27] For the same reason several other cases were closed: those of Ignacy Gutman, a chief of the construction department of the Lodz Jewish Council, close collaborator and a personal friend of Chaim Rumkowski; Hersz Goldsztajn, a policeman from Międzyrzec Podlaski; David Gertler, a former chief of the Lodz ghetto police; and there were others.[28]

Many cases were discontinued for various reasons. Michał Suess, a member of the *Judenrat* in Radziechów, who helped the Ukrainian police organize anti-Jewish roundups, became an important Communist Party activist after the war.[29] Henryk Jakubowski, an employee of the Bendzin *Judenrat,* who was in charge of a card index of all the people living in the ghetto, was declared free of any crime and therefore innocent.[30] The same reasoning was used in the cases of Karol Pohoryles-Buczyński, the president of the *Judenrat* in Tarnopol;[31] Karol Peczenik, a commander of the Jewish police in one of the sections of the Warsaw ghetto;[32] Majer Pinkus, a *Judenrat* member from Łokacze in Volhynia;[33] and Stanisław Murzyński, an employee of the Jewish Council in Żelechów.[34] Documents of many cases do not include an explanation of why they were discontinued, even though portions of them do indicate that a given person was involved in criminal collaboration. This was so in the cases of Benjamin Lubicz, an eager commander of the Jewish Police in Międzyrzec;[35] Majer Nichler (Piotr Wilczyński after the war), the cruel president of the *Judenrat* in Skałat;[36] Henryk Nowogrodzki, an officer of the Jewish police in the Warsaw ghetto;[37] and Chanan Pakin, a former beadle in the Lodz ghetto.[38] Alfred Merbaum proved that he accepted the presidency of the Horodenka Jewish Council because he was threatened with execution.[39] Several cases had already been investigated by Polish prosecutors or were transmitted to them by the People's Court.[40]

The history of the Holocaust is one of the most important elements in an understanding of the Jewish diaspora experience, and the *Judenräte* problem is crucial to a better understanding of the Holocaust.[41] Jewish public opinion was deeply troubled with the abbreviated treatment of the Holocaust by the International Military Tribunal in Nuremberg.[42] But the results of the courts of honor in Western Europe, the People's Court in Poland, and the Israeli courts in trying Jewish collaborators are disappointing as well. The important historical problem of the *Judenräte* and other forms of the wartime ghetto administration has not been resolved yet. Many similar questions appear when we study the Holocaust, and most of them have no satisfactory answer. The history of the Holocaust is still far from settled.

NOTES

1. Isaiah Trunk, *Judenrat: The Jewish Councils in Eastern Europe under the Nazi Occupation* (New York: Macmillan, 1972); Yehuda Bauer, "The Ju-

denräte—Some Conclusions," in *Patterns of Jewish Leadership in Nazi Europe, 1933–1945: Proceedings of the Third Yad Vashem International Historical Conference, Jerusalem, April 4–7, 1977* (Jerusalem: Yad Vashem, 1979), p. 399.

2. Trunk, op. cit., pp. xvi–xvii; Meir Teich, "New Editions and Old Mistakes," and Nathan Eck, "Historical Research or Slander?" *Yad Vashem Studies* 6 (1967): 375–430.

3. Edward Alexander, *The Holocaust and the War of Ideas* (New Brunswick and London: Transaction, 1994), pp. 161–6.

4. Léon Poliakov, *Harvest of Hate: The Nazi Program for the Destruction of the Jews of Europe* (Syracuse, N.Y.: Syracuse University Press, 1954), pp. 88–9.

5. Aharon Weiss, "The Historical Controversy Concerning the Character and Functions of the Judenrats," in *The Historiography of the Holocaust Period: Proceedings of the Fifth Yad Vashem International Historical Conference, Jerusalem, March 1983,* ed. Yisrael Gutman and Gideon Greif (Jerusalem: Yad Vashem, 1988), p. 679.

6. Trunk, op. cit., p. xxxv.

7. Bauer, "Judenräte," p. 393.

8. Léon Poliakov, "Human Morality and the Nazi Terror," *Commentary* 10, no. 2 (August 1950): 111.

9. *Siedem wyroków Najwyższego Trybunału Narodowego* (Seven Sentences of the Supreme National Tribunal), ed. Tadeusz Cyprian and Jerzy Sawicki (Poznan: Instytut Zachodni, 1962), p. v.

10. Leni Yahil, "Historians of the Holocaust: A Plea for a New Approach," *Wiener Library Bulletin* 21, no. 1 (1967/68): pp. 2–3.

11. Joseph Michman, "The Controversy Surrounding the Jewish Council of Amsterdam from Its Inception to the Present Day," in *Patterns of Jewish Leadership in Nazi Europe, 1933–1945: Proceedings of the Third Yad Vashem International Historical Conference, Jerusalem, April 4–7* (Jerusalem: Yad Vashem, 1979), pp. 242–5; *Encyclopedia Judaica* (Jerusalem: Macmillan, 1971), vol. 8, p. 901, s.v. "Holocaust."

12. Trunk, op. cit., p. 549.

13. Ibid.; "Holocaust," op cit., p. 902.

14. Trunk, op. cit., pp. 549–61.

15. Ibid., pp. 562–7; *Jerusalem Post,* 6 January 1952, p. 1, and 8 April 1952, p. 3

16. *Jerusalem Post,* 20 January 1952, p. 1.

17. Trunk, op. cit., p. 568.

18. Rezsö (Rudolf) Kasztner, a Zionist leader from Hungary, negotiated with Adolf Eichmann and the Nazis during the war, started an operation called "Blood for Goods," and saved over 1,600 Hungarian Jews. In

1954, in Israel, he was accused of being a traitor and causing the deaths of many Jews. During the trial he was murdered by national extremists. See *Jerusalem Post*, 23 June 1955, pp. 1–3, and 22 June 1955, p. 2.

19. I consider it my pleasure to be able to thank Ms. Alina Skibińska from the Warsaw branch of the United States Holocaust Memorial Museum in Washington, D.C., for her contribution in this part of my research.

20. Archives of the Jewish Historical Institute in Poland (Archiwum Żydowskiego Instytutu Historycznego w Polsce), Sądy Społeczne (People's Court) 313, file 145, no pagination.

21. Ibid., 313, file 153, p. 49.

22. Ibid., files 147–54.

23. Ibid.

24. Ibid., file 2.

25. Ibid., file 109.

26. Several departments of the Warsaw ghetto administration were controlled by, and working for, the Gestapo. They were called "the 13" because their address was 13 Leszno Street. See Adam Rutkowski, "O agenturze gestapowskiej w getcie Warszawskim" (About a Gestapo agency in the Warsaw ghetto), *Biuletyn Żydowskiego Instytutu Historycznego,* nos. 12–20 (July–December 1956): 38–59.

27. Archives of the Jewish Historical Institute in Poland, Sądy Społeczne (People's Courts), 313, file 30.

28. Ibid., files 33, 39, 64, 103.

29. Ibid., file 114.

30. Ibid., file 10.

31. Ibid., file 99.

32. Ibid., file 92.

33. Ibid., file 71.

34. Ibid., file 85.

35. Ibid., file 69.

36. Ibid., file 86.

37. Ibid., file 90.

38. Ibid., file 91.

39. Ibid., file 78.

40. Ibid., files 27, 48, 116.

41. Ismar Schorsch, *On the History of the Political Judgment of the Jew,* Leo Baeck Memorial Lecture 20 (New York: Leo Baeck Institute, 1977), p. 4; Trunk, op. cit., p. xviii.

42. Jacob Robinson, "The International Military Tribunal and the Holocaust: Some Legal Reflections," *Israel Law Review* 7, no. 1 (January 1972), pp. 1–13.

IV. S·E·X·U·A·L·I·T·Y

Marion Kaplan

Gender
A Crucial Tool in Holocaust Research

FEMINIST SCHOLARSHIP, WHICH USES GENDER ANALYSIS, MUCH AS CLASS or ethnic analyses are used by traditional historians, has been crucial to my work on German-Jewish daily life under the Nazis. Gender—the culturally and hierarchically constructed differences between the sexes—made a difference in the way Jews were treated by the oppressors. Gender also made a difference in the ways Jews perceived and reacted to daily events. A gender analysis reveals dimensions in private life otherwise untouchable—the decision-making process between husbands and wives regarding emigration, for example, or the way fathers and mothers reacted to the persecution of their children at school.

It is clear to scholars who study the Holocaust, that Jews were persecuted *as Jews* and murdered *as Jews*. But feminist scholars look beyond this general truth to ask more complicated questions. As Carol Rittner and John Roth have pointed out: "much that happened to men and women during the Holocaust was devastatingly alike. *But,* much that happened was devastatingly different, too."[1] There were differences between men and women, in how they were treated as well as how they reacted. Mary Felstiner insists that "along the stations toward extinction . . . each gender lived its own journey."[2]

Let me be a bit more specific. Although the calamity that hit German Jews affected them as Jews first, they also suffered based on gender. First of all, racism and sexism were intertwined in the minds of the torturers. The Nazis attacked Jewish men first, demolishing their careers and businesses. Nazi propaganda put the emphasis on Jewish men—"the Jew" or *der Jude*—usually strangely distorted males with huge noses and stomachs. Hence, Jewish men and "Jews" were usually conflated. For example, at a dinner party in late 1933, the vice mayor of Berlin assured the Jewish journalist Bella Fromm that "I am only against Jews, not against Jewish women. Especially not against charming Jewesses."[3] Jewish men were also far more vulnerable to physical assault and arrest. (Even in mixed marriages, the Nazis privileged the marriage of "Aryan" men to Jewish women over Jewish men to "Aryan" women—a situation that made Jewish women safer than Jewish men, for the short run, at least.) Women were often left to carry the burden of maintaining their homes and families, of keeping their households and communities together. Even if ultimately Jewish women, the procreators, were also enemies doomed to perish in the Nazis' "race war," at the beginning of the Nazi era Jewish women saw their men's status slip precariously and tried to alleviate the distress, saw their men endangered and tried to rescue them.[4]

Not only was early Nazi racism and persecution gendered, so, too, were the victims' survival strategies in both practical and psychological terms. The victims *reacted* not always and not only as Jews, but as Jewish women and men. A focus on women led me to recognize, for example, that most women took the early warning signals of Nazism far more seriously than most men. Women eagerly trained for jobs and crafts useful abroad, whereas men continued to hope that they would be able to maintain their careers or professions. And women "made do" on smaller budgets, shopped in hostile stores, and tried to create cheer in cramped spaces, while at home, husbands were asked only to limit their expectations.

Gender made an enormous difference in deciding between fight and flight. In the early years, Jewish women were more sensitive to discrimination, more eager to leave Germany, more willing to face uncertainty abroad rather than discrimination and ostracism at home. Jewish men thought they had—and in fact did have—a great deal more to lose by leaving Germany. They had to tear themselves away from their life work, whether a business or professional practice. As long as they made a living, many breadwinners were unwilling to face poverty abroad. In light of men's primary identity with their occupation, they often felt trapped into staying. Women, whose identity was more family oriented, struggled to preserve what was central to them by fleeing with it.[5]

Men and women also led relatively distinct lives and often interpreted daily events differently. Women were more integrated into their community. There were the daily interactions with neighbors, regular exchanges with the grocer, and, often, participation in local women's organizations. As women were raised to be sensitive to social situations, their social antennae were not only more finely tuned than men's, but directed toward more unconventional—what men might have considered more trivial—sources of information: what the baker said, whether the neighbor gave her usual greeting. A widespread assumption that women lacked political acumen—stemming from their primary role in the domestic sphere—gave women's warnings less credibility. Many men insisted that they were more attuned to political realities: "You're a child" said one husband. "You mustn't take everything so seriously. Hitler used the Jews . . . as propaganda to gain power—now . . . you'll hear nothing more about the Jews."[6] Men claimed to see the "broader" picture, to maintain an "objective" stance. They mediated their experiences through newspapers and broadcasts. Politics may have remained more abstract to them, whereas women's "narrower" picture—the minutiae (and significance) of direct everyday contacts—brought politics home.

Gender differences in perceiving danger do not mean that gender roles remained static. On the contrary, in what Raul Hilberg has described as communities of "men without power and women without support,"[7] we find, for the most part, active women who, early on, greatly *expanded* their traditional roles. We see anxious but highly energetic women, taking note of the political and social environment and strategizing ways of responding to it. Many experimented with new behaviors rarely before attempted by *any* middle-class German women: interceding for their men with the authorities; seeking paid employment for the first time; and after the pogrom, rescuing men from concentration camps, sending off children on *Kindertransporte*, selling their homes on their own, and deciding on countries of refuge by themselves.

Even in desperate circumstances, women's dignity was not merely a proclamation of female strength to counter the stereotype of female "frailty." Emphasis on composure also resulted from the decorum stressed in Jewish bourgeois upbringing. Moreover, it asserted Jewish pride in the face of "Aryan" savagery, human dignity in the face of general dishonor.[8] But women's perseverance is also more than the sum of its parts, suggesting a new role for women. Traditionally men had publicly guarded the honor of the family and community; now suddenly women found themselves in the difficult position of defending Jewish honor. Often taking on "male" roles both within and outside the family, women transformed their own female identities—at least for the duration of the crisis—while seeking to save their families.

Even though women transcended certain gender roles, gender as such continued to have serious consequences in emigration, in forced labor, and in hiding. Gender made a difference in matters of life and death. For example, more women than men remained trapped in Nazi Germany. While there are many explanations for this—including male deaths in World War I, a higher number of widows, and so on[9]—it is also clear that more men got out before the doors were tightly shut: through connections, capitalist visas, or because they were in physical danger earlier than women and the women sent them out first. The disproportionate number of elderly women whom the Nazis murdered, suggests that gender and age were a lethal combination.

And just as gender made a sharp difference in the destiny of German Jews, it also plays a role in how the Nazi era is remembered. There is a relationship between gender and memory in the memoirs, diaries, letters, and interviews I have used. Women and men offer different perspectives, often on the same events. Women and men remember differently. Their original experiences, gendered as they were, provide for the different perspectives they offer. Women's memories tend to focus on family and friends, on the ways in which a variety of Jews coped within the privacy of their homes or in public, while men's tend to focus on their work, business, or political environments. In fact, women typically depict themselves in relationships, drawing sketches of partners, children, and friends, describing events that befell others as well. Men, on the other hand, more frequently see themselves as independent actors, so that women are often rather shadowy figures.[10] A good case in point is the recently published diary of Victor Klemperer, a Jewish professor married to an "Aryan" woman in Dresden. Between 1933 and 1945, Klemperer wrote in elaborate detail about his academic projects, his political and personal fears, his acquaintances, and his daily routine. He also noted in passing how his wife scurried for food from morning until night and gave piano lessons in exchange for food. He described his terror when she was taken ill, since his very existence depended on his marriage to her. Still, she remained a shadowy figure. He related her physical ailments far more than her thoughts or feelings.[11]

Women's memoirs also highlight entirely new dimensions of history. For example, men write of the public spectacle of the November Pogrom, the night of broken shop windows and burning synagogues, the lasting images of broken glass from which the Nazis cynically extracted the name "Crystal Night." A powerful, if more mundane image, mentioned often in Jewish women's memoirs, is that of flying feathers—feathers covering the internal space of the home, hallway, and front yard or courtyard. As in pogroms in Russia at the turn of the century, the marauders tore up goose feather blankets and pillows, shaking them into the rooms, out the windows, down the stairways.[12] German Jews were thus bereft of their bedding, and with that, of the kind of physical and psychological security and comfort that this represented and that they had once known. In addition, not only were these items expensive, but they could no longer be readily replaced, in part because of their cost and also because, in the looming war economy, linens were severely limited.[13] Broken glass in public and strewn feather beds in private spelled the end of Jewish security in Germany.

To conclude:

Feminist scholarship has two interrelated goals: to give women a voice long denied them *and* to offer a perspective long denied us. Examining women's experiences during the years of persecution and genocide raises the question: why, until recently, have we looked primarily at men in studying the Holocaust? And why do some historians of the Holocaust accept a gender analysis only with the greatest reluctance, while others shun it entirely?[14] In part, this has to do with the broader perspective of Jewish history in general. Gender analyses have not been seen as vital by the majority of Jewish historians, although a productive minority has stepped forward to challenge the mainstream at every turn.[15] Traditional historians have focused on men's public and communal activities, their philosophical, religious, or political contributions, neglecting women's powerful and sustained influence on European Jewry in the family and in the culture of Jewish and national communities. This reluctance to address gender continues with Holocaust studies, although here old as well as new roadblocks can be seen: the old ones—"what of importance can we really learn by studying women?"—are reinforced by new ones—

"are women's historians (read: feminists) trying retrospectively to divide Jews during the most tragic moment in modern Jewish history?"[16] My own answer is as follows: to raise the issue of gender does not place it above racism in some hierarchy of horrors. We know, to quote Hannah Arendt, that the Nazis did not want "to share the earth with the Jewish people."[17] To raise the issue of gender also does not place blame on other survivors for the disproportionate deaths of Jewish women. Blame rests with the murderers. Rather, gender helps us to tell a fuller and more nuanced story, to emphasize the multiplicity of voices and experiences in the war against the Jews. Gender mattered, maybe especially, in extreme situations.

NOTES

1. Carol Rittner and John Roth, eds., *Different Voices: Women and the Holocaust* (New York, 1993), p.3. Although my work focuses on Germany and German Jews, the issue of gender in the Holocaust throughout Europe has also been raised by Joan Ringelheim, whose research shows that "being male or female mattered during the Holocaust. Antisemitism, racism and sexism were not separated in the theory of the Nazis or in their practice— nor was sexism absent from the responses of the Jewish community. Sexism, the division of social roles according to biological function, placed women at an extreme disadvantage during the Holocaust. It deprived them of skills that might have enabled more of them to survive. At the same time, the group that was supposed to protect them—men—was not able to do so." From her essay "Women and the Holocaust: A Reconsideration of Research," in *Different Voices,* p. 400.

2. Felstiner, *To Paint Her Life: Charlotte Salomon in the Nazi Era* (New York, 1994), pp. 204–7. For further investigations into women and the Holocaust, see Lenore Weitzman and Dalia Ofer, *Women in the Holocaust* (New Haven, 1998); Cynthia Crane, *Divided Lives: The Untold Stories of Jewish-Christian Women in Nazi Germany* (New York, 2000); Ingrid Strobl, *Die Angst kam erst danach: Jüdische Frauen im Widerstand 1939–1945* (Fear came afterward: Jewish women in the Resistance, 1939–1945) (Frankfurt am Main, 1998); S. Lillian Kremer, *Women's Holocaust Writing: Memory and Imagination* (Lincoln, Nebr., 1999); Judith Tydor Baumel, *Double Jeopardy: Gender and the Holocaust* (London, 1998).

3. Fromm, *Blood and Banquets: A Berlin Social Diary* (London, 1942), pp. 119–20.

4. For a fuller, more detailed history of this period, see my *Between*

Dignity and Despair: Jewish Life in Nazi Germany (New York, 1998), in which I use gender as an important analytical perspective in describing Jewish daily life under the Nazis.

  5. For examples, see Else Gerstel, memoirs, Leo Baeck Institute, New York (hereafter cited as LBI), p.71, and John Foster, ed., *Community of Fate: Memoirs of German Jews in Melbourne* (Sydney, London, Boston, 1986), pp. 28–30.

  6. G. W. Allport, J. S. Bruner, and E. M. Jandorf, "Personality under Social Catastrophe: Ninety Life-Histories of the Nazi Revolution," *Character and Personality: An International Psychological Quarterly* 10, no. 1 (September 1941): 3.

  7. *Perpetrators, Victims, and Bystanders* (New York, 1992), p. 127.

  8. Erna Albersheim, memoirs, p. 33, Harvard University, Houghton Library, memoirs in Collection BMS GER 91, written for contest "Mein Leben in Deutschland vor und nach dem 30. Januar 1933." Publication of citations is by permission of the Houghton Library. Hereafter cited as Harvard ms.

  9. See my "Between Dignity and Despair: Jewish Women in the Aftermath of November 1938," Leo Baeck Memorial Lecture, Leo Baeck Institute, New York, 1996. Archival form.

  10. The diaries of Victor Klemperer, published to much acclaim in Germany and translated into English, exemplify this. His wife's existence— her "Aryan" status as well as her bravery in working for and finding food— saved his life, but we learn little of her thoughts and see only snippets of her actions as he reports on the books he's read, the conversations he's had with others, his forced labor, or the books he is writing. *Ich will Zeugnis ablegen bis zum letzten: Tagebücher*, vols. 1 and 2 (Berlin, 1995), and *I Will Bear Witness: A Diary of the Nazi Years 1933–1941,* trans. Martin Chalmers (New York, 1998); vol. 2, *I Will Bear Witness, 1941–1945: A Diary of the Nazi Years* (New York, 2000).

  11. Klemperer, *Ich will Zeugnis,* vols. 1 and 2.

  12. For feathers during the November Pogrom, see Frances Henry, *Victims and Neighbors: A Small Town in Nazi Germany Remembered* (S. Hadley, Mass., 1984), pp. 116–8; Erna Albersheim, Harvard ms., p. 28; Elsie Axelrath, Harvard ms., p. 43; Alice Baerwald, Harvard ms., p. 72.

  13. Erna Albersheim, Harvard ms., p. 28; Elsie Axelrath, Harvard ms., p. 43; Alice Baerwald, Harvard ms., p. 72.

  14. Ringelheim, "Reconsideration," p. 400. At a "Women and the Holocaust" conference at the Hebrew University, Jerusalem, in June 1995, several participants thought a gender analysis was "obscene" in the face of the destruction of the Jewish people.

  15. There is a growing literature in this field. See for example Paula

Hyman, *Gender and Assimilation in Modern Jewish History: The Roles and Representation of Women* (Seattle and London, 1995); Judith R. Baskin, ed., *Jewish Women in Historical Perspective* (Detroit, 1991); Marion Kaplan, *The Making of the Jewish Middle Class: Women, Family, and Identity in Imperial Germany* (New York, 1991).

16. Although there is no broad-based critique on issues of gender and the Holocaust, Gabriel Schoenfeld's article in *Commentary* of June 1998, titled "Auschwitz and the Professors" (pp. 44–6), singled out such scholarship as part of its attack on Holocaust studies. *Lilith* magazine responded to Schoenfeld a few months later.

17. Arendt, *Eichmann in Jerusalem: A Report on the Banality of Evil* (New York, 1965), p. 279.

Atina Grossmann

Trauma, Memory, and Motherhood
*Germans and Jewish Displaced Persons
in Post-Nazi Germany, 1945–1949*

I. INTRODUCTION: DIFFERENT VOICES
ON "*ARMES DEUTSCHLAND*"

8. Mai: Deutschland hat kapituliert. Gegen eine Welt von Feinden hat es sich sechs Jahre gehalten, es wird auch wieder hochkommen.... Lieber Gott—Berlin hat so viel aushalten müssen, laß es vorübergehen.

18. Mai. Im übrigen wird jetzt Kesseltreiben gegen die Nazis veranstaltet. In der "Täglichen Rundschau" groß Berichte über das Todeslager von Auschwitz. Selbst, wenn nur ein kleiner Teil davon wahr wäre und ich fürchte, es ist alles wahr, wäre die Wut der ganzen Welt auf die Nazis zu verstehen. Armes Deutschland!

IN MAY 1945 A MIDDLE-AGED WOMAN PHYSICIAN WITH EXCELLENT ANTI-fascist credentials, veteran of the Weimar campaigns for birth control and abortion reform, faces the defeat of Nazi Germany and the first press reports about Auschwitz and the death camps. She is not shocked or disbelieving; she can imagine and would not try to deny the horrors of which the Nazis were capable. Her response: to sigh for "poor Germany" *(armes Deutschland)*—an apparent victim—and look forward to the day when Germany—and especially her beloved metropolis Berlin—would revive *(wieder hochkommen)*.[1]

Five years later, in a 1950 report for the American Jewish journal *Commentary* titled "The Aftermath of Nazi Rule," Hannah Arendt diagnosed in Germans' "absence of mourning for the dead, or in the apathy with which they [Germans] react, or rather fail to react, to the fate of the refugees in their midst . . . a deep-rooted, stubborn, and at times vicious refusal to face and come to terms with what really happened." Now a visitor from the United States, the land of the victors, Arendt lamented the pervasive self-pity that allowed no reaction to her insistent revelation that she was a German Jew and that continually invoked the image of *armes Deutschland* as the miserable and sacrificial victim—*Opfer* in its double sense—of history.[2]

As Arendt pointed out with her customary acerbity, most Germans after 1945 understood themselves as victims and not as victimizers. The persecution and extermination of Jews, while initially widely and graphically documented in the German (albeit occupier-licensed) press, often in reportage on early trials of Nazis, seems nonetheless absent, or at best obscured and distorted, in immediate postwar public and private discourse.[3] This putative lack of memory or "amnesia" has become a truism for the "silent fifties" in West Germany, the years of nation building and economic miracle, supposedly broken only by the sea change of the 1960s.[4] In the early occupation period from 1945 to 1946—often described as the "zero hour" and the "hour of the women"—processions past naked, emaciated corpses in liberated camps, denazification procedures, press reports and film images of "death mills," and the Nuremberg trials, ensured that the immediate past of Nazi crimes remained highly present. But despite the lack of "silence"—indeed the remarkable amount of discussion about precisely the issues of memory, commemoration, guilt, and complicity that continue to agitate historical and public debate in (and about) Germany—for most Germans, the more powerful impressions, the stuff of which memories were made, derived from other more direct experiences of war and defeat.

In the midst of a ruined physical and political landscape, and in the absence of a legitimate national past or clear national boundaries, or for that matter, legitimated rulers or markets, female experiences such as rape, abortion, childbirth, caring for malnourished and sick children, and grief over the dying and dead, as well as relations with occupiers and returning German soldiers and prisoners of war, became especially powerful markers of German victimization and defeat. They signaled also the urgent need for healthy reconstruction.

Clearly, rapidly constructed and tenaciously remembered narratives of victimization worked, not only to block confrontation with recent Nazi crimes but most importantly (and efficiently), to manage the chaos of the immediate postwar years, and eventually to authorize reconstruction of German nationhood and national identity. (Ernst Renan in his famous 1882 disquisition "What Is a Nation" had already noted that "the essence of a nation is that all individuals have many things in common, and also that they have forgotten many things.")[5] But, during the early "pre- or non-national," or at least nonstate, years of military occupation from 1945 to 1949,[6] these narratives competed with, and were contested by, those posed by other protagonists who shared territory with defeated Germans, such as the Soviet and American victors or Jewish survivors gathered in displaced persons (DP) camps. Given the lack of a sovereign German state, and the unclarity about what it might mean to identify as German, it seems especially important to analyze stories of victimization from a vantage point that is not exclusively "German." Moreover, as our understanding of post-Nazi Germany has finally become more gendered,[7] it becomes all the more necessary to consider the notion of "the hour of the women," and the particular association of postwar victimization with female experience, from multiple non-German as well as German perspectives. If the history of postwar Germany is, as we have increasingly acknowledged, not only a story of men, it is also not only a German story.

I aim then, in this article, to reflect on two separate but inextricably interwoven and highly gendered stories about the meanings of sexuality, motherhood, and childbirth in the wake of National Socialism, war, and genocide. These are stories about the reconstruction of identity and community, maybe even desire, in the wake of violence and trauma in which—to put it crudely or polemically—Germans appear as victims and Jews as survivors (and Allies as victors). But they are also stories in which the binaries of those categories emerge as highly complicated and mixed up. In order to illustrate these points, I focus on two "multinational" sites where post-Nazi occupied Germany presents itself as a highly diverse and contradictory terrain of "bordercrossers" *(Grenzgänger):* the DP camps for Jewish survivors in the American and British zones of occupation, and Berlin, the former Reich capital, occupied by the four Allied victors.

II. BORDERCROSSERS *(GRENZGÄNGER)* IN BERLIN, 1945–1948

My initial focus is on Berlin, certainly not typical but exemplary for my purposes, and located usefully at an intersection of East and West. Conquered by the Soviets in April/May 1945, Berlin became after July 1945 a polyglot city of bordercrossers in four sectors; a kind of laboratory of international understanding, as U.S. Military Government officials initially preferred to put it, in which the precarious relations among the victorious powers and the management of the incoming refugee tide commanded virtually as much attention as the occupied Berliners themselves.[8] The *größter Trümmerhaufen der Welt*, as its inhabitants sarcastically dubbed it,[9] was a city of women, refugees, and foreigners. Of a population of about three million (2,600,000 in May), over 60 percent was female in 1945/46. Berlin was filled with returning soldiers and prisoners of war, liberated slave laborers from many different countries, German expellees and refugees from the East, repatriated political exiles (especially Communists returning to work with the Soviet Military Administration, SMAD), Jews emerging from hiding, forced labor, or concentration camps, and Allied troops (including a highly visible handful of former German Jews).[10]

By July 1945, huge numbers (some estimates as high as half a million) of displaced persons of multiple nationalities were streaming into some fifty transit camps in Berlin. Some fifteen thousand mostly ethnic German refugees from Soviet and Polish occupied territories in the East poured into the city daily, at the same time as Allied officials struggled to repatriate freed foreign laborers, prisoners of war, and concentration camp inmates.[11] It is worth remembering that by 1945 the presence of foreigners in Berlin was nothing new; after all, 7.5 million non-Germans had been mobilized and coerced into the Nazi war economy before May 1945.[12]

There were also some six to seven thousand Jews (or "partial" Jews) in Berlin (a high proportion of the 15,000 who survived within the entire Reich, but only a fraction of the 160,000 who had been registered in Berlin in 1932).[13] Their ranks were soon swelled by the "illegal infiltration" of Polish Jewish refugees fleeing renewed persecution. Starting in November 1945, the flight of East European Jewish survivors reached a high point after the pogrom in Kielce, Poland, on 4 July 1946 in which a charge of ritual murder led to the massacre of at least forty Jews who had tried to return to their hometown. About 250 arrived in the U.S. sector daily via the open secret of the underground Zionist *Bricha* network, seeking routes out of Europe and especially to Palestine.[14] Indeed the apparent presence of so many Jews, the formerly hidden and the newly arrived, so soon after the end of the regime that had promised to make Germany *judenrein,* so unnerved the journalist Margaret Boveri that already on 9 May, one day after the unconditional surrender, she commented in a surprised and somewhat irritated tone on her encounter with a young *rabbi* bicycling through the ruins: "Es ist also auch kein Wunder, daß es jetzt überall von Juden in leitenden Stellen wimmelt, sie sind einfach aus der Verborgenheit hervorgekommen. Zuzug soll aber auch aus Osteuropea kommen, vor allem aus Polen,—solche, die sich mit den Flüchtlingszügen hierher schmuggelten."[15]

Within the next months and years U.S.- and British-occupied Germany would become a temporary home for some quarter of a million Jewish survivors, leading to many more such unexpected and difficult encounters. Astonishingly, between May and September, the victors had managed to repatriate about six million of the seven million displaced persons they had faced in the occupied areas; a significant number of those who remained uprooted were Jewish survivors.[16] As numerous contemporary observers had already noted, it belonged "to the ironies of history that Germany, of all places, became under the occupation of the Allied powers a sheltering haven for several hundred thousand Jews."[17]

During this liminal interregnum of occupation and military government from 1945 to 1949, and particularly in the turbulent first two years, defeated Germans, together with hundreds of thousands of their former enemies and victims, became, as they were often called, bordercrossers *(Grenzgänger)* on the surreal stage of a broken country. This was especially evident in carved-up and bombed-out Berlin. Ruth Andreas-Friedrich titled her diary of war's end *Schauplatz Berlin,* and Curt Riess, a Berlin Jew who had returned as an American journalist, depicted his former hometown as "gar nicht mehr wie eine Stadt, sondern eher wie eine Bühne, auf der Kulissen herumstanden."[18] The U.S. diplomat Robert Murphy recorded his impressions when U.S. forces moved into the city in July 1945: "Two months after their surrender, Berliners still were moving about in a dazed condition. They had endured not only thousand-plane raids for years, but also weeks of Russian close-range artillery fire. In addition to three million Germans in Berlin, thousands of displaced persons were roaming around the shattered city."[19]

After accusing his Soviet allies of having created in Berlin "another Nanking, with Russians instead of Japanese doing the raping, murdering, and looting," Colonel Frank Howley, the American commander, remembered in 1950:

> Berlin in late July was still a shambles from the effects of Allied bombing, especially incendiary raids, and of Russian street fighting, but the Russians already had put large squads of German women to work clearing the rubble in various parts of the city. As the women wearily passed the fallen bricks from hand to hand, in a long human chain, they presumably were spurred on to heroic efforts by the great posters the Russians had erected to assure the Germans that they had not been conquered but "liberated" by the Communists from their Fascist oppressors.[20]

Inhabitants moved between Allied occupation sectors and their varied models of denazification, democratization, and reconstruction. Germans in Berlin moved also between identities as victims or perpetrators, liberated or conquered people. They appeared as rightfully subjugated former citizens of a criminal regime, or as hapless victims of Nazi betrayal, Anglo-American bombings, and Soviet plunder and rape. Rather quickly, they also surfaced as plucky survivors fascinated with the number of cubic centimeters of ruins to be methodically cleaned up, cheering the premiere of the Philharmonic, or the reopening of the much worried-about Berlin zoo. Especially in the early occupation period through 1947, much that would seem settled by the 1950s after the formation of the Federal Republic and the German Democratic Republic was still open and fluid; nothing about the postwar order was fixed.

At a moment when survival and reinvention of national and ethnic communities had such high political and cultural priority, women were especially visible, and issues of reproduction—literally birth and death—were foregrounded, both in public policy and in personal accounts. Moreover, given the indeterminacy of viable categories of citizenship or identity (as continually reworked, for example, in rationing or denazification classifications), reproduction, motherhood, and sexuality loomed intriguingly large as crucial discourses for organizing the past, understanding the present, and imagining the future.[21]

III. WOMEN'S WORK: RAPE AND MOTHERHOOD: VICTIMS AND VICTORS

I begin with the example of rape, probably the most dramatic form of gendered victimization, and one which has—after years of remarkable inattention—begun to receive a good deal of notice.[22] Let me just reiterate briefly that, whatever the numbers, and they vary wildly—perhaps one out of every three of about one and a half million women in Berlin—it is unquestionably the case that mass rapes of civilian German women by the Red Army signaled the end of the war and the defeat of Nazi Germany.[23] The notorious days of mass rapes from 24 April to 8 May 1945 were an integral part of the final bitter battle for Berlin. The continuing (if not as massive) experience, and fear, of rape for at least months and probably several years thereafter, as well as the often repeated recollections, inscribed indelibly in the memory of many German women (and of the men who were unable or unwilling to protect them) a firm conviction of their own victimization. At the same time they retained a sense of their superiority over the vanquisher from the East who came to "liberate" them.[24]

Rape of German women by Red Army soldiers also secured a particularly potent place in postwar memories of victimization because they represented the one, and certainly in Berlin the only, instance in which Goebbels's relentless anti-Bolshevik propaganda turned out to be substantially correct. As Berliners emerged from their cellars during the piercingly beautiful spring of 1945, the Soviets did not kill everyone on sight, deport them to Siberia, or burn down the city. As the musician Karla Hoecker reported, with genuine surprise, in one of the many diaries composed by women at war's end, "daß die Russen, die uns doch hassen und fürchten müssen, die Mehrheit der deutschen Zivilbevölkerung ganz unbehelligt leben lassen—daß sie uns nicht scharenweise abtransportieren!"[25] In fact, the SMAD moved quickly and efficiently to organize municipal government, restore basic services, and nurture a lively political and cultural life.[26] In regard to violence against women, however, the Nazi *Gruelgeschichten* (horror stories) were largely confirmed.

Women's continuing (and undeniable) sense of unjust victimization was exacerbated by a nagging perception that the experience of massive sexual assault on women was quickly and lastingly silenced or tabooized—as anticommunist propaganda, as the normal by-product of a vicious war, or in the "antifascist" narrative, downplayed as understandable retribution.[27] However, there was after May 1945 no lack of speech or documentation about rape. If anything, we find a plethora of speech in many different voices: detailed police and medical reports, statements by Communist Party, SMAD, and then U.S. authorities. Most concretely, the Communist- and Soviet-dominated Magistrat already on 20 May recognized the problem and its public health consequences by authorizing a moratorium on the long-standing and controversial antiabortion paragraph 218 of the penal code (as well as instituting harsh venereal disease surveillance and treatment). This liberalized abortion policy was instituted despite some grumbling on the part of doctors and clear but irrelevant protest from Walter Ulbricht, the new KPD (Communist Party) leader who had flown into the embattled and smoldering city from Moscow on 1 May: "Die Herren Ärzte müssen darauf aufmerksam gemacht werden, in dieser Frage etwas mehr Zurückhaltung zu üben," he remarked laconically. But the very statement shows how widespread the practice already was.[28]

Drawing on a mixed legacy of Weimar and National Socialist maternalist population policy, and racial discourses, as well as occupation policy, women seeking to terminate pregnancies told their stories in highly specific terms, and by the thousands, to authorities in medical commissions attached to district health offices which then sanctioned abortions, right up to the very last months of pregnancy. Women also retold rape stories in diaries and memoirs in astonishing quantity; never before had German women put pen to paper as copiously as they did in April and May 1945 when—and in many cases only when—they faced defeat. Both in private statements and official affidavits, women deployed a wide range of direct and indirect vocabulary—*Schändung* (violation), *Vergewaltigung* (rape), *Übergriff* (encroachment), *Überfall* (attack)—to denote the "it" *(es)* that had been endured.[29] Sometimes they recounted stories of surprising escape or reprieve; often they resorted to generalities and passive voice ("the awful scenes went on all night"; "we all had to submit")—or referred specifically to the horrific experiences of neighbors, mothers, sisters, which they themselves had supposedly been spared.[30] "Aber es entkamen viel weniger, als später behaupter wurde," Curt Riess asserted a few years later.[31]

Public conversation about rape, common in the early postwar period, was indeed curtailed in both West and East once conditions had normalized. But rape stories continued to circulate, indeed were repeatedly invoked or alluded to by contemporary chroniclers, both German and occupier.[32] Moreover, the importance of Berlin as the conquered capital, and the millions of refugees from the East who poured into western Germany, assured the centrality of rape stories in memories of defeat even in areas where there had never been a Red Army soldier.

In the Berlin stories that I work with, maternal and rape experiences were often closely connected; in these stories of victimization the terminology of *Opfer* clearly carries the double meaning absent in the English term: the negative connotation of victim but also the more positive, redeeming, and even heroic sense of sacrifice. Women reported offering themselves in order to protect their young daughters: "Mein damals 10 jähriges Mädchen wollten sie mir nehmen. Welche Mutter aber hätte das getan. So konnte ich mich also nur selbst dafür opfern."[33] Or; "Mir schlug das Herz, doch ich glaube, meine Seele war abgestorben. Er riß die Tür auf, legte einen Revolver auf den Nachttisch und legte sich zu mir ins Bett. Die Sorge um mein Kind, das schlief, ließ mich alles ertragen."[34] In another oft-repeated but somewhat different scenario, women recounted trying to take advantage of the Soviet troops' repeatedly observed kindness to children by clutching a young child to their body, or taking children along wherever they went. In one version, a mother remembered that she pinched her baby in the behind to make him cry piteously, said the child was very ill, and the soldiers let her go.[35] And sometimes women explicitly interpreted the rapes as a kind of revenge; the soldiers, they recollected, called: "Dawai, Dawai. Dein Mann wollen Krieg, drum deutsche Frau wollen, was wir wollen."[36]

Rape stories came, however—and this is central to the "not only a German story" aspect of my project—not only from these victims, but from those marked (in other contexts) as survivors and victors, that is, from Jews and antifascists who welcomed the Red Army. As Gabrielle Vallentin, the sister of the executed Jewish Communist Judith Auer, wrote bitterly: "Was ist aus Goebbels 'Gruelmärchen' geworden? Wirklichkeit! . . . Viele überzeugte Kommunisten drehten nun der Partei den Rücken zu. Auf diese Willkür der Russen waren sie nicht gefaßt gewesen!"³⁷ Disappointment and disillusionment with the Red Army *Befrier* and their clear connection to rape are surprisingly explicit in the complaints of communist activists about the damaging effect Soviet soldiers' behavior was having on an otherwise not unreceptive (and indeed somewhat relieved) local populace. One unhappy comrade wrote: "Männer und Frauen aus der arbeitenden Bevölderung sagen uns immer und immer wieder: Wir haben so gehofft, daß es jetzt endlich besser wird, wir haben uns gefreut, daß die Rote Arme kommt und jetzt benehmen sie sich so, wie es uns die SS und die NSDAP immer vorher gesagt hat. Wir können das nicht verstehen. Die Hoffnung, daß es besser werden wird, wie wir ihnen immer und immer wieder sagen, haben die meisten nicht mehr."

Or even, as frustrated communist organizers reported: "Die Stimmung unter der Bevölkerung ist jetzt in letzter Zeit durch diese Vorfälle wieder sehr schlecht geworden.... Eine Frau äußerte mir gegenüber heute auf der Strasse, als sie mir erzählte, wie nachts wieder die Rote Armee bi ihnen im Hause war und die Frauen vergeweltigt hat: 'Da hatten wir es ja mit der SS besser, die hat uns Fruaen doch in dieser Bezichung in Ruhe gelassen.'"³⁸

Antifascist activists, many of them recently released from Nazi concentration camps, despaired of their potentially promising political work, as the Soviets' liberator image was rapidly dismantled: "Für uns, die wir zwölf Jahre lang den Faschismus bekämpft haben, waren die Konzentrationslager keine Erholungsheime und wenn wir jetzt sehen müssen, wie die Arbeiterschaft immer mehr und mehr enttäuscht wird, so könnte auch uns die Verzweifelung packen..., wenn wir nicht den starken Glauben an die Parteileitung der KPD hätten."³⁹

Rank-and-file Communists pleaded with their leaders "daß auch die Rotarmisten, nachdem der Krieg schon 8 Wochen beendet ist, unbedingt Disziplin halten müssen."⁴⁰ But they presented themselves as motivated less by outrage at the crime than by bitterness over the problems it posed for their political organizing. In their desperation, one group of comrades helpfully suggested that the army set up brothels staffed with "bourgeois" and Nazi women to relieve the pressure.⁴¹ Party documents also make perfectly clear that rape by Red Army forces presented very concrete material problems. The much-needed harvest was endangered, not only by the plunder of farm animals and equipment, but because women were afraid to work in the fields. Female activists were even so bold as to counter SMAD criticism of women's inadequate political involvement by protesting that women did not attend meetings because they were simply afraid to be on the street after dark.[42]

Far from imposing a total silence, Communists and Soviet military authorities—certainly in the immediate postwar years 1945 to 1947—did find many ways of talking about and acknowledging the massive incidence of rapes. They tried simultaneously to deny, minimize, justify, shift responsibility for, and contain them. Beyond the public health response—organizing abortion and venereal disease treatment—KPD and SMAD officials also deployed a wide range of rhetorical and political strategies, freely admitting violations, "excesses," "abuses," "unfortunate incidents" *(Auswüchse, Übergriffe, unglückliche Vorfälle),* and vowing to get them under control (or to demand that the Soviet army do so). But they also trivialized rape as an inevitable part of normal brutal warfare, as comparable to Allied excesses, and as understandable if not entirely excusable in view of the atrocities perpetrated on the Russians by the Germans: "Wir können und werden nicht etwa versuchen zu rechtfertigen, wenn wir auch Erklärungen haben und die Frage damit beantworten könnten, was Hitler alles in der Sowjetunion angerichtet hat."[43]

Despite all efforts at containment, rapes figured prominently as public relations and political control problems because they provoked anti-Soviet sentiment, especially among women, youth, and dedicated anti-Nazis, precisely those groups considered most likely to support a new socialist and democratic peace-loving Germany. Such protestations notwithstanding, it was generally if not explicitly acknowledged that the KPD's embarrassing loss to the SPD (Social Democratic Party) in Berlin's first open elections in 1946 was due in no small part to a majority female electorate remembering and responding to the actions of the Soviet *Freunde*.[44]

For their part, German Communist leaders and the SMAD continually complained about German unwillingness to focus on their own guilt or complicity, noting that calls for *Wiedergutmachung* (referring to reparations to the Soviet Union) or discussions of responsibility and guilt were met with "geradezu eisiges Schweigen."[45] The clear implication was always that the Germans should be happy to have gotten off as easily as they did. Even in regard to rape, both

SMAD and KPD/SED (Sozialistische Einheitspartei [Socialist Unity Party]) contended that women would have had more of a right to complain if only, rather than senselessly battling the Red Army to the bitter end right into the center of Berlin, the German working class had fought fascism for even a day or two, thereby preserving some German honor and credibility vis-à-vis the Soviets. One communist leader petulantly remarked that those who supported the war and the attack on the Soviet Union could not stand there later and cry "Pfui." He proceeded to add: "Der Krieg ist kein Erziehungsinstrument."[46] But there was little popular sympathy for Ulbricht's perhaps irrefutable logic in an early leaflet promising swift punishment for "excesses": "Wäre gleiches mit gleichem vergolten worden, deutsches Volk, was wäre mit Dir geschehen?"[47]

Even three years later, in 1948, when two overflowing meetings were held in the "Haus der Kultur der Sovietunion" to discuss the ever sensitive subject "about the Russians and about us" ("über die Russen und über uns"), the subject most on the predominantly female audience's mind was Soviet soldiers' violations. The SED argued that the memory of rape as the most dramatic example of abuse by the victors was whipped up and kept alive by Western propaganda.[48] In a standard construction, used both negatively and positively, of the Soviets as more impulsively "natural" and primitively "hot-blooded" than the defeated Germans, the SED ideologue Wolfgang Harich insisted that the Soviet rapes were mere expressions of "victor's excess" ("Überschwung des Sieges"), as compared to German crimes, which were "cold-blooded actions of master-race consciousness."[49] The topic was abandoned after two crowded four-hour-long meetings threatened to get out of control. Discussion of the topic could be publicly restrained, but not closed.

The continuing prominence of rape in German narratives of victimization was, however, certainly not, as suggested by the SED, due to cold war propaganda by the Western allies. The Americans had their own problems with rape by GIs, and, more importantly, with fraternization and casual prostitution. Indeed, there is a remarkably similar rhetoric of anxiety in the American debate about the negative and corrupting effects of servicemen's looting, brawling, raping, and general "sexual antics," on both occupier and occupied.[50] In the early occupation years, U.S. officials were far from seizing on rape stories to discredit their Soviet allies and competitors, whom they described in 1946 as "hard bargaining, hard playing, hard drinking, hard bodied, and hard headed."⁵¹ The Soviets were viewed as not only barbarian rapists, but also as tough fighters and exotic celebrators who could drink, eat, and copulate prodigiously—often to the frustration of U.S. colleagues unable to match their levels of consumption.⁵² Noting that "[o]ur army has done a little on occasion," William Shirer remarked in his *End of a Berlin Diary* on 2 November 1945 that "taking into account that the Soviet troops had been in the field constantly fighting for two to three years and that capturing Berlin was a costly operation and that some of the Russian divisions were made up of very inferior material not to mention a weird assortment of Asiatic troops, then the amount of raping by Russian troops here apparently was not above the average to be expected.⁵³

The U.S. occupiers in Berlin downplayed German anxieties about hunger, homelessness, suicide, and disease, and especially crime and disorder (including a high level of violence by returning German soldiers against their families, as well as assaults by Soviets, Poles, and Ukrainians). The Americans noted with a touch of sarcasm that the crime rate per capita in 1945/46 Berlin was lower than that of most cities in the United States, especially New York!⁵⁴ Indeed, the threat of violence and epidemics was generally identified with "outsiders" and refugees clamoring for entry into Berlin.⁵⁵ This process of official marginalization and privatized retelling left much space for rape stories to proliferate and shape memories. As one women wrote for an essay contest sponsored by the Berlin Senate in 1976 on "Berlin 1945: Wie ich es erlebte": "Darüber mehr zu schreiben, hieße schreckliche Erlebnisse wieder wachzurütteln, die man zwar gern vergessen möchte, die aber im tiefsten Innern doch immer wieder wach bleiben."⁵⁶ In immediate reports and in later memoirs, women reported over and over that the cry "Frau komm" still rang in their ears.⁵⁷

Rape was, of course, by no means the only traumatic event that contributed to German women's perceptions of victimization. In some ways, rape came as just one more (sometimes the worst, but sometimes not) in a series of horrible deprivations and humiliations of war and especially conquest; for mothers, not comparable to the loss of children. Rape—itself signified by a variety of generalized expressions—was integrated into a whole range of other violations and abuses (the ubiquitous term *Mißrauch*), in particular plunder and vandalism, hunger, homelessness, disease, especially infant and child mortality, the harsh treatment of German prisoners of war in the Soviet Union, the perceived arbitrary injustices of denazification, and the expulsions from the eastern territories. "Flucht ist Frauensache ebenso wie der Krieg Männersache war," Ilse Langner noted in her postwar novel *Flucht ohne Ziel* (Flight without end).[58]

After the initial burst of reporting on rape and despair, many accounts of German (and especially Berlin) women's experience at war's end have portrayed sturdy, fresh-faced women, wielding shovels and clad in trousers and kerchiefs (think of Hildegard Knef in postwar films). Or reporters presented young "furlines" driven by material need and moral degeneration, eager to fraternize, providing quite apocalyptic accounts of Berlin's wild trade in rumors, sex, and black market goods.[59] Only in the last several years have these rather heroic or salacious versions been displaced by the early stories of German women as victims of mass rape. Indeed in most immediate postwar sources, the *Trümmerfrauen* are hardly heroines; they appear as resentful and reluctant conscript labor tainted with having been Nazis or Nazi wives, or as hungry mothers desperate to escape the so-called *Himmelfahrt* (journey to heaven) category of the ration card system assigned to "unproductive" housewives.

Just as the city landscape itself was marked by theatrical contrasts between the utterly destroyed and the eerily intact, official reports by occupiers and German authorities stressing how remarkably quickly Berlin began to work again (in large part due to women's valiant housecleaning efforts) contrasted sharply with women's accounts. Memoirs and diaries related bitter experiences of rape, lack of fuel and food, suicide, and disease, such as dysentery, typhus, typhoid, and diphtheria, which particularly claimed children as its victims.[60] Berliners cherished images of themselves as plucky, good-humored survivors; "Berlin lebt auf!" (Berlin revives) the *Berliner Zeitung* already proclaimed on Monday, 21 May 1945, and other headlines announced, "Berlin ist wieder da" (Berlin is back). The sometimes still irrepressible Berliner *Schnauze* reported in a tone of ironic suffering: "Deutschland, Deutschland ohne alles, ohne Butter, ohne Fett und das bißchen Marmelade frißt uns die Besatzung weg."[61] But despite all efforts to revive the legendary *Berliner Luft* of the Golden Twenties,[62] the pervasive picture was one of relentless misery. Municipal officials themselves frequently emphasized how needy the city was in order to argue for improved occupation conditions; so much so that U.S. military authorities countered what they deemed to be persistent German "whining" by labeling fears about starvation as "bushwah."[63]

Contemporary reports (whether by foreign observers, occupiers, or Berliners themselves) present a virtually unanimous portrait of a thoroughly "whipped and beaten" population, self-pitying, broken, in the grip of what one today might identify as a mass clinical depression. A major symptom was the inability or unwillingness to bear children—as reflected in high abortion and low birth rates.[64] Berliners were described as listless and apathetic; they were dully, sullenly willing to clean up and rebuild, to "look forward," but neither insightful into the root causes of their misery nor remorseful about their own agency or responsibility.[65] Amazingly, the *Berliner Zeitung*, published by the Magistrat, felt it necessary already in June 1945 to instigate a readers' forum on the topic, "Zu viel oder zu wenig. Soll das die Zeitung bringen?" asking whether the Berlin daily press was overreporting news about concentration camps and Nazi crimes.[66] Just weeks after the collapse of the Third Reich, a major daily in the Soviet zone published (among others) responses that invoked *armes Deutschland:* "Wir haben ein schweres Erbe übernommen und müssen ieder gut machen, was diese Verbrecher getan haben. Dazu müssen wir aber vorwärts blicken, dann bauen wir auf und nicht, wenn wir zurückblicken auf häßliche vergangene Zeiten." In a rhetoric more commonly associated with the 1980s and 1990s, readers called for a *Schlußstrich* (concluding line) to the discussion of the Nazi era.[67] As one American Military Government official observed in his diary in 1945: "The Germans in Berlin . . . were on very short rations, had only what shelter they could find . . . and looked beaten physically and in spirit. But what they were going through as they toiled, clearing up bricks and rubble, did not compare with the hell of Belsen and Buchenwald. Still, I doubted that they knew that."[68]

IV. VICTIMS AND SURVIVORS: JEWS

Like the U.S. occupation officer interjecting the experience of the concentration camps into his narrative of German victimization, I too want at this juncture to insert another parallel story that mixes up categories of victims and survivors. The high suicide and abortion rate among German "victims," the sense that having to bear and care for children was somehow an intolerable burden in the months after the defeat, contrasts sharply with the remarkable fertility among the approximately 250,000 Jewish "survivors" or "victims" living in DP camps. In some kind of supreme historical irony, at the same time as Germans bemoaned the high incidence of suicides, infant and child mortality, and abortion, and German women were desperately seeking to keep alive the children they already had,[69] Jewish DPs in occupied Germany were producing a record number of babies. In 1946, occupied Germany, far from being *judenrein,* counted the highest Jewish birth rate in the world.[70]

The "steady rush of weddings"[71] in the DP camps, sometimes within days to neighbors in the next barracks, without necessarily knowing or loving them very well, and the resulting "population explosion," had little to do with the reconstruction of "normal" family life and self-sacrificing maternalism demanded by West Germany (or pronatalist calls for renewing the health of the *Volk* in the East). Neither among Germans nor in the DP camps, could one really speak of orderly family life. Indeed the Jewish DPs were often characterized by a vocabulary similar to that defining the Berliners, whom their occupiers had quickly judged "shocked and apathetic . . . concerned almost exclusively with problems of food and shelter."[72] Jewish relief workers and American military authorities, as well as German observers, saw the DPs as depressive, afflicted with "inertia" and "an air of resignation," unsuited to any kind of normal life. They regularly and graphically bemoaned the "uncivilized" state of the survivors, oblivious to the most elementary rules of hygiene, uninhibited in regard to the opposite sex, unwilling to work or take any sort of active initiative. Other reports cited symptoms that today are clearly associated with post-traumatic stress disorder: DPs were labeled "jittery, excitable, anxiety prone."[73] Echoing his Military Government colleagues' gloss on the Berliners, Irving Heymont, the American (and as he later revealed, Jewish) commander of Landsberg DP camp in Bavaria, portrayed his charges: "With a few exceptions, the people of the camp themselves appear demoralized beyond hope of rehabilitation. They appear to be beaten both spiritually and physically with no hopes or incentives for the future."[74]

Particularly the young mothers in the DP camps were in many ways utterly unsuited for motherhood and domesticity (in any case limited in the camps). They had come into Nazi ghettos and death camps, partisan encampments, or hiding as teenagers, and had been given no time in which to grow up. Their own mothers were generally dead (often killed or selected for death before the survivors' eyes), or they had once had children, now lost and murdered. As a shocked American Army rabbi reported back to Jewish agencies in New York: "Almost without exception each is the last remaining member of his entire family. . . . Their stories are like terrible nightmares which make one's brain reel and one's heart bleed."[75]

In some widely publicized cases, children had been appropriated by Christian rescuers who would not give them up or, most painfully, the children themselves did not want to give up their new identities. Some women had simply picked up other families' lost children and made them their own, at least for the duration of the displacement: "Women who have lost entire families . . . , one woman who came in with three children not hers nor related to each other—she merely picked them up in route—one in one place, one in another—all three had lost their parents."[76]

Relief workers consistently noted this desperate need to re-create some kind of familial as well as group bonds in a situation where "[t]he overwhelming majority of the Nazi camp survivors are *single* survivors of exterminated families,"[77] Meyer Levin, in his searching memoir *In Search,* bitterly reflected on the sentimentalization of the desperate search for lost children:

> There were heartbreaking stories of children seeking their mothers; in a few cases they found them, and these cases were so endlessly overplayed in the radio dramas of American Jewish organizations for the next few years that Europe and its DP camps must have seem [*sic*] to the mind of the American Jew to be one large happy reunion center where every half-hour another distracted mama called out a long-forgotten childish pet name, whereupon a curly haired five-year-old who had disguised her dark eyes for blue eyes in order to survive as a Polish child under the name of Wanda, rushed to the call of Bubaleh into mama's arms.[78]

His own vision was different: remarking on a young woman survivor he encountered as he drove through devastated Europe in his U.S. Army jeep, he wrote: "She hadn't been able to save her child, nobody had been able to save the child in this place. And somehow her tragedy seemed more terrible than that of the mothers who went into the gas chambers with their babies clutched to their breasts."[79]

V. *MASCHIACHSKINDER*

The veritable baby boom of 1946/47 was, however, a phenomenon much more complicated and remarkable than the "manic defense" against catastrophic experience and overwhelming loss diagnosed by contemporary psychiatrists and social workers.[80] "In the midst of the depressed desert life" of the DP camps, "a noticeable change occurred: people who had survived singly in all age groups were struck with a strong desire to be married."[81] Levin too sensed that survivors' primary need was "to seek some link on earth. . . . This came before food and shelter."[82]

The rapid appearance of babies and baby carriages in the dusty streets of DP camps throughout the American and British zones served as a conscious and highly ideologized reminder that *mir szeinen doh* (Yiddish for "we are here"). A *She'erit Hapleita* (surviving remnant, or more literally, leftover remnant of a remnant) of the Jewish people had survived the Nazis' genocide and seemed determined to replace the dead at an astonishingly rapid rate.[83] Despite everything, women who only weeks or months earlier had been emaciated, amenorrheic "living corpses" became pregnant and bore children.[84] They were not deterred by the knowledge that for purposes of *Aliyah* to Palestine and emigration elsewhere, pregnancy and young children were only an obstacle.[85] Major Heymont noticed "that the use of contraceptives is highly frowned upon by the camp people. They believe it is everyone's duty to have as many children as possible in order to increase the numbers of the Jewish community."[86] The American Jewish Distribution Committee (Joint) found itself having to scramble to build Jewish ritual baths for brides *(Mikveh)*, and to produce gold wedding rings as well as wigs for Orthodox wives.[87]

It is plausible then to suggest that this rash of marriages, pregnancies, and babies represented a conscious affirmation of Jewish life. This was true for both men and women; in his memoir *Risen from the Ashes,* Jacob Biber poignantly described the birth of his son, the first baby in Föhrenwald camp near Munich: Chaim Shalom Dov was named in honor of the first son who had been murdered in his father's arms as the family fled to the forest in the Ukraine, and in celebration of peace and life. While on the run and in hiding, after the death of their son, Biber and his wife had "lived like brother and sister," not daring to risk pregnancy, and now this "pleasant surprise was a sign of the continuity of life."[88]

Women especially were determined to claim domestic reproductive roles that they had once been promised in some long ago and now fantastic past. Women survivors of the death camps, sometimes of medical experiments, were anxious to reassure themselves of their fertility, as a way of establishing that they had indeed survived.[89] Observers were shocked by a kind of hypersexuality among the mostly youthful inhabitants of the DP camps, and noted with a certain astonishment that the "appearance of numbers of new-born babies has become a novel feature of the Jewish DP camps."[90] As many survivors have articulated, they were young and finally freed from constant fear; they wanted to live, to taste the pleasures of youth long denied: "our young bodies and souls yearned to live."[91]

In one major displaced persons camp in October 1945, there were only nine babies among 1,281 inhabitants. The majority of the survivors were young, and men outnumbered women (approximately sixty to forty); young children and their mothers, along with the elderly, had been automatically marked for death in the Nazi camps. But within several months almost a third of the camp's 2,000-strong population were children, most of them newborn infants. On the grounds of Bergen-Belsen, the former concentration camp that became the center of Jewish life in the British zone, fifteen Jewish babies were born every week; in early February 1948, the birth of the thousandth Belsen baby was celebrated.[92] Marriages were a daily ritual: "By the winter of 1946, a thousand [Jewish] babies were born each month" in the American zone.[93]

Fertility and maternity worked, if you will, as a mode of reidentifying and reconstructing, both of claiming an intact individual body, and of constructing a viable new community—after extraordinary trauma, and even in transit. Supported by the traditional religious imperatives of the East European Jewish community in the camps, the reproductive behavior of the *She'erit Hapleita* could not offer any redemptive meaning to the catastrophe *(Churban)* that had been experienced. But it did perhaps offer a possible means to "redeem the future,"[94] or at least to begin the regenerative work of making and imagining one. In that sense, the quick construction of new families could also be interpreted as a kind of genealogical and biological revenge;[95] Jewish infants, born on territory that had been declared *judenrein* to women who had been slated for extermination, were literally dubbed *Maschiachskinder* (children of the Messiah).[96]

Marriage, pregnancy, and childbirth clearly represented a possible reconstruction of collective or national, as well as individual, identity for the Jewish DPs—the battered survivors of the death camps, ghettos, and partisan groups in Eastern Europe as well as those tens of thousands of mostly Polish Jews who had spent the war years in the Soviet Union. Such practices offered a means of establishing a new order and a symbolic sense of home, even and especially in the approximately sixty refugee camps in the U.S. and British zones and in the American sector of Berlin.[97] Despite the overcrowding, the unappetizing rations, the sometimes humiliating and uncomprehending treatment by military and relief workers who "looked down on us . . . as if we were some kind of vermin or pests,"[98] the DP camps and the new families they housed provided a makeshift therapeutic community for survivors who had been "liberated from death" but not yet been "freed for life."[99] Magda Denes, who had survived in hiding with her mother in Czechoslovakia, remembered her reaction to the chaotic, depressing DP camp where "[b]eing processed was a protocol to which we were subjected again and again." She asked a friend: "'Do you think we live in a madhouse?' She looked at me sadly. 'No, my dear,' she said. 'You have never been in a concentration camp. This is normalcy. This is practically heaven.'"[100]

VI. JEWISH DPS IN TRANSIT STATION BERLIN

In Berlin also, despite the best efforts of American occupation officials to stem the flow of Jewish refugees, and especially to evacuate pregnant women and mothers with young children to the ostensibly better-equipped DP camps in West Germany, the numbers of Jewish DPs continued to grow. U.S. Military Government had initially resisted forming DP camps in Berlin, particularly since "the Jewish population resident in Berlin in the main did not desire to have a camp created for them, stating that they had seen enough of camps."[101] Starting in November 1945, however, about 250 to 300 Jewish survivors arrived in the officially closed city every day, creating what one U.S. officer termed a "red-hot" crisis.[102] By 1947, over a thousand Jewish infants and children were housed in camps in the American sector. The Soviets forced the *Bricha* underground network to curtail its "flight and rescue" missions in fall 1946, but altogether, some 32,000 Polish Jews would pass through Berlin from November 1945 through January 1947.[103]

American policy was pressured by an eagle-eyed press and public opinion campaigns at home. The Harrison Report, commissioned in summer 1945 by General Eisenhower, who had been deeply shaken by what he had seen at the liberated death camps, alerted especially American Jewish organizations that "we appear to be treating the Jews as the Nazis treated them except that we do not exterminate them."[104] Much to their annoyance, the U.S. Military Government authorities could not as easily, guiltlessly, and unilaterally ban all Jewish DPs from their zone in Berlin as the British and French, and certainly the Soviets, did. The British, preoccupied with the crisis in Palestine, flatly said no; the French, typically, pleaded poverty and lack of resources; and the Soviet general, with "a puckish smile on his face," rather gleefully noted that the refugees all snuck out of their sector into the West anyway.[105] In fact, squabbles about the "Polish Jewish problem held center stage" at a surprising number of Allied *Kommandatura* sessions. The U.S. Military Government officer responsible recalled: "Everyone was irked by the way we were being browbeaten into assuming responsibility for all of the Polish Jews, regardless of what sector of Berlin they were in."[106]

The Americans, in cooperation with UNRRA (United Nations Relief and Rehabilitation Administration), eventually made the commitment, as they did throughout their zone, that "reasonable care be taken of these unfortunate people."[107] But they did so with great reluctance and resentment; as Irving Heymont confessed in his memoir about running Landsberg camp, "[w]hen I raised my right hand and took the oath as an officer, I never dreamed that there were jobs of this sort."[108] In the characteristic rapid turnaround of sentiment in the postwar years, it was the victims of Nazism, still displaced and unruly, who came to be seen, even by the victors, as the disreputable villains. The Germans, miserable and depressed but trying to rebuild—with their "clean German homes and pretty, accommodating German girls"[109]—came to be viewed as victims, pathetic but appealing, and later, with the airlift in Berlin, even heroic.[110] Frustrated by Allied indifference to the particular trauma of their experience and what they perceived as favorable treatment for the more orderly Germans, DPs tartly observed that "it is better to be a conquered German than a liberated Jew,"[111] and joked among themselves: "The Germans will never forgive us for what they did to us."[112]

DPs existed within the "historic triangle" of occupiers, Germans, and Jews,[113] and as the impact of the Harrison Report faded into cold war politics, it seemed to many that "[t]he guilt of the Germans was forgotten." A worried Zorach Wahrhaftig informed the American and World Jewish Congress that, six months after liberation, the Jewish DPs "are looked upon as intruders, the Germans as the autochthonic population suffering from the plague of DPs."[114] It was directly in response to the mass influx of East European Jewish DPs that in December 1945, the liberal U.S.-licensed *Tagesspiegel* editorialized: "So darf man hoffen, daß die millionenfachen Opfer der Juden nicht umsonst gebracht worden sind, sondern daß es nach jahrhundertelangen Bemühungen heute möglich sein wird, das jüdische Problem in seiner Gesamtheit zu lösen [*sic*] und zwar einerseits durch Auswanderung der heimatlosen Juden und andererseits durch vollständige Assimilation der Juden, die in Europa zu verbleiben wünschen."[115]

Indeed, Allied and German anxieties about a "flood[ing] by Jews from the East," into "countries [Germany and Austria], made Judenrein by the Nazis,"[116] and then exacerbated by their high birth rate and obvious lack of assimilation, reveal a great deal about when and how Jews were specifically defined as victims of Nazi genocide, assigned roles (either uncomfortable or valorized, and differing whether one looks West or East) as victims of fascism, or, most prominently, subsumed in the larger category of unwelcome war refugees.[117]

By 1948/49, currency reform, blockade, and airlift sealed the division of Berlin and fundamentally changed its status from vanquished Nazi capital to plucky cold war ally (this too is a highly gendered process that requires further analysis). Ironically, it was the final division of the city into East and West that also basically eliminated the Jewish DP problem for Berlin. Almost all of the stubbornly remaining DPs in Berlin (about 6,500) were flown out into the Western U.S. zone in empty airlift planes returning to their base at Rhine-Main: another step toward the normalization of divided Berlin.

While Berlin had been a crucial entry point, the "vorgeschobene... Landzunge für diese jüdische Wanderung aus Ost-Mitteleuropa,"[118] the center of Jewish DP life in occupied Germany had been shifting to large camps near Munich and Frankfurt.

VII. GERMANS AND JEWS

Writing about the same transitional period of occupation and adjustment, a German woman in Berlin wrote not at all untypically: "1947 kam unser kleiner Junge zur Welt und mit ihm für mich eine große Sorge mehr. Es war unverantwortlich, daß ich in dieser furchtbaren Notzeit noch ein Kind in die Welt gesetzt habe."[119] Certainly, young Berlin women reported excitedly on their encounters with well-fed fraternizing GIs, but even the *Fräuleins,* Curt Riess caustically noted, "waren nur noch Ruinen dessen, was sie einmal gewesen waren, ganz wie die Häuser, in denen sie ihr Leben fristeten."[120] Women's stories were more likely to highlight rape, or the terrible hardships of motherhood at war's end; nursing a child through typhoid or diphtheria, the virulent dysentery epidemic of the first winter that killed sixty-five of every hundred newborns,[121] pushing a wheelbarrow with a dead child in a cardboard box (for lack of coffins) through a bombed-out street, and sometimes, most horrifically, accounts of mothers and children separated on the trek west, on the road, or in the packed refugee trains. Gabrielle Vallentin's 1955 account poignantly recalled the Berlin streetcars where "man so manches traurige Bild [sah], Mütter, die stumm und starr dasassen, auf ihrem Schoß ein Pappkarton, darin sie ihr totes Kind aus dem Krankenhaus abgeholt hatten."[122]

In compelling counterpoint to the response of Jewish survivors, it seems that for German women really quite brief but vivid experiences of victimization, narrated over and over again, so dominated all memory as to seemingly block out all knowledge of what went before. Another classic testimony: "Die Bomben im Winter 1944/45 waren schlimm, doch die Tage die jetzt kamen, waren kaum zu ertragen."[123] Such sentiments were of course also interpreted more cynically: "What they claim not to have known yesterday they wish to forget again today!" a Jewish observer commented in 1950.[124] The *Frauenleben* page of the *Tagesspiegel* conveyed the ubiquitous despair about the condition of infants and children: "Es ist ja so, daß wir uns den berühmten Blick in jeden Kinderwagen, den angeblich keine Frau sich versagen mag, schon abgewöhnt haben, weil uns das, was wir sehen, oft so traurig macht."[125]

A few statistics can serve to provoke discussion about the different meanings attached to childbirth and babies by Germans and Jews in the time immediately after war's end. Berlin births, which had reached a quite unprecedented height early in the war in 1940 of 74,903 (17.2 per 1,000 population), plummeted in 1946 to 22,894 (7.3 per 1,000 population), a circumstance that provoked much anxiety in the press and among medical and social welfare officials (agonizing about the need to rebuild a healthy *Volk*).[126] In Bavaria, where there had "never been as many Jews as there were one year after the destruction of European Jewry,"[127] the 1946 Jewish birth rate was 29 per 1,000, in contrast to 7.35 per 1,000 for Germans. The death rate for Jews was also much lower, 1.6 versus 8.55, and at a rate of 27.7 versus 2.8, there were also many more Jewish weddings. The recorded Jewish birth rate in Germany for 1948, right before the proclamation of the state of Israel on 16 May 1948 and the easing of U.S. immigration regulations eventually reduced the "problem" to small but highly visible proportions, was a whopping 35.8 per 1,000, far exceeding anything the Germans had managed in this century.[128]

The point here is not to make facile comparisons on the basis of statistics that describe two very different populations who had undergone such different and incommensurate experiences and now lived under quite different circumstances. I am indeed talking about two groups—"Aryan" Germans (themselves hardly homogenous) and mostly East European Jewish survivors—whose social histories were dramatically different, but who quite unexpectedly (and ironically) found themselves in the same war-torn territory after May 1945. All these striking demographic markers can be related to empirical data, such as the opposite "alarming disparity"[129] of sex ratios among Jewish survivors and the general German population (preponderance of males among Jews and of women among Germans), the different age structure (most Jewish survivors were young), and the higher rations (some 2,500 calories a day) and guaranteed (if primitive) housing for Jews. Having sex and making babies was also a good way to deal with the boredom and loneliness of leading a waiting life—*auf dem Weg* (on the way)—in the transit camps, and the disappointment at the reality of the long-yearned-for liberation, where, as was often and loudly pointed out by the DPs and their advocates, Jewish survivors were once again consigned to living in barracks behind barbed wire.[130]

The radically different reproductive and sexual patterns of Germans and Jews—unsurprising as they may be in light of the divergent social histories and circumstances—were at the time saturated with, and represented as carrying, highly charged political meaning and memory: a process that bears examination for all of us interested in gender, nation, and memory.[131] I would insist that these glaring statistics, and the intense scrutiny to which they were subjected by Germans, Allies, and Jews, do speak to the blurred and complicated categorizing of victim, victor, and survivor in consciousness and memory after war and Holocaust.

Certainly, many Germans conceived of their experience as that of *Opfer*, and they did so in gendered and sexualized terms that focused on birth and abortion rates, infant and child mortality, on female victimization and rape (and on male impotence—one would have to look here at the competing images, for example, of the "poor infantryman" [*armer Lanzer*] and broken POW that populated the postwar era). Jews, I would argue—certainly in the published record and in political representations—looked to pregnancy and maternity as emblems of survival, as signs that they were more than just victims and precisely did not dwell obsessively on the traumatic recent past. DP culture placed a premium on collecting personal histories, on bearing witness for the future. But in its preoccupation with the mundane everydayness of camp life and political association, it also fostered a kind of productive forgetting. Bearing children worked to mediate this continuous tension between remembering and forgetting. Babies, in their names and in their features, bore the traces of the past, of those who were dead and lost. But imaginatively, and in their ever present demandingness, they also represented futurity. As the first issue of the DP newsletter *Unzre Hoffnung* stated: "Wir müssen zum Heute übergehen und ein besseres Morgen vorbereiten, ein schönes, ein gesundes Morgen."[132]

In a sense, the aborting German women carried within their bodies a huge question mark about the future of the nation: would Germany—as nation, as *Volk*—go on *(wieder kochkommen),* would it be reconstituted and how? None of that was clear at war's end. The question of national identity was indeed on the agenda. Mass rape at the point of defeat of course exacerbated such worries with all their nationalist and racial implications; the attempt to restore German women's bodily (and genetic) integrity via abortion seemed a necessary precondition for national integrity. If German women were expressing uncertainty about the possibility of a viable nation, Jewish women survivors, living in a kind of extraterritoriality on both German and Allied soil, were prefiguring on their pregnant bodies a kind of imaginary nation that they hoped—at least this is the message of the sources—to realize in Palestine/*Eretz Yisroel*. Their babies had "red-hot" political valence, not only for the Allies, but also for the Zionists, who dominated political and cultural life in the DP camps. The DP press and political actions demanding open emigration from Germany to Palestine invariably foregrounded images of babies and baby carriages.[133] The DP camp newsletters, which reported on cultural life in the camps and on progress toward a Jewish state—written in Yiddish, but printed in Roman characters because no Hebrew typesetting equipment was available in occupied Germany—drove their message home with pages of marriage and birth announcements (along with notices searching for lost relatives). Meyer Levin was particularly struck by the hectic din of the streets in Berlin, Vienna, or Munich, where DPs congregated and "DP women paraded their babies."[134] It is also crucial to keep in mind that this Jewish baby boom did not simply go on behind the gates of the DP camps, and unnoticed by Germans. As the survivors settled in, both inside and outside the camps, Jews gave birth in German hospitals where they were treated by German physicians and nurses; some Jews hired German women as housekeepers and nannies; they sometimes (especially given the surplus of men) dated, had sex with, and even (in a much stigmatized minority of cases) married German women. DP mothers crisscrossed the streets of German towns with their baby carriages; the many Jewish marriages and births in the DP camps were registered in the German *Standesämter* (marriage bureaus).[135]

What are we to make then of these contrasting statistics and reports, about birthing Jews and aborting Germans—especially if direct comparisons are not appropriate? This leads me to some concluding speculations on the continually vexed questions of remembering and forgetting, and their relationship to (gendered) nation making, especially the particular issues raised by the (increasingly acknowledged) prominence of women's voices in defining the "difficult legacy" of the early postwar period. In a context in which female bodies—raped, aborting, pregnant, mothering—are so clearly both public and private and where neither public nor private is clearly defined or bordered, these German and Jewish stories, taking place, after all, on the same territory, if not really in the same (nonexistent) nation, must, I think, be told together. They must be examined as contrasting survival strategies and differing responses to different wartime traumas (which were in turn given different public meanings by Germans, Allies, and Jews). But they also raise similar and provocative questions about the place of sexuality, pregnancy, childbirth, and motherhood in furnishing possible reconstructions of ethnic or national identity in the wake of Nazism and World War II (or other violent trauma, either individual or collective).

Both Germans and Jews turned to narratives and metaphors of fertility and maternity (in terms of both loss and possibility) to comprehend victimization and survival and to conceptualize and imagine future identities as nation or *Volk*. By looking comparatively at these disparate experiences and the discourses they generated, we could begin to usefully complicate our understanding of gender as a historical category, "de-Germanize" a German history in which multiculturalism or heterogeneity is too often seen as an invention of the very recent past, and cut through the persistent division between German history and history of Jews in Germany that still characterizes our work on gender, nation, and memory.

NOTES

Atina Grossman's essay has appeared in *Archiv für Sozialgeschichte* 38 (1998): 230–54.

1. Anne-Marie Durand-Wever, "Als die Russen kamen: Tagebuch einer Berliner Ärztin," unpublished diary, with kind permission of Dr. Madeleine Durand-Noll, pp. 36, 51 ("May 8: Germany has capitulated. It held out six years against a world of enemies, it will recover again. . . . Dear God—Berlin has had to endure so much, let this be over with." "May 18: And now witch-hunts against the Nazis are being orchestrated. In the 'Täglichen Rundschau' big reports about the death camp in Auschwitz. Even if only a small part is true, and I fear it is all true, then the rage of the entire world against the Nazis is understandable. Poor Germany!").

2. Hannah Arendt, "The Aftermath of Nazi Rule: Report from Germany," *Commentary* 10 (1950): 342–3. Here Arendt obviously anticipates

Alexander and Margarete Mischerlich's famous discussion of the German "inability to mourn" *(Die Unfähigkeit zu trauern)* (Munich, 1967).

3. See for example the extensive coverage in the daily press during the fall and winter 1945/46 of the Belsen trial in Lüneberg in the British zone, the Dachau trial in the American zone, and the Hadenar Clinic trial in Nuremberg (on charges of "euthanasia"), culminating in the headline-making Nuremberg trials beginning in November 1945. For Berlin and a representative sampling of reportage in both the Soviet and the American sectors, see especially *Tägliche Rundschau, Berliner Zeitung,* and *Tagesspiegel.* For a highly problematic analysis of divergent occupier and German interpretations of the war and its aftermath, see Dugmur Barnouw, *Germany 1945: Views of War and Violence,* (Bloomington, 1996).

4. See Wolfgang Benz, "Postwar Society and National Socialism: Remembrance, Amnesia, Rejection," in: *Tel Aviver Jahrbuch für deutsche Geschichte* 19 (1990): 1–12. The impression of "amnesia" in the 1950s has now been forcefully challenged by a host of scholars. See among many others Michael Geyer and Miriam Hansen, "German-Jewish Memory and National Consciousness," in *Holocaust Remembrance: The Shapes of Memory,* ed. Geoffrey H. Hartman (Cambridge, Mass., 1994), pp. 175–90; Alf Lüdtke, "'Coming to Terms with the Past': Illusions of Remembering, Ways of Forgetting Nazism in West Germany," *Journal of Modern History* 65 (1993): 542–72; Jeffrey Herf, *Divided Memory: The Nazi Past in the Two Germanys* (Cambridge, Mass., 1997).

5. Ernst Renan, "What is a Nation," in *Nation and Narration,* ed. Homi K. Bhabha (London, 1990), p. 328.

6. For a useful discussion of the ambiguities and vagueness of the term "nation," see Clifford Geertz, *Die Welt in Stücken: Kultur und Politik am Ende des 20. Jahrhunderts* (Vienna, 1996), pp. 37–67.

7. Two recent outstanding examples, from American historians, are Elizabeth Heineman, "The Hour of the Woman: Memories of Germany's 'Crisis Years' and West German National identity," *AHR* 101 (1996): 354–95, and Robert G. Moeller, "War Stories: The Search for a Usable Past in the Federal Republic of Germany," *AHR* (American Historical Review) 101 (1996): 1008–48. See also the volume *Stunde Null: Kontinuitäten und Brüche,* in *Ariadne: Almanach des Archivs der deutschen Frauenbewegung* 27, Mai-Heft (1995).

8. American Military Government officer John Maginnis referred in February 1947 to "a record of successful international adjustments and sympathetic understanding." Major General John J. Maginnis, *Military Government Journal: Normandy to Berlin* (Amherst, 1971), p. 345.

9. *Berlin: Kampf um Freiheit und Selbstverwaltung 1945–1946* (Berlin, 1961), p. 10 ("the greatest collection of rubble in the world").

10. See for example Hans Speier, *From the Ashes of Disgrace: A Journal from Germany, 1945–1955* (Amherst, 1981).
11. See Maginnis, pp. 278 ff. See also Landesarchiv Berlin (hereafter cited as LAB) OMGUS 4/24-1.4.
12. By the end of the war foreigners composed almost a quarter of the wage labor force in Germany. See Mark Roseman, "World War II and Social Change in Germany," in *Total War and Social Change,* ed. Arthur Marwick (Basingstoke, 1988), pp. 63, 71. For a vivid picture of the immediate postwar period in Berlin, see the many microfilms of the Zeitgeschichtliche Sammlung of the LAB.
13. These figures, taken from Frank Stern, "Antagonistic Memories: The Post-War Survival and Alienation of Jews and Germans," in *Memory and Totalitarianism,* International Yearbook of Oral History and Life Stories, vol. 1, ed. Luisa Passerini (New York, 1992), p. 23, are necessarily imprecise. To the total of about 15,000 Jews (of a pre-1933 Jewish population of about half a million) who survived within the Reich must be added perhaps 50,000 Jewish forced laborers who were liberated on German territory at the end of the war. Andreas Nachama, "Nach der Befreiung: Jüdisches Leben in Berlin 1945–1953," in *Jüdische Geschichte in Berlin: Essays und Studien,* ed. Reinhard Rürup (Berlin, 1995), pp. 268 ff., quotes other reports estimating that there were about 7,000 Jews in Berlin: 1,500 had survived the camps, 1,250 had been "U-boats" in hiding, and about 4,250 had been spared deportation because they lived in mixed marriages; of these, 2,250 were "starwearers," while the rest were privileged due to their Christian-identified children. Stern's corresponding figures are 1,155 camp survivors, 1,050 "illegals," 2,000 mixed-marriage partners, and another 1,600 exempted from wearing the star. Nachama also counts the pre-Nazi Jewish population of Berlin as about 200,000, which presumably includes those not officially registered as Jews.
14. See Nachama, p. 272; Angelika Königseder, "Durchgangstation Berlin: Jüdische DPs 1945–1948," in *Überlebt und unterwegs: Jüdische Displaced Persons im Nachkriegsdeutschland,* ed. Fritz Bauer Institut, Jahrbuch 1997 zur Geschichte und Wirkung des Holocaust (Frankfurt am Main, 1997), pp. 189–206. See also Maginnis, pp. 323–9, for a detailed (and candid) discussion of the Polish Jewish refugee crisis and the considerable problems it posed for the Allied *Kommandatura* and especially the American occupiers. On Kielce, see Abraham J. Peck, "Jewish Survivors of the Holocaust in Germany: Revolutionary Vanguard or Remnants of a Destroyed People?" *Tel Aviver Jahrbuch für deutsche Geschichte* 19 (1990): p. 35. On the *Bricha* network that transported Jews into the American zone of Germany and Italy for eventual *Aliyah* to Palestine, see especially Yehudah Bauer, *Flight and Rescue: Bricha* (New York, 1970).

15. Margaret Boveri, *Tage des Überlebens: Berlin 1945* (Munich, 1968), p. 128. Remarkably, Boveri opted to leave this section in her revised diary when she published it in 1968 ("So it is no wonder that important positions are crawling with Jews, they have simply crawled out of obscurity. Reinforcements however are also supposedly coming from East Europe, especially from Poland—those who are smuggling themselves in with the refugee treks").

16. Zorach Wahrhaftig, *Uprooted: Jewish Refugees and Displaced Persons after Liberation,* From War to Peace 5 (New York: Institute of Jewish Affairs for the American Jewish Congress and World Jewish Congress, 1946). Altogether, Allied armies had to cope with over seven million DPs in occupied territories, plus some twelve million ethnic German expellees. See also Leonard Dinnerstein, *America and the Survivors of the Holocaust* (New York, 1982).

17. Michael Brenner, "East European and German Jews in Postwar Germany, 1945–50," in *Jews, Germans, Memory: Reconstructions of Jewish Life in Germany,* ed. Michal Y. Bodemann (Ann Arbor, 1996), p. 50.

18. Ruth Andreas-Friedrich, *Schauplatz Berlin: Tagebuchaufzeichnungen 1945 bis 1948* (Frankfurt am Main, 1984); Curt Riess, *Berlin 1945–1953* (Berlin, n.d. [presumably 1952]), p. 174 ("hardly like a city anymore, more like a stage on which the backdrops are just standing around"). The notion of Berlin in ruins as a kind of surreal theatrical or operatic stage set was invoked by many observers—and filmmakers—at war's end; see the large number of films made in the ruins; exemplary perhaps are Roberto Rossellini's *Germania Anno Zero* and Billy Wilder's *A Foreign Affair.*

19. Robert Murphy, *Diplomat among Warriors* (New York, 1964), p. 264.

20. Frank Howley, *Berlin Command* (New York, 1950), p. 65. An extraordinary number of Berlin's occupiers published memoirs.

21. For a fine general discussion of the West German case, see Heineman.

22. See, for example, Helke Sander and Barbara Johr, eds., *Befreier und Befreite: Krieg, Vergewaltigungen, Kinder* (Munich, 1992). For earlier feminist analyses, see Ingrid Schmidt-Harzbach, Eine Woche im April Berlin, 1945; "Verbewaltigung als Massenschicksal," in *Feministische Studien* 5 (1984): 51–62; Erika M. Hoerning, "Frauen als Kriegsbeute, der Zwei-Fronten Krieg: Beispiele aus Berlin," in *"Wir kriegen jetzt andere Zeiten": Aud der Suche nach der Erfahrung des Volkes in nachfaschisischen Ländern,* ed. Lutz Niethammer and Alexander von Plato (Berlin, 1985), pp. 327–344; Annemarie Tröger, "Between Rape and Prostitution: Survival Strategies and Chances of Emancipation for Berlin Women after World War II," in *Women in Culture and Politics: A Century of Change,* ed. Judith

Friedlander (Bloomington, 1986), pp. 97–117. On the thorny problems of historicizing rape at war's end, see Atina Grossmann, "A Question of Silence: The Rape of German Women by Occupation Soldiers," in *West Germany under Construction: Politics, Society, and Culture in the Adenauer Era,* ed. Robert G. Moeller (Ann Arbor, 1997), pp. 33–52.

23. Barbara Johr, "Die Ereignisse in Zahlen," in *Befreier und Befreite,* pp. 48, 54 ff., 59. See also Erich Kuby, *Die Russen in Berlin 1945* (Bern, 1965), pp. 312 ff., and especially Norman Naimark, *The Russians in Germany: A History of the Soviet Zone of Occupation, 1945–1949* (Cambridge, Mass., 1995), pp. 69–90.

24. Naimark, p. 88, suggests that the Red Army rapes continued "at least through 1947."

25. Karla Hoecker, *Beschreibung eines Jahres: Berliner Notizen 1945* (Berlin, 1984), p. 42 ("that the Russians, who must hate and fear us, leave the majority of the German civilian population entirely alone—that they don't transport us off in droves!"). See also Susanne zur Nieden, *Alltag im Ausnahmezustand: Frauentagebücher im zerstörten Deutschland 1943–1945* (Berlin, 1993).

26. See Wolfgang Schivelbusch's engaging study of postwar and pre–cold war cultural politics, *Vor dem Vorhang: Das geistige Berlin 1945–1948* (Munich, 1995).

27. This was certainly expressed in the lively discussions surrounding Helke Sander's film *Befreier und Befreite,* which explicitly claimed to "break the silence" around Soviet rapes of German women. See the special issue of *October 72* (spring 1995) on "Berlin 1945: War and Rape, 'Liberators Take Liberties.'"

28. BA (SAPMO), NL 182 (Nachlass Walter Ulbricht)/246, Besprechung Gen. Ulbricht mit je einem Genossen aus jedem Verwaltungsbezirk, Berlin, 20 May 1945, p. 47 ("The gentlemen doctors should be reminded to exercise a bit of restraint in this matter"). See also LAB rep. 12, acc. 902/NR 5, Dienstbesprechungen der Amtsärzte 1945/6.

29. See zur Nieden, especially pp. 74, 95 ff.

30. A wide range of literature about wartime rape, including from the recent conflict in former Yugoslavia, makes similar observations about the ways in which women describe and circumscribe their experiences. See, for example, Shana Swiss and Joan E. Giller, "Rape as a Crime of War: A Medical Perspective," in *Journal of the American Medical Association* 270 (1993): 612–5.

31. Riess, p. 10 ("But many fewer escaped than was later claimed").

32. Howley, p. 11, referred to the "atrocious crimes" of the Soviets. For a rather melodramatic summary of many such accounts of destroyed Berlin, see Douglas Botting, *In the Ruins of the Reich* (London, 1985).

33. LAB 240/2651/655/1, report by Erna Köhnke ("They wanted to take my then 10 year old girl. What mother would have done such a thing. So I could only sacrifice myself instead"). The following three texts are from an essay contest sponsored by the Berlin Senat in 1976: "Preisausschreiben: Berlin 1945: Wie ich es erlebte." Eight hundred twelve contributors, most of them women, wrote about the period from May 1945 to the end of the blockade in June 1949.

34. LAB 240/265/131/1, report by Gertrud Strubel ("My heart was pounding, but I believe my soul was dead. He ripped open the door, placed the revolver on the night table and lay down beside me in bed. The anxiety about my sleeping child let me endure everything").

35. LAB 240/265/83/1, report by Erna Beck.

36. LAB 240/265/644/4, report by Elli Fallner ("Dawai, dawai [Russian for 'Get going']. Your man wanted war, then German women want what we want").

37. LAB acc. 2421, report by Gabrielle Vallentin: "Die Einnahme von Berlin durch die Rote Armee vor zehn Jahren: Wie ich sie selbst erlebt habe" [1955], p. 30 ("What came of Goebbels's 'horror-stories'? Reality! . . . Many committed Communists turned their back on the party. They were not prepared for this random vindictiveness").

38. BA (SAPMO), NL 182/853, p. 30 ("Men and women from the working population say to us over and over again: We had so hoped that it would finally become better, we were so happy that the Red Army was coming, and now they are behaving just like the SS and the NSDAP always told us they would. We cannot understand this. The hope that things will get better, which we have promised people over and over again, most of them no longer have that hope." "The mood in the population has become very bad due to these incidents. . . . One woman on the street said to me today, while telling me how at night the Red Army had again been at their home, raping women, 'In that regard we had it better with the SS, at least in that respect they left us women alone'").

39. Ibid., NL 182/853. p. 97. See also report from Köpenick, 842, p. 132 ("For us, who fought against fascism for twelve long years, the concentration camps were no sanitoria and when we now have to watch as the workers are more and more disappointed, we too could despair . . . , if we did not have our strong faith in the party leadership of the KPD").

40. Ibid., NL 182/852, p. 134. Report from the comrades in Köpenick ("even the Red Army soldiers, now that the war is already over for 8 weeks, absolutely must discipline themselves").

41. BA (SAPMO), NL 182/852, p. 132, KPD Tegel-Süd to ZK, 29 June 1945. Naimark, p. 119, also cites this example.

42. See ibid., DFD (Demokratischer Frauenbund Deutschlands)

BV 1, Gründung des zentralen Frauenauschuss beim Magistrat der Stadt Berlin, p. 102. See also ibid., NL 182/853, p. 105; Naimark, pp. 116–21.

43. Ibid., NL 182/856, p. 27, Der Funktionär: KPD-Bezirk Thüringen, October 1945 ("We cannot and will not try to provide justifications [for rape], even if we do have explanations and could answer the question by referring to all the havoc that Hitler wreaked in the Soviet Union").

44. See, among many sources, Naimark, pp. 119–21.

45. BA (SAPMO), NL 182/853. p. 39 ("icy silence").

46. Wolfgang Hurich in *Die Tägliche Rundschau* no. 291, 12 December 1948, p. 3 ("war is not a socializing tool").

47. BA (SAPMO), NL 182/853, p. 10, Aufruf der KPD, n.d. ("Had they [the Soviets] taken equal revenge, German *Volk*, what would have happened to you?").

48. *Die Tägeliche Rundschau* no. 291, 12 December 1948, p. 3. I am indebted to Norman Naimark's work for steering me to this source.

49. Ibid.

50. Harold Zink, *The United States in Germany, 1944–1955* (New York, 1957), p. 138. Among many contemporary sources on relations between American occupiers and German women (rape, fraternization, and venereal disease), see also Julian Bach Jr., *America's Germany: An Account of the Occupation* (New York, 1946), especially the chapter "GIs between the Sheets," pp. 71–83; Bud Hutton and Andy Rooney, *Conqueror's Peace: A Report to the American Stockholders* (Garden City, N.Y., 1947); Earl F. Ziemke, *The U.S. Army in the Occupation of Germany, 1944–1946,* Army Historical Series, Center of Military History, United States Army, (Washington, D.C., 1975); Hans Hube, *Our Love Affair with Germany* (New York, 1953).

51. *Six Month Report, 4 January–3 July 1946: U.S. Army Military Government, Report to the Commanding General U.S. Headquarters Berlin District* (n.p., n.d.), p. 8. By 1950, with the cold war in full swing, Frank Howley, who had been the American commander in Berlin, had changed his view of the Soviets: "We went to Berlin in 1945, thinking only of the Russians as big, jolly, balalaika-playing fellows, who drank prodigious quantities of vodka and liked to wrestle in the drawing room. We know now—or should know—that we were hopelessly naive." Howley, p. 11.

52. Howley, Maginnis, and Murphy, among others, all make this point.

53. William L. Shirer, *End of a Berlin Diary* (New York, 1947), p. 148. It was clearly acknowledged, however, that the incidence of outright rape (as opposed to various levels of sexual "fraternization") was much lower among U.S. occupiers. See, for example Hutton and Rooney, and Zink.

54. *Six Month Report,* p. 8. See the detailed Berlin police reports on

rape, prostitution, drug addiction, and especially family suicides and murders in LAB rep. 9/241, Polizeipräsident 1945–1948.

55. LAB rep. 12, acc. 902/no. 5, Dienstbesprechungen der Amtsärzte 1945/46, demonstrate clearly the anxiety about refugees and displaced persons, the attempts to deny them entry or at least limit the resources available to them, as well as to blame them (rather than "legitimate" Berliners) for the spread of social disorder and infectious diseases.

56. LAB rep. 240/2651/655/1, report by Erna Köhnke ("To write more about this would mean to reawaken terrible experiences that one would like to forget but that in fact are constantly reawakened in one's deepest inner self").

57. See for example, LAB rep. 2651/2/184/1, report by Erna Kadzloch on the cry "Frau komm und Uri Uri."

58. Ilse Langner, *Flucht ohne Ziel: Tagebuch-Roman Frühjahr 1945* (Würzburg, 1984), p. 123 ("Flight is women's work just as the war was men's work"). See also Heineman, Moeller.

59. For a summary (and good bibliography) of such dramatic versions, see Botting.

60. There were at least fifteen thousand deaths from epidemic diseases from May to December 1945 (plus a very high VD rate). Municipal and occupation officials were more likely to stress the rapidity and efficacy of public health measures such as mass immunizations, examinations, and disinfection. For a brief overview, see Dieter Hanauske, ed., *Die Sitzungsprotokolle des Magistrats der Stadt Berlin 1945/46* (Berlin, 1995), p. 74.

61. The quote is from the diary of Frau Heidleberg in LAB/rep. 240, acc. 2651/748 ("Germany, Germany, without everything, without butter, without fat, and the little bit of marmalade is eaten up by the occupiers").

62. See, among others, Schivelbusch, on efforts to bring back into the public the stars and successes of Weimar culture.

63. Howley, p. 85.

64. Botting, p. 109, summarizes many reports: "The wish to have a child is waning. Instead of wanting a child many women are now succumbing to a deep despondency."

65. This portrayal of whining self-pity is especially evident in reports by occupiers and only really changes to the spunky *Berlin ist wieder da* image with the blockade and the airlift. For an insightful analysis of this "depression" (and the distinctions in the psychoanalytically oriented literature between melancholia and *Trauerarbeit*) see Eric L. Santner, *Stranded Objects: Mourning, Memory, and Film in Postwar Germany* (Ithaca, N.Y., 1990), especially pp. 1–56.

66. *Berliner Zeitung*, no. 35, 24 June 1945, p. 3 ("Too much or too little. Should the newspapers report this?").

67. *Berliner Zeitung,* no. 39, 29 June 1945, p. 3 ("We have taken on a difficult legacy and must make good again what these criminals [the Nazis] have done. For that, however, we must look forward, only then can we rebuild, and not if we look back on ugly past times").

68. Maginnis, pp. 258 ff.

69. This rhetoric of despair complements the pronatalist rhetoric immediately deployed in both East and West Germany (only partially but carefully reworked from the Nazi version) in which self-sacrificing motherhood was key to restoring "humanity and culture" to the German *Volk.* For excellent samples, see BA (SAPMO) DFD (Demokratischer Frauenbund Deutschlands) BV 7, Zeitungsausschnittsammlung, "Probleme der Frauen im Nachkriegsdeutschland, 1945/46."

70. See among numerous sources, Peck, p. 38; Michael Brenner, *Nach dem Holocaust: Juden in Deutschland 1945–1950* (Munich, 1995), p. 36; Margarete L. Myers, "Jewish Displaced Persons Reconstructing Individual and Community in the U.S. Zone of Occupied Germany," *Leo Baeck Institute Yearbook* 42 (1997): 306–8.

71. Jacob Biber, *Risen from the Ashes* (San Bernardino, 1990), p. 49.

72. *Berlin Sector: A Report by Military Government from July 1, 1945 to September 1, 1949* (n.p., n.d.), p. 113.

73. Quoted in Alex Grobman, *Rekindling the Flame: American Jewish Chaplains and the Survivors of European Jewry, 1944–1948* (Detroit, 1993), p. 57. See also Dinnerstein.

74. Jacob Rader Marcus and Abraham J. Peck, eds., *Among the Survivors of the Holocaust—1945: The Landsberg DP Camp Letters of Major Irving Heymont,* Monographs of the American Jewish Archives, vol. 10 (Cincinnati, 1982), p. 5 (letter to Heymont's wife, 19 September 1945). Heymont graphically describes the camp residents' unwillingness or inability to use the latrines properly and the lack of sexual privacy.

75. Letter to Stephen S. Wise, 22 June 1945, in *The Papers of the World Jewish Congress 1945–1950: Liberation and the Saving Remnant,* ed. Abraham J. Peck, Archives of the Holocaust, vol. 9 (New York, 1990), p. 30. On the important role of U.S. military rabbis in dealing with Jewish DPs, see Grobman; and Louis Barish, *Rabbis in Uniform* (New York, 1962).

76. Memorandum from Kaiman Stein, 7 December 1945, in Peck, p. 146. The problem of reclaiming perhaps ten thousand Jewish orphans who had been saved by Christians was prominently discussed in the immediate postwar period. Altogether about 150,000 children outside Russia were estimated to have survived. See Wahrhaftig, p. 121.

77. Wahrhaftig, p. 44. Polish Jews who had fled to the Soviet Union and who later entered DP camps in the American zone after experiencing postwar persecution when they returned to Poland were more likely to ar-

rive in intact family groups than were survivors of the death camps, ghettos, or partisan groups.

78. Meyer Levin, *In Search: An Autobiography* (New York, 1950), p. 245. This is precisely what happens in the American film *The Search* (1948, directed by Fred Zinnemann), in which Montgomery Clift plays a U.S. GI who picks up a lost and speechless child, clearly a victim of unspeakable brutality, wandering in the German ruins. At the movie's conclusion, the child is reunited with his concentration camp survivor mother who has been walking the assembly centers of Europe looking for him. She finally spies him walking past her in a row of children being prepared for *Aliyah* for Palestine. "Karel," she cries; "Mamischka," he calls out and runs toward her, and the movie fades out. There is, however, a twist familiar to Levin, who railed against the universalization and de-Judaization of the Holocaust: while the other orphans being prepared for emigration out of Europe are Jewish, little blond Karel is the child of anti-Nazi Czech intelligentsia.

79. Levin, p. 270.

80. For a fine analysis of this literature, see Isidor J. Kaminer, "'On razors edge'—Vom Weiterleben nach dem Überleben," in *Auschwitz: Geschichte, Rezeption, und Wirkung*, ed. Fritz Bauer Institut, Jahrbuch 1996 zur Geschichte und Wirkung des Holocaust (Frankfurt am Main, 1996), pp. 146 ff., 157.

81. Biber, p. 37.

82. Levin, pp. 183 ff.

83. See Juliane Wetzel, "Mir szeinen doh, München und Umbegung als Zeflueht von Überlebenden des Holocaust 1945–1948," in *Von Stalingrad zur Währungsreform: Zur Sozialgeschichte des Umbruchs in Deutschland*, ed. Martin Broszat, Klaus-Dietmar Henke, and Hans Woller (Munich, 1988), pp. 327–64. See also Angelika Königseder and Juliane Wetzel, *Lebensmut im Wartesaal: Die jüdischen DPs (Displaced Persons) in Nachkriegsdeutschland* (Frankfurt am Main, 1994), pp. 104 ff., 187. The term *She'erit Hapleita* derives from reworkings of Biblical references to the survivors of the Assyrian conquest.

84. See Zalman Grinberg, "We are Living Corpses," in *Aufbau*, Ausgabe vom 24. 8. 1945. For a strong argument against the view of survivors as "living corpses" and for the agency, and what Peck has called "the revolutionary ideology" of the *She'erit Hapleita* (which focuses on political organization rather than reproduction), see Ze'ev Mankowitz, "The Formation of *She-erit Hapleita:* November 1944–July 1945," *Yad Vashem Studies* 20 (1990): 337–70; Mankowitz, "The Affirmation of Life in *She'erit Hapleita*," *Holocaust and Genocide Studies* 5 (1990): 13–21.

85. "And the urge to arrive in time for the birth of the child in Eretz was real on every vessel that left for Palestine with its host of pregnant women, some of whom were smuggled onto the ships in their ninth month despite the Haganah regulation making the seventh month the limit." Levin, p. 360. See also Wahrhaftig, pp. 52–4.

86. Heymont, p. 44.

87. Judith Tydor Baumel, "DPs, Mothers, and Pioneers: Women in the *She'erit Hapleita,*" *Jewish History* 11, no. 2 (1997): 103. See also Baumel, *Kibbutz Buchenwald: Survivors and Pioneers* (New Brunswick, 1997).

88. Biber, p. 1.

89. It is worth noting how many "Holocaust memoirs" actually include (or conclude with) time in the DP camps and experiences of marriage, pregnancy, and childbearing. See, among many memoirs, Sonja Milner, *Survival in War and Peace* (New York, 1984); Sala Pawlowicz (with Kevin Klose), *I Will Survive* (London, 1947). In general, see Lenore Weitzman and Dalia Ofer, eds., *Women in the Holocaust* (New Haven, 1998); Sybil Milton, "Gender and Holocaust—ein offences Forschungsfeld"; Sara R. Horowitz, "Geschlechtsspezifische Erinnerungen an den Holocaust"; and Atina Grossmann, "Zwei Erfahrungen im Kontext des Themas 'Gender und Holocaust,'" all three in *Forschungsschwerpunkt Ravensbrück: Beiträge zur Geschichte des Frauen-Konzentrationslagers,* ed. Sigrid Jacobeit and Grit Philipp (Berlin, 1997), pp. 124–46.

90. Wahrhaftig, p. 54. Occupation and relief officials, as well as Germans, were often caught between disbelief at the horror and magnitude of the extermination and incomprehension of the fact that there remained, after all, hundreds of thousands of survivors who resisted repatriation and for whom there had to be found not just "relief" but a new life (what was still called "a final solution") outside Europe. See report by Zorach Wahrhaftig, 27 November 1945: "Life in Camps Six Months after Liberation," in Peck, p. 130.

91. Biber, p. 46.

92. See also Myers, *Jewish Displaced Persons,* pp. 306–8.

93. Grobman, p. 17. This baby boom is well portrayed in the American documentary film *The Long Way Home,* Simon Wiesenthal Center, Los Angeles, 1997.

94. Mankowitz, *Formation,* p. 351.

95. We might consider this gendered view of "revenge" in light of current discussions about the relative lack of vengeful actions by survivors. See John Sack, *An Eye for an Eye* (New York, 1993).

96. I am grateful to Samuel Kassow, History Department, Trinity College, for this reference.

97. Comparative anthropological literature is useful in this context. See especially Lisa Malkii's analysis of the ways in which refugee camp settings encourage "construction and reconstruction of [their] history 'as a people'" and the importance of children in that process, in *Purity and Exile: Violence, Memory, and National Cosmology among Hutu Refugees in Tanzania* (Chicago, 1995), p. 3.

98. Biber, p. 14.

99. Wahrhaftig, *Uprooted,* p. 86.

100. Magda Denes, *Castles Burning: A Child's Life in War* (New York, 1997), pp. 304, 316. A recent letter to the editor of the American Jewish magazine *Moment* recalled DP Camp Föhrenwald as "a vibrant Jewish community. . . . we needed this transition time after Nazi hell." *Moment,* June 1997, p. 21.

101. Lt. Col. Harold Mercer, chief of Displaced Persons and Welfare Section (OMG), 5 February 1946, LAB OMGUS 4/20–1/10.

102. Maginnis, p. 326.

103. Nachama, p. 272. See also Königseder, *Durchgangstation Berlin.* All these numbers are inexact. The Berlin Sector/Public Welfare Branch of the Office of Military Government estimated on 20 June 1947 that there were 8,000 German Jews in Berlin receiving aid from the American Joint Distribution Committee, plus 6,300 Polish Jews in two DP camps. Another memorandum on 20 June 1947 for the Jewish Agency for Palestine counted 8,000 persons in Düppel and 4,000 in Wittenau camps.

104. Among many sources see Brenner, *Nach dem Holocaust,* p. 18.

105. Maginnis, p. 327.

106. Ibid., 326.

107. Lt. Col. Harold Mercer, chief of Displaced Persons and Welfare Section (OMG), 5 February 1946, LAB OMGUS 4/20–1/10.

108. Heymont, *Among the Survivors,* p. 38.

109. Samuel Gringauz, "Our New German Policy and the DPs: Why Immediate Resettlement is Imperative," *Commentary* 5 (1948): 510.

110. Among many other sources on shifting American policy, see ibid., pp. 508–14; in general, see also Dinnerstein.

111. Quoted in the documentary *The Long Way Home.*

112. Norbert Mühlen, *The Return of Germany: A Tale of Two Countries* (Chicago, 1953), pp. 154 ff.

113. Frank Stern, "The Historic Triangle: Occupiers, Germans, and Jews in Postwar Germany," *Tel Aviver Jahrbuch für deutsche Geschichte* 19 (1990), pp. 47–76.

114. Wahrhaftig, "Life in Camps," p. 134. For case studies of relations between Jewish DPs and a local German population in Landsberg, see Angelika Eder, "Jüdische Displaced Persons im deutschen Alltag: Eine Re-

gionalstudie 1945–1950," in *Überlebt und unterwegs,* pp. 163–87; Dietrich Kohlmannslehner, "Das Verhältnis von Deutschen und jüdischen Displaced Persons im Lager Lampertheim 1945–1949" (unpublished paper, Fritz Bauer Institut Archives, Frankfurt am Main).

115. K.[t]E., "Juden in Deutschland," in *Tagesspiegel,* no. 39, 5 December 1945, p. 3 ("So one may hope that the millions of sacrifices [*Opfer*] by the Jews have not been brought in vain, but that rather after hundreds of years of effort it will finally be possible today to solve the Jewish problem in its totality [*sic*]; namely, on the one hand, through emigration of the homeless Jews and, on the other hand, through the complete assimilation of those Jews who wish to remain in Europe").

116. Wahrhaftig, "Life in Camps," p. 133.

117. The reconstituted Jewish community in Berlin engaged in tense discussions with the SMAD about whether Jews could be classified as resistance fighters, and not just as "victims of fascism" *(Opfer des Faschismus).* See Nachama, p. 279.

118. Wolfgang Jacobmeyer, "Jüdische Überlebende als 'Displaced Persons': Untersuchungen zur Besatzungspolitik in den deutschen Westzonen und zur Zuwanderung osteuropäischer Juden 1945–1947," *GG* 9 (1983): 432 ("first frontier for this Jewish migration from East-Central Europe").

119. LAB rep. 240/2651/98/3, report by H. Gnädig ("1947 our younger son was born and with him for me yet another great worry. It was irresponsible that in this terrible time of need I would put another child into the world").

120. Riess, p. 34 ("were only ruins of their former selves, just like the houses in which they now lived out their days"). This view contrasted with more cheerful portrayals of women in western Germany, and surely had to do with the experience of mass rape. For fraternization stories, see the interviews in Heimatmuseum Charlottenburg, *Worüber kaum gesprochen wurde: Frauen und allierte Soldaten: Katalog zu der Ausstellung vom 3. September bis 15. Oktober 1995* (Berlin, 1995).

121. Maginnis, p. 344, makes this point. On the toll exacted by epidemics see *Berlin: Kampf um Freiheit und Selbstverwaltung 1945–1946* (Berlin, 1961), p. 10.

122. LAB acc. 2421, report by Gabrielle Vallentin, p. 28 ("one saw many such sad pictures; mothers who sat silent and rigid, on their lap a cardboard box, in which they had picked up their dead child from the hospital").

123. LAB, rep. 240/2651/131, report by Gertrud Strubel, p. 1 ("The bombs in winter 1944/45 were bad, but the days that came now were almost impossible to bear").

124. B. Sagalowitz, "Report on Trip to Germany, April 1950," in Peck, p. 377.

125. *Tagesspiegel,* no. 29, 23 November 1945, p. 3 ("It is after all the case that we have already broken the habit of the famous glance into the baby carriage, which supposedly no woman would deny herself, because what we see there so often makes us so sad").

126. LAB OMGUS 4/24–1/4; see also *Berlin in Zahlen 1947* (Berlin, 1949), p. 128. In 1946, 166 marriages in which the man was Jewish, and 109 in which the woman was Jewish, were celebrated (out of a total 20,903). Ibid., p. 122.

127. Brenner, "East European," pp. 49 ff. He adds, "Ironically, some places that the Nazis never had to make *judenrein* because Jews had never lived there were eventually populated by several hundreds, if not thousands, of Jews."

128. Jacobmeyer, p. 437. See also Brenner, *Nach dem Holocaust,* p. 36. For comparative purposes: the German birth rate in 1933 stood at 14.7 (9.9 in Berlin); in the aftermath of World War I it had reached 25.9 in 1920. Two-thirds of Jewish DPs eventually ended up in Israel; altogether about 100,000 went to the United States and 250,000 to Israel. On the reaction in Israel, see Tom Segev, *The Seventh Million: Israel Confronts the Holocaust* (New York, 1993).

129. Wahrhaftig, *Uprooted,* p. 54. As noted earlier, the approximate sex ratio in the DP camps was 60 percent male and 40 percent female; in Berlin at war's end, approximately the opposite ratio (over 60 percent female) applied.

130. See the poignant depictions in the feature film *Lang ist der Wege,* a German/Polish coproduction (1947). For a critical analysis, see Cilly Kugelmann, "*Lang ist der Wege:* Eine jüdisch-deutsche Film-Kooperation," in *Auschwitz,* ed. Fritz Bauer Institut, pp. 353–70.

131. Anthropologists have reminded us that "children are a crucial element in the representation of refugees"; Malkii, p. 11. Literary scholars are increasingly admonishing us to interrogate discourses of reproduction as responses to experiences of mass death and crises of futurity. Pressured by the AIDS crisis, queer theory has provided some of the most insightful analyses of cultures of reproduction in relation to loss and death. See Michael Warner, "Repro-Culture" (unpublished paper, Rutgers University, 1995).

132. Dieter E. Kesper, "Unsere Hoffnung: Die Zeitung Überlebender des Holocaust im Eschweger Lager 1946," Eschwege 1996. Newspaper of the UNRRA camp in Eschwege, discovered in Heimatarchiv Eschwege, Nv. 1, 4.6. 1946. The published text is a translation of the original Yiddish ("We must turn to today and prepare a better tomorrow, a beautiful and a healthy tomorrow").

133. See the extraordinary photo collection in Jacqueline Giere and Rachel Salamander, *Ein Leben aufs neu: Das Robinson Album: DP-Lager, Juden auf deutschem Boden 1945–1948* (Vienna, 1995).

134. Levin, p. 398.

135. See Eder.

V. P·R·O·X·I·M·I·T·Y

Tomasz Kranz

Between Planning and Implementation
The Lublin District and Majdanek Camp in Nazi Policy

THE NAZI OCCUPATION OF POLAND AIMED AT THE MAXIMUM UTILIZAtion of the material and human resources of the country, and regarding the population featured the utmost severity and total terror, especially toward the Polish Jews. This applied in a particular way to the Government General (GG), a central and southern part of Poland that was not incorporated into the Reich and covered an area of more than ninety thousand square kilometers and encompassed a population of twelve million. These lands were treated by the Nazi leaders as a temporary dwelling place for the Poles, a kind of colony and reservoir of cheap manpower where they put into effect the most ruthless demographic strategies. According to the concepts developed and elaborated by various institutions—mainly by the Reich Security Main Office (RSHA) and the Race and Settlement Office (RuSHA), which were closely linked with and subordinate to the Reichsführer-SS, Heinrich Himmler, who in turn was also the Reich Commissioner for the Consolidation of German Nationhood (RFK)—the Government General perfectly suited the purpose of intermediary between the Reich and the East, which was to be conquered and to serve as an economic hinterland, supply base, and site for the realization of the colonization and extermination plans.

A unique role with regard to the displacement of population, its course and intensity, as well as the scope and character of the killing operation, was played by the Lublin District, one of the five administrative units of the GG. It must be stressed that this area featured the two fundamental goals of Nazi ideology and policy: the establishment of a new ethnic order in the East and the destruction of European Jewry.[1] This is reflected by the fact that before the outbreak of war, about 2,400,000 people inhabited the Lublin region, and as a result of German colonization and extermination operations, approximately another 900,000 were deported to this region, while some 250,000 were transported away.[2] In the years 1939 to 1944 about 1,500,000 people, most of them Jews, died or were killed there. They perished in numerous ghettos, labor and POW camps, were murdered in death camps, or killed in mass executions.[3] The harsh treatment of this part of Poland is explained primarily by its geographical position—proximity to the Ukraine and large settlements of Jews and the personality of the SS and police leader of the Lublin District, SS-Brigadeführer Odilo Globocnik, one of the most ruthless SS officers, who was closely allied to Himmler and commissioned by him to prepare and carry out many important programs. The most significant of these were two far-reaching operations concerning the Jews and Poles, namely, the extermination of the Jews, carried out under the code name *Aktion Reinhardt,* and the establishment of the first German settlement area within the Government General. The Lublin District, which served to a high degree as the laboratory in which the Nazi population and extermination policies were verified, also featured significantly in the administration and cohesion of both operations, which were devised almost simultaneously by the same apparatus.[4]

The Lublin District had an important place in Nazi political and economic plans, and this role intensified with the invasion of the Soviet Union in June 1941; at this time the region became a transit and staging area for German troops. This was regarded as the first stage in the implementation of the *Generalplan Ost* (General Plan East), a gigantic concept that would radically change the demographic structure of the populations living in Eastern Europe and would create there a "New Order." This long-term colonization plan—if we consider its various versions as a whole—provided for the expulsion of the native population of about thirty or forty million "racially unnecessary" people, including twenty million Poles, and the resettlement of *Volksdeutsche,* ethnic Germans, in their place. Only about fourteen million people were to be allowed to remain and be turned into modern-day slaves. The twenty million Poles considered unsuitable for Germanization were to be deported to western

Siberia, scattered over as wide an area as possible, and intermingled with the local population. The majority, in fact, were destined for death. The German ethnic frontier was to be extended by some 1,000 km to the southeast, and the vast areas lying further to the east were to become an enormous German "sphere of influence" extending deep into the heart of Asia. The implementation of this plan was to be facilitated by the creation of a network of SS and police strongpoints *(Stützpunkte)* in the occupied Polish and Soviet territories as "settlements for entire families of SS and police officers," and as the nucleus of the future economic empire. Six such bases were planned in the Lublin District.[5]

The city of Lublin and its environs were to perform the functions of important Germanization centers, and the plans for Lublin itself provided for the establishment of a military base and supply depot for the higher SS and police leader of South Russia, a military economic depot, and the construction of a huge housing district for sixty thousand SS men. Thus, the city was to constitute an economic support for the SS strongpoints in the occupied Soviet territories and develop into a nucleus for the German eastward expansion *(Drang nach Osten)*. The entire Lublin region was to be turned into a "German protective wall" and serve therefore as a future ethnic bridge between the Germanized Baltic countries and Transylvania.[6]

The General Plan East—an undertaking on an unprecedented scale—was to be carried out gradually over a period of about thirty years, but the realization of this demographic strategy was postponed until after the victorious conclusion of the war. Some attempts at Germanization were made in the Government General during the war, however, and were regarded as experiments to test the methods to be used in the future resettlement operations, and to gauge the reaction of the Polish population. For these experiments the Nazis selected the counties in the southeastern part of the Lublin region, an area known as Zamojszczyzna. This area was chosen for its geographical position, agrarian character, and fertile soil, and the existence of small German minorities. As early as June 1941 it was officially announced that a "purely German settlement area" would be established there, the first one in the Government General. A month later, on 17 July 1941, SS-Brigadeführer Globocnik was appointed plenipotentiary for organization of the SS and police strongpoints in the new eastern territories and entrusted with the colonization program. To cope with this task, a special staff *Umwandererzentralstelle* (Central Resettlement Office) in Lodz established a branch in Zamość to work out guidelines for the eviction of native Poles. The expulsion of the Polish population from the Zamość region lasted—with interruptions—from November 1941 until August 1943, during which time almost one hundred thousand peasants, including some thirty thousand children, were affected by these operations. These brutal resettlements followed a prearranged plan. Usually at night or in the early morning, SS and police troops, who were often accompanied by Wehrmacht units, surrounded a village and allowed the people only a few minutes to pack some clothes and food before being evicted from their homes. The operations were accompanied by rape, terror, and looting. The evicted people were transported or marched on foot to transit camps where harsh living conditions prevailed. They were next examined by a commission appointed by the Race and Settlement Office, subjected to "racial tests," and divided into four racial groups. Those found to have Germanic features were assigned to Group I, while those assigned to Group II consisted of people considered suitable for Germanization. According to Nazi estimates, these two groups made up about 5 percent of the total population. Group III consisted of persons capable of work, 74 percent, and Group IV was made up of persons classified as "undesirable elements," 21 percent. Those included in Group III were sent to Germany for forced labor, and those in Group IV to concentration camps. Children up to the age of fourteen years who were separated from their parents, the elderly, and the sick were accommodated in "pensioner villages." The fate of the Zamość children was particularly tragic. About five thousand of them were carried away to the Reich for Germanization. Others were transported to various localities in Poland, but in fact, many died of cold and hunger en route. A substantial percentage were brought with their parents to Auschwitz and Majdanek and murdered there in gas chambers or with phenol injections.[7]

Despite the detailed preparations, the first stage of the resettlement operation was a failure, and the Nazis succeeded in rounding up less than 30 percent of the population. They also managed to resettle only one-third of the total of twenty-seven thousand German colonists; the rest remained in transit camps. This was due to the chaos that prevailed during the evacuation operation and resistance on the part of the Polish peasants. The second stage of the operation began in June 1943. During its implementation—in conjunction with combating Polish "bandits," as the Nazis termed the partisans— many localities suffered the same fate as Lidice: in "pacification" operations, dozens of villages were burned down and destroyed and their inhabitants killed on the spot: machine-gunned, killed with hand grenades or bombs, or burned alive. Thus, the atrocities committed in the Zamość region are generally considered to be among the most horrible Nazi crimes.[8]

Apart from the colonization program, during the course of the Nazi policy the Lublin region also became one of the largest extermination centers for European Jews. As early as October 1939, Berlin planned to send about five million Jews from the Reich and annexed western Polish territories to the Lublin reservation. This gigantic project was never put into effect, however, and only some twenty-five thousand Jews were actually resettled there. The plan was abandoned in March 1940, due to objections by the German civil authorities. Although the creation of the reservation had little chance of success, there can be no doubt that the underlying idea was the first step in solving the "Jewish problem" through extermination, as the London *Times* recognized on 24 October 1939: "Herr Hitler now proposes to concentrate the three million Jews of Poland in a State which is to be cut out of the body of Poland and will have Lublin for its centre.... To thrust 3,000,000 Jews, relatively few of whom are agriculturists, into the Lublin region and to force them to settle there would doom them to famine. That, perhaps, is the intention."[9] The Lublin reservation was a testing ground for ad hoc race policy solutions accentuated by the extraordinary zeal of SS-Brigadeführer Globocnik, who, from the very beginning, had attempted to take all Jewish problems under his control, and advocated the harshest treatment for Polish Jews. The concept of the reservation found a peculiar continuity in the concentration of the Jewish population in the system of forced labor camps that had expanded rapidly since the spring of 1940. Interned in an extensive network of camps, the inmates created a vast reservoir of manpower and were employed in military and economic projects such as the construction of the so-called *Ostwall,* road building, and river regulation. Between 1939 and 1941, about a hundred forced labor camps for Jews were established in the Lublin District, and by 1940 about fifty to seventy thousand Jewish workers were involved in projects within the scope of SS-Brigadeführer Globocnik's plans.[10]

The persecution of the Jews in the Lublin District reached its peak in the spring of 1942, when Globocnik was charged with the coordination of *Aktion Reinhardt*—part of the Final Solution. This mass murder was mainly carried out in the three camps—Bełżec, Sobibór, and Treblinka. They were built on the eastern frontier of the Government General, and while they had good rail communications, their isolation from populated areas ensured the secrecy of the extermination operation. It was also of prime importance that they were located on the border between two main areas of Jews—about 2,300,00 in the Government General and 3,500,00 in the Ukraine—and close to the numerous ghettos and forced labor camps of the Lublin District. They were also not far from the *Aktion Reinhardt* headquarters in Lublin: Bełżec 110 km, Sobibór 80 km, and Treblinka 160 km. The geographical location of the death camps also made it possible to give the impression that the victims were being deported to ghettos or forced labor in the East.[11]

Functionally and administratively the *Action Reinhardt* death camps came under several authorities, with the whole operation being coordinated by SS-Brigadeführer Globocnik and his staff. Globocnik in turn was subordinate to the Reichsführer-SS, Himmler. The first commandant at Bełżec, and from 1 August 1942 the inspector of the three SS-*Sonderkommandos* at Bełżec, Sobibór, and Treblinka, Kriminalkommissar Christian Wirth, received his orders, however, from Section II of the Kanzlei des Führers (KdF) in Berlin. The direct involvement of the KdF in the mass murder was hidden behind a cover organization known by the code name "T4," the organization that had previously supervised the killing operation in the "euthanasia" institutions. The personnel at the death camps consisted on average of about thirty men, aged twenty-five to thirty, many of whom were former male nurses from psychiatric institutions or civilian employees recruited through local labor offices. Several were members of the SS, and some, like Christian Wirth and Gottlieb Hering at Bełżec and Franz Stangl at Sobibór (and later Treblinka), were police officers. All of them had previously been employed in killing the mentally ill in the "euthanasia" institutions. The guard company at each death camp consisted of *Trawnikimänner* (Trawniki men) or "Hiwis" (*Hilfswillige*—volunteers)—Ukrainian, Russian, Lithuanian, Latvian, and Byelorussian POWs who had gone over to the German side and had been trained by German SS and police officers at the SS training camp for foreign volunteers at Trawniki, near Lublin. About 120 of them served in each death camp. The last group essential for the functioning of the camps consisted of Jewish prisoners who were selected upon arrival. They were assigned to various tasks directly connected with the killings: unloading the transports, cutting off the women's hair, grave digging, unloading the gas chambers, burial and cremation of the corpses, and sorting the effects of the victims. Some also worked in the administration section of the camps. They were generally allowed to live for only a few weeks before being killed and replaced from the next transports. The extent of the work carried out by these Jewish work brigades is demonstrated by the fact that about a thousand were employed in each camp.[12]

From the beginning, *Aktion Reinhardt* was directed through Himmler. He visited Lublin on 14 March 1942, that is, shortly before the start of the mass killings, returned on 20 July and inspected the Jewish property depot (*Effekten-Lager*) and valuables store, and had a conversation with SS-Hauptsturmführer Hermann Höfle, Globocnik's chief of staff and the administrative head of *Aktion Reinhardt* in Lublin, and with commandant Wirth from the Bełżec death camp. On 21 August he again visited Lublin, evidently also in connection with the mass murder of the Jews. He also visited the death camps on several occasions in 1942 and 1943.[13]

The camps were built under primitive conditions. The construction of Bełżec was begun in October 1941, and it became operational in mid-March 1942; construction of Sobibór was begun in March 1942, and it became operational at the beginning of May 1942; while construction at Treblinka started in May 1942, and it began operating in the second half of July 1942. At first, each camp was provided with only three primitive gas chambers, but in the summer of 1942 a reorganization of the camps was carried out that included the construction of bigger gassing installations. They were never equipped with technical installations such as existed in Birkenau, however, and consequently never achieved the efficiency wished for by SS-Brigadeführer Globocnik: 15,000 a day at Bełżec, 20,000 at Sobibór, and 25,000 at Treblinka. Their temporary and primitive character—as the well-known American historian Raul Hilberg has stated—was due to the fact that no budget was allocated for their construction;

lack of finance and building materials thus forced the *Aktion Reinhardt* architects to improvise and economize.[14]

The *Aktion Reinhardt* camps were all organized in a similar way. They were compact and consisted of four areas: the reception and administration section, in which were located the railway platform and barracks for storing the clothing and luggage of the victims, workshops, provisions stores and kitchens; the economics section, where the looted belongings were sorted; the extermination area, with the gas chambers and mass graves; and the SS living quarters. The entire area of each camp was surrounded by high, camouflaged fences. The transports of Jews arrived in the camps by rail; only in infrequent cases, for example, in Sobibór, did the victims arrive on foot or in farm carts. After arrival in the camps the Jews were told that they were in a *Durchgangslager* (transit camp), and were first ordered to undress to have a bath. The women then had their hair cut off while the men were being gassed. All the victims, with the exception of the old, sick, and infirm, were killed by the exhaust fumes from internal combustion engines. The old, sick, and infirm were shot separately.[15]

In *Aktion Reinhardt* over 1,500,000 Jews were murdered in the death camps run by SS-Brigadeführer Globocnik. The overwhelming majority of victims were Polish Jews. The number of victims in Treblinka is estimated at 800,000, in Bełżec 500,000, and in Sobibór 200,000. About 80,000 Jews were killed in the Majdanek concentration camp, Lublin, as this camp too functioned as an extermination center, if not within the ranks of *Aktion Reinhardt,* then at least on the periphery of this operation. In addition, many thousands more perished from starvation, illness, or shooting in various other places in the Lublin region.[16]

An important adjunct in the extermination operation—in parallel with the liquidation of the ghettos and deportation of the Jews to the death camps—was the utilization by the SS of the remaining Jews as forced labor. On Himmler's initiative Oswald Pohl, head of the SS Economic-Administrative Main Office (SS WVHA), seized installations and machinery in the factories of the liquidated Warsaw ghetto. But the removal of the Jewish workforce from Warsaw to the Lublin District ordered by the Reichsführer-SS was delayed and the SS and police leader in Lublin, SS-Brigadeführer Globocnik, saw a chance to increase his influence: he would have control of the remainder of the Jews capable of work, who would be transferred to his factories and workshops. On 12 March 1943 Globocnik founded the *Ostindustrie* (Osti) with himself as managing director. Osti aimed to exploit the Jewish workforces in the labor camps in Poniatowa and Trawniki, to seize "former" Jewish property, and to utilize machinery, tools, and products of "former" Jewish property. About six thousand Warsaw Jews were transferred to Trawniki to work for the Schulz firm, about fifteen thousand to Poniatowa to work for the Toebbens firm, and several thousand more to Majdanek concentration camp, as well as to other, smaller SS-run camps. By early 1943, the SS and police leader in Lublin had created an economic empire, whose factories helped supply the demands of Germany's war economy. This economic empire was an enormous source of revenue for the SS as an institution, as well as for individual SS officers, among them SS-Brigadeführer Globocnik. According to a note by Globocnik of 21 June 1943, there were forty-five thousand Jews under his control in the Lublin District.[17] But the development of the SS enterprises was immobilized by one of the bloodiest massacres of World War II, code-named *Erntefest* (Harvest Festival), in which during the course of two days, on 3 and 4 November 1943, about forty-two thousand Jews were shot in the Lublin District. The killings were carried out in three camps, Majdanek concentration camp, and in the Poniatowa and Trawniki labor camps. Only about three thousand Jews in the Budzyń camp who worked for the Heinkel aircraft firm, and other small *Julags* (Jewish camps), were spared. The important reasons for this wave of killing were events in the death camps—a revolt in Treblinka at the beginning of August 1943, and in mid-October a mass breakout by prisoners in Sobibór. Another reason for the *Erntefest* was Himmler's ambition: he did not want to hand over the Jews employed in the SS-run labor camps to the civil armament authorities.[18]

In the course of *Aktion Reinhardt* in 1942, the Lublin region was the biggest extermination center of the Jews, but from 1943 the focal point of the extermination operation shifted to Auschwitz-Birkenau; nevertheless, *Aktion Reinhardt* claimed more victims than the Birkenau gas chambers. Although mainly Polish Jews were killed—more than 90 percent of those murdered were Polish Jews—the nationality of the victims of the death camps was not restricted to the area of Poland. The Lublin region alone was the final destination for almost fourteen thousand Czech Jews, nearly ten thousand from Austria, and several thousand from France and Germany.[19]

Before the war the Lublin region had a population of about 2,400,000, of whom the Jewish population made up about 10 percent. In the course of the colonization operations, forced labor service, and the Nazi extermination policy against the Jews, between 1939 and 1943 over 600,000 Jews were deported to the Lublin region, which, with the indigenous population, brought the total number of Jews to almost 900,000. Only a small part, about 50,000, were taken away from this area. The majority of the others, more than 800,000 people, were killed there in the ghettos, labor camps, and death camps. The total number of Jewish victims in the Lublin region is therefore comparable with the total number murdered in Auschwitz-Birkenau. Not only is the extent of the crime proof of the special position of this region in the planning and execution of the Holocaust; the development of the *Judenpolitik* in the Lublin region is at the same time an example of the most important objectives of the Nazi leadership concerning the Jews—dispossession, concentration, exploitation of the labor force, and extermination often ran parallel and overlapped. It is also striking that the "Final Solution of the Jewish Question" in this part of Poland, in territorial respects the broadest and most complex, was realized in the shortest time. For these reasons the Lublin District was the central scene of the crime of mass murder committed by the Nazis against the Jews of Europe.[20]

In the context of the aforementioned projects, special attention should be paid to Majdanek concentration camp, as it reflects the main features of the Nazi policies in the East, including colonization and extermination, and with regard to its location and character has no analogy in the system of camps administered by the SS state. During the time of its existence, from October 1941 to July 1944, Majdanek fulfilled various functions. In the beginning it was called a POW camp of the Lublin Waffen-SS; on 16 February 1943 it was officially renamed as a concentration camp. For the authorities in the Lublin District it became a convenient instrument and reflected to a high degree the character and scope of their activities.[21] In many cases, however, the development of the camp was the result of policies based on improvisations created by the multiplicity of functions and tasks allocated to it. In this respect Majdanek, as the German historian Wolfgang Scheffler has correctly stated, belonged among the most intolerable camps.[22]

The decision for the construction of Majdanek was made by

Himmler on 20 July 1941. From the endorsement of his order, the SS authorities made the leading decisions about the construction of the concentration camp in Lublin mainly out of economic necessity. The camp was to be a reservoir of manpower for the economic colonization program. The construction of the camp did not begin immediately. The acceleration of the preparations first occurred in the final days of September 1941, according to an order from the head of Department II in the SS Budget and Construction Main Office, Hans Kammler. On 22 September, with reference to Himmler's order, Kammler ordered the immediate construction in Lublin of a concentration camp for 5,000 prisoners. This was the first section in the area provided for the later construction of a concentration camp for 50,000 prisoners. A few days later, on 27 September, he issued a new order: that from 1 October a camp with a capacity of 50,000 POWs should be immediately established.[23] The change of the official character of the camp was due to two underlying factors. According to an agreement between the SS and the commander-in-chief of the army, the SS was to take over 325,000 Soviet POWs, 100,000 of them to be handed over for the purpose of employment in construction work at the Auschwitz and Majdanek camps.[24] The Reichsführer-SS wanted to exploit the situation to his best advantage: at that time the use of Soviet POWs as a workforce for German industry was out of the question on racial grounds; therefore, they could be transferred to SS concerns without further ado. An important reason for the official change of function of the Majdanek camp was also that it was easier for the SS to build a POW camp that would be independent from the civil administration, which in the Lublin District was not without serious consequences because of a rift between SS-Brigadeführer Globocnik and civil governor Ernest Zörner.[25]

Altogether, six construction orders were issued and the capacity of the camp enlarged each time. In six months the capacity was increased sixfold, if one takes the Himmler order of 20 July 1941 as the lowest limit. The dynamic expansion of building projects and the immediate and extravagant breadth of planning were typical of the original phase of the organization of the Majdanek concentration camp. After this, the mania for size had no limit, and on 23 March 1942 the camp commandant, Karl Koch, approved a general construction plan with a capacity for 250,000 inmates. According to this plan, the camp complex was to be divided into three areas: the POW camp, the expansion of the POW camp, and the clothing workshops of the Waffen-SS. Majdanek would thus become the biggest camp in Nazi-occupied Europe.[26]

There was a certain air of unreality in these plans, however, especially as they did not take into consideration the existing situation or the actual materials and transport possibilities. It is therefore surprising that this plan was ever approved, especially as only a month earlier the recently formed SS Economic-Administrative Main Office had canceled the construction order of 22 September 1941 because of the difficult situation on the raw materials market.[27]

Due to the difficulties in procuring building materials, as well as the reduced transport capabilities—as a result of troop reinforcements and provisions transports for Operation Barbarossa, and also by reason of the impending transports to the Bełżec and Sobibór death camps, and to some extent also as a result of the strained relations between the SS and the civil administration—the plan for the enormous camp complex quickly fell through. On 14 April 1942, Himmler communicated to the Reich transport minister that from the beginning of the year he had given up the plan for the final construction of the camp, and that the camp had been reduced to a capacity of fifty thousand. This decision coincided with his letter of 27 March 1942 to SS-Brigadeführer Globocnik, in which he released the SS and police leader of the Lublin District from his order of July 1941 that charged him with the task of organizing SS and police strongpoints.[28]

The decision made in the spring of 1942 not only reduced the construction project, but meant that the plan for the SS economic empire, in which Majdanek should have played an important part, had also broken down. Shortly afterward, the construction plans were again revised, and on 14 May it was decided to reduce the camp to eight fields; but these plans, too, foundered, and up until July 1944 only six fields were completed, of which five were for housing prisoners. The final capacity of the camp amounted to about 25,000 prisoners, with an average of 250 to a barrack, only 10 percent of the intended general construction plan.

During the construction period Majdanek rated its original designation as a POW camp, but this did not last long. In addition to the first big transports in October 1941, Soviet POWs arrived only sporadically. In autumn 1941, the Nazi leadership, in consideration of the increasing lack of manpower in Germany, decided to transfer Soviet POWs to German concerns. The agreed-upon transfer by the Wehrmacht of the 325,000 prisoners to the SS existed only on paper, which caused Himmler on 26 January 1942 to instruct the future inspector of concentration camps, Richard Glücks, that the Russian POWs destined for the concentration camps should be replaced by German Jews.[29]

A high proportion of prisoners at Majdanek were from the rural population. At the turn of the year 1941–1942, Majdanek began to serve as a penal camp for Poles, primarily for village inhabitants who were sent there because of failure to meet their agricultural quotas, or as a reprisal for the activities of the resistance movement. They were classified as "hostages," a category of prisoners that did not exist in most other Nazi camps. The overwhelming majority imprisoned there came from the Lublin District because of the significance of the region for the Government General as the agricultural hinterland in which quota policies were enforced. The large number of peasants was also connected with the further function of Majdanek as a transit camp for the victims of the evacuation and "pacification" operations carried out in the Zamość region, and for the inhabitants of the occupied territories of Byelorussia, the Ukraine, and Russia, where similar repressions followed the course of activities of the *Einsatzgruppen*. Altogether, about fifty-seven thousand peasants from Poland, the Ukraine, Byelorussia, and Russia—about 20 percent of the total number of prisoners—were confined in Majdanek.[30]

Of prime significance in the history of KL Lublin was its incorporation in the extermination of the Jews, camouflaged as "resettlement." Following the Wannsee Conference of 20 January 1942, there arrived in Majdanek men classified as fit for work to build the camp; in the beginning they came from Slovakia, the *Reichsprotektorat* of Bohemia and Moravia, and from the Reich. Later on, they came also from the Lublin District, the Warsaw and Białystok ghettos, and some, too, from Holland. The influx of Jewish prisoners to Majdanek, however, from the second half of 1942, resulted primarily from two orders from Himmler, dated 19 July 1942 and 16 February 1943. The first determined the closing date for the "resettlement" of the Jewish population of the Government General, and ordered that the Jews there were to be allowed to stay only in collection camps in Warsaw, Cracow, Radom, Częstochowa, and Lublin. According to the second order, a concentration camp was to be established in the Warsaw ghetto, the "Gęsiówka," and then, together with its equipment and inmates, transferred to Lublin and neighboring labor camps.[31] Initially, Majdanek was for the Jews primarily a labor camp, but considering the harsh conditions prevailing there, inadequate provisions, and the tremendous tempo of work, it also had the function of a place of extermination.[32] With the construction of gas chambers in the camp in the autumn of 1942, Majdanek played a vital role as a place for the concentration and, in part, extermination, of the Jews, since of the roughly ninety thousand Jews who passed through the camp, some eighty thousand died.[33]

With the completion of the greater part of the camp structures in mid-1942 the role of Majdanek as a labor camp was enlarged, as inmates were employed in the workshops and enterprises of the SS, especially in the Deutsche Ausrüstungswerke (DAW) [the German Armaments Works], clothing factories, and Osti dealing in the looted Jewish belongings. These firms were engaged in meeting requirements for the front, such as ammunition baskets, straw shoes, and furs, and in the utilization and processing of Jewish property. These products, however, had little strategic importance. Due to this fact, and the lack of industrial concerns in the Lublin region, Majdanek main camp was not an important component in the Nazi economy; in spite of its initial large-scale planning, Majdanek actually had a surplus of prisoner labor, unlike camps in the Reich. The economic role of the camp, as of the whole of the Lublin District, was subordinate to the extermination plans.[34]

From the beginning of 1943, Majdanek rose to prominence as a typical concentration camp, as an instrument of terror and intimidation in the struggle against the Polish resistance movement. In connection with Himmler's order of 14 December 1942 concerning the transfer of thirty-five thousand able-bodied prisoners from prisons to concentration camps, forty thousand Polish political prisoners were delivered to Majdanek within twelve months.[35]

From 1942, parallel with its listed functions, Majdanek assumed the especially tragic role of a death camp and place of political executions. The distinction between the two forms of extermination had important consequences for the camp, and accordingly Majdanek is classified as a special case in the system of Nazi camps. With regard to function, it often was compared with Auschwitz and was perceived as similar by the Polish resistance movement during the occupation. In the case of Auschwitz, however, the organized mass exterminations took place in Birkenau, a segregated part of the camp complex, whereas in Majdanek they were carried out inside the base camp. A peculiarity of Majdanek is that the camp also served at the same time as a place for mass executions and mass gassings. In this respect it appears to be an exception. The majority of mass executions were carried out at the beginning of 1942 and in the first half of 1944, when Majdanek was the execution site for Polish political prisoners; in other periods the executions took place rather sporadically. The executions also included Soviet POWs and Jews. The total number of victims of the shootings was about forty thousand.[36]

It should be emphasized that Majdanek was also a site of the biggest mass execution in the history of Nazi concentration camps—the *Erntefest* (Harvest Festival) massacre of 3 November 1943 in which about eighteen thousand Jews were killed, among them eight thousand prisoners from the camp.[37]

The function of Majdanek concentration camp as a death camp is connected mainly with the construction of the gas chambers. The preserved source material unfortunately does not unequivocally answer the question of what connection they had with the mechanism of *Aktion Reinhardt*. Their construction was begun at the latest in August 1942, and therefore it may be plausible that they go back to Himmler's order issued in Lublin on 19 July 1942 concerning the conclusion of the "resettlement" of the Jews in the Government General by the end of the year. It is also possible that the origin of the gas chambers in Majdanek was connected with the reorganization of the death camps at Bełżec and Treblinka, and the beginning of the second phase of *Aktion Reinhardt*. It appears most likely that altogether seven gas chambers were constructed, of which three were used for mass killing in the period from September 1942 to October 1943. The main wave of gassings took place in the summer of 1943, and the victims included Jews from the ghettos in Warsaw and Białystok. In addition to the Jews selected for death by gassing in the "Rose Garden," the selection area in Majdanek, sick and emaciated prisoners were also selected and gassed. According to information from the Polish resistance movement, such selections took place in Majdanek concentration camp once or twice a month. The number of victims of mass gassings in Majdanek may be estimated at no more than fifty thousand.[38]

The staggering death rate at Majdanek was due to the appalling conditions in the camp. This is reflected in Oswald Pohl's report to Himmler, in which he states that the highest death rate in August 1943 occurred in the Lublin concentration camp.[39] This state of affairs was caused, among other things, by the temporary and, in comparison with other camps, particularly squalid living conditions. The camp was of makeshift character: the inmates were accommodated in wooden stablelike barracks without proper sanitary amenities, the food rations kept down to a minimum. The prisoners suffered greatly from the cold, plagues of vermin, overcrowding, and shortage of water. Halina Birenbaum, a Holocaust survivor, recalled, "We had to fight for everything in Majdanek: for a scrap of floor space in the hut on which to stretch out at night, for a rusty bowl without which we could not obtain the miserable ration of nettle-soup with which they fed us, or yellow stinking water to drink."[40] All these conditions contributed to the typhus epidemics that broke out frequently, decimating the prisoner population. As stated by many historians, 60 percent of the victims in Majdanek died as a result of starvation, forced labor, maltreatment, and illness.[41]

The various functions of the Majdanek concentration camp had an exceptional influence on the number of victims which, it has been estimated, amounted to about 200,000 to 250,000 people.[42] Still this number could be too high. One can estimate the total gross number as around 170,000.[43] It is certain that more prisoners were killed there than in other concentration camps, but fewer than in the permanent death camps like Bełżec, Treblinka, and Birkenau.

In 1941 to 1944, the Majdanek concentration camp served a variety of functions related to the political, economic, and racial goals of the Nazi authorities: a POW camp, a penal camp, a transit camp, a labor camp, and an extermination camp. A place of martyrdom and extermination, it never did develop into the camp complex originally planned. Its internal structure and development were largely marked by a lack of stability and a high degree of improvisation. It is additionally apparent that by early 1942 Himmler's interest in this camp waned, in spite of its original concept. External circumstances, especially the situation on the Eastern Front and the appointment of the Lublin District as the center for the extermination, prevented the full development of Majdanek. It became, nevertheless, one of the most significant places of Nazi genocide and a symbol of crimes committed in the Lublin region in the course of Nazi efforts at creating a "New Order."

NOTES

1. Z. Mańkowski, "Strategiczne znaczenie Lubelszczyzny i polityka represyjna okupanta" (Strategic role of the Lublin region and occupiers' reprisals), *Zeszyty Majdanka* 4 (1969): 9–20; Mańkowski, *Między Wisłą a Bugiem: Studium o polityce okupanta i postawach społeczeństwa* (Between the Vistula and Bug: A study of the occupiers' policy and attitudes of society) (Lublin, 1978).
2. See J. Kiełboń, *Migracje ludności w dystrykcie lubelskim w latach 1939–1944* (Displacements of population in the Lublin District 1939–1944) (Lublin, 1995).
3. Cz. Madajczyk, "Lubelszczyzna w polityce okupanta" (The Lublin region in the occupiers' policy), *Zeszyty Majdanka* 2 (1966): 5–21; Madajczyk, *Polityka III Rzeszy w okupowanej Polsce* (The Third Reich's policy in occupied Poland) (Warsaw, 1970).
4. The problem of the synchronization between the Final Solution and the General Plan East has been raised by the leading Polish historian Cz. Madajczyk in "Besteht ein Synchronismus zwischen dem 'Generalplan Ost' und der Judenfrage?" in *Der Zweite Weltkrieg,* ed. W. Michalka (Munich, 1989), pp. 844–57.
5. For details of this planning see one of the recent publications with new documents concerning the General Plan East: M. Rössler, S. Schleiermacher, and M. v. Tollmien, eds., *Der "Generalplan Ost": Hauptlinien der nationalsozialistischen Planungs- und Vernichtungpolitik* (Berlin, 1993).
6. J. Marszałek, "Geneza i początki budowy obozu koncentracyjnego na Majdanu" (Genesis and beginning of construction of the Majdanek concentration camp), *Zeszyty Majdanka* 1 (1965): 15–75; B. Wasser, "Die 'Germanisierung' im Distrikt Lublin als Generalprobe und erste Realisierungsphase des 'Generalplans Ost,'" in *"Generalplan Ost,"* pp. 271–93.
7. See R. Hrabar, Z. Tokarz, and J. Wilczur, *The Fate of Polish Children during the Last War* (Warsaw, 1981).
8. Cz. Madajczyk, ed., *Zamojszczyzna—Sonderlaboratorium SS: Zbiór dokumentów polskich i niemieckich z okresu okupacji hitlerowskiej* (Zamość region—Special SS laboratory: Collection of Polish and German documents from the Nazi occupation period) (Warsaw, 1977); Z. Mańkowski, "Hitlerowska akcja wysiedleń i osadnictwa na Zamojszczyźnie" (Nazi de-

portation operations and resettlement of the Zamość region), in *W kręgu polskich doświadczeń historycznych XIX i XX w.* (In the circle of Polish historical experience XIX and XX), T. Berenstein and A. Rutkowski, eds. (Lublin, 1986), pp. 210–40.

9. Cited in G. Aly, *Endlösung: Völkerverschiebung und der Mord an den europäischen Juden* (Frankfurt am Main, 1995), p. 35.

10. For details see D. Pohl, *Von der "Judenpolitik" zum Judenmord: Der Distrikt Lublin des General-gouvernements 1939–1944* (Frankfurt am Main, 1993); J. Marszałek, *Obozy pracy w Generalnym Gubernatorstwie w latach 1939–1945* (Labor camps in the Government General in the years 1939–1945) (Lublin, 1998).

11. J. Marszałek, "System obozów śmierci w Generalnym Gubernatorstwie i jego funkcje 1942–1943" (The system of death camps in the Government General and their functions), *Zeszyty Majdanka* 17 (1996): 17–38.

12. Y. Arad, "'Operation Reinhardt': Extermination Camps of Bełżec, Sobibór, and Treblinka," *Yad Vashem Studies* 16 (1984): 205–40; M. Tregenza, "Christian Wirth a pierwsza faza 'Akcji Reinhardt'" (Christian Wirth and the first phase of "Aktion Reinhardt"), *Zeszyty Majdanka* 14 (1992): 7–37; Tregenza, "Christian Wirth: Inspekteur der SS-Sonderkommandos 'Aktion Reinhardt,'" *Zeszyty Majdanka* 15 (1993): 7–57.

13. Tregenza, "Christian Wirth: Inspekteur," pp. 22–5.

14. In E. Jäckel and J. Rohwer, eds., *Der Mord an den Juden im Zweiten Weltkrieg: Entschlußbildung und Verwirklichung* (Stuttgart, 1985), pp. 129–30.

15. Arad; Tregenza, "Christian Wirth a pierwsza faza," passim.

16. An overview of the number of victims is cited in: I. Arndt and W. Scheffler, "Organisierter Massenmord an Juden in nationalsozialistischen Vernichtungslagern: Ein Beitrag zur Richtigstellung apologetischer Literatur," *Vierteljahrshefte für Zeitgeschichte*, no. 24 (1976): 105–11; W. Benz, ed., *Dimension des Völkermordes: Die Zahl der jüdischen Opfer des Nationalsozialismus* (Munich, 1991); J. Marszałek, "Stan badań nad stratami osobowymi ludności żydowskiej w Polsce oraz nad liczbą ofiar obozów zagłady w okupowanej Polsce" (State of investigation into the losses of Jewish people in Poland, together with the number of victims of death camps in occupied Poland), *Dzieje Najnowsze* 2 (1994): 33–44.

17. See H. Grabitz and W. Scheffler, *Letzte Spuren: Ghetto Warschau, SS-Arbeitslager Trawniki, Aktion Erntefest* (Berlin, 1988); D. Pohl, "Rola dystryktu lubelskiego w 'ostatecznym rozwiązaniu kwestii żydowskiej,'" *Zeszyty Majdanka* 18 (1997): 21–2.

18. See F. Karay, "Spór władz niemieckich o żydowskie obozy pracy w GG" (Dispute between the German authorities about Jewish labor camps in the Government General), *Zeszyty Majdanka* 18 (1997): 27–47.

19. Kiełboń, passim.
20. Pohl, *Von der "Judenpolitik,"* passim.
21. There is an abundant literature about the history of the Majdanek concentration camp. See: T. Kranz and J. Kiełboń, "Archival Sources and the State of Research Concerning the History of the Camp at Majdanek," in *Les archives de la Shoah,* ouvrage collectif sous la direction de J. Fredj (Paris, 1998), pp. 521–40.
22. Cf. E. Fechner, *Proces: Obóz na Majdanku w świetle wypowiedzi uczestników rozprawy przed Sądem Krajowym w Düsseldorfie* (The trial: The camp in Majdanek in the light of statements by participants before the court of assizes in Düsseldorf), trans. and with an introduction and explanation by T. Kranz (Lublin, 1996), p. 47.
23. T. Kranz, "Das KL Lublin—Zwischen Planung und Realisierung," in *Die nationalsozialistischen Konzentrationslager—Entwicklung und Struktur,* ed. U. Herbert, K. Orth, and Ch. Dieckmann (Göttingen, 1998), pp. 363–89; here p. 367.
24. J. Marszałek, *Majdanek: The Concentration Camp in Lublin* (Warsaw, 1990), p. 21.
25. This is also confirmed by the statement of the leader of the SS Central Construction Office in Lublin, Naumann: "The designation of POW camp must be used for camouflage reasons as permission for a concentration camp cannot be reckoned on from the side of the Governor General." Cited in G. Schwarberg, *Der Juweiler von Majdanek: Geschichte eines Konzentrationslagers* (Hamburg, 1981), p. 18.
26. Details of this plan in Marszałek, "Geneza," passim.
27. Archive of the State Museum at Majdanek (hereafter cited as APMM), photo no. 164, p. 14, letter from the SS-WVHA to the Construction Inspectorate of the Waffen-SS and Police in Cracow, dated 7 February 1942.
28. Marszałek, "Geneza," p. 51, footnote 140.
29. Himmler's telegram to Glücks, cited in *Faschismus—Ghetto—Massenmord: Dokumentation über Ausrottung und Widerstand der Juden in Polen während des Zweiten Weltkrieges* (Berlin, 1961), p. 268.
30. Cz. Rajca, "Chłopi w obozie koncentracyjnym na Majdanku" (Peasants in the concentration camp at Majdanek), in *Studia z dziejów ruchu ludowego* (Warsaw, 1971), pp. 47, 48, 60, 62.
31. A. Eisenbach, *Hitlerowska polityka zagłady Żydów* (Nazi policy of the extermination of the Jews) (Warsaw, 1961), pp. 314, 431.
32. APMM, I d 19, according to the death book, in September 1942 alone 2,531 prisoners, or one-third of the total camp population, died.
33. More than 8,000 came from Slovakia, about 35,000 from different localities in the Lublin region, over 20,000 from the Warsaw ghetto,

over 11,000 from the Białystok ghetto. Assume that 20 percent of the Jews deported to the Lublin District were selected for the construction of Majdanek, including about 3,000 Czech, 4,000 German, and 1,000 Austrian Jews. Cf. Y. Büchler, "The Deportation of Slovakian Jews to the Lublin District of Poland in 1942," *Holocaust and Genocide Studies* 6 (1991): 159; J. Kiełboń, *Migracje ludności w dystrykcie lubelskim,* pp. 148, 153, 154, 174. According to T. Berenstein and A. Rutkowski, eds., op cit., p. 19, the total number of Jews delivered to Majdanek amounted to 130,000. But the number of Jews from Slovakia quoted by Berenstein and Rutkowski (12,000), those deported from Warsaw in spring 1943 (about 40,000), and those deported from Białystok in summer 1943 (about 24,000), is evidently too high.

34. For details of prisoner assignments in Majdanek, see A. Wiśniewska, "Problem pracy więźniów w obozie koncentracyjnym na Majdanku" (The problem of prisoners' work at Majdanek concentration camp), *Zeszyty Majdanka* 5 (1971): 59–117.

35. Z. Leszczyńska, "Transporty więźniow do obozu na Majdanka" (Prisoner transports to the camp at Majdanek), *Zeszyty Majdanka* 4 (1969): 174–236.

36. Kranz, *KL Lublin,* p. 378.

37. T. Kranz, "Egzekucja Żydów na Majdanku 3 listopada 1943 r. w świetle wyroku w procesie w Düsseldorfie" (The execution of Jews at Majdanek on 3 November 1943 in the light of the verdict of the trial in Düsseldorf), *Zeszyty Majdanka* 19 (1998): 139–50.

38. Kranz, *KL Lublin,* p. 379–80.

39. Cf. J. Billig, *Le camps de concentration dans l'économie du reich hitlerien* (The concentration camps in the economy of the Nazi Reich) (Paris, 1973), p. 96.

40. H. Birenbaum, *Hope Is the Last to Die,* trans. from the Polish by D. Welsh (Armonk, N.Y., and London, 1996), p. 79.

41. Thus Marszałek, *Majdanek,* p. 142; W. Scheffler, "Chełmno, Sobibór, Bełżec und Majdanek," in *Mord an den Juden,* p. 148.

42. There are considerable discrepancies concerning the number of victims at Majdanek. R. Hilberg, for example, quotes in R. Hilberg, *Die Vernichtung der europäischen Juden* (Frankfurt a.M., 1990), p. 602, the minimum number of Jews killed there as being 50,000, while L. Dawidowicz, in *Der Krieg gegen die Juden 1939–1945* (Wiesbaden, 1979), p. 199, gives the very high figure of 1,380,000. The court of assizes in Düsseldorf determined that at least 250,000 people were killed in Majdanek. This total is also accepted by the authors of the *Enzyklopädie des Holocaust* (Berlin, 1993), vol. 2, p. 918, s.v. "The Persecution and Murder of the European Jews." According to Scheffler's estimates, the number of victims at Maj-

danek was 200,000; see "Chełmno, Sobibór," p. 148. In the Polish historiography the highest estimate is given by Z. Łukaszkiewicz, "Obóz koncentracyjny i zagłady Majdanek," *Bulletin of the Main Commission for the Investigation of Nazi Crimes in Poland* 4 (1948): 63–105, in which he states the number of victims as 360,000. The Lublin historian Cz. Rajca arrived at the figure of 235,000 in "Problem liczby ofiar w obozie na Majdanku" (The problem of the victims number in the camp at Majdanek), *Zeszyty Majdanka* 14 (1992): 127–32.

43. Cf. Kranz, *KL Lublin,* p. 388, footnote 73.

Geoffrey J. Giles

Confirming Their Prejudices
German University Students and Himmler's Resettlement Program

IN ONE OF MY EARLY ESSAYS, I WAS STRUCK BY THE LACK OF ENTHUSIASM for Nazi ideology among university students after the initial turbulence of the early months of the Third Reich, and wrote of the "failure of political education."[1] I conceded in my book on the Nazi Students' Association that anti-Semitic sentiments had long been endemic to the German student body, but in analyzing the frequent complaints by Nazi student leaders, I concluded that the anti-Semitism of the student body overall was passive, and certainly not proactive. Many German students did not go out of their way in the 1930s to be unpleasant to or about Jews.[2] In light of new evidence concerning the activities of wartime students in the Nazi-occupied territories, I have to revise that overly optimistic assessment.

The Nazi Party had found a high level of support in crucial elections in the eastern border areas, and set about strengthening it after 1933 by playing on fears of invasion by the "Slavs," as the populations east of the German border were vaguely termed. The student leadership encouraged students to study at the so-called border universities in Breslau, Danzig, and Königsberg with special scholarships. The main precursor of the students' extramural Eastern Deployment *(Osteinsatz)* program, with which this paper is principally concerned, was the Rural Service *(Landdienst)* scheme of the mid-1930s.[3] By 1938 some forty thousand students had answered the call for volunteers, admittedly under varying amounts of pressure and outright coercion from local student leaders.

There were several reasons for the deployment of students in the border areas, and later captured territories:

- to give the local population a highly visible demonstration of the German determination to introduce greater order and thus to improve conditions of work and life in the region;
- to expose German students to the backwardness of areas distant from the main center of German nationality;
- to encourage the students to rise to the challenges here by settling in the region after graduation, and forming the new, German, professional elite;
- to reinforce racial stereotypes in the students' encounters with "foreign" peoples and cultures.

After the outbreak of war in September 1939, fewer students were available (most having been called up for military service), but the scope of the activities mushroomed, especially after Himmler's SS agencies began the massive resettlement of ethnic Germans into the captured territories.[4] The Reichsführer-SS was very clear, once the *Einsatzgruppen* had begun their grisly work of ethnic cleansing, what the goal was: "It is our task to Germanize the East, not in the old sense, that is, to teach German language and German laws to the people living there, but to ensure that only people of really German, Germanic blood live in the East."

Professor Otto Reche of the University of Leipzig hurriedly drew up extensive plans for population clearance operations in the East only a couple of weeks after the German attack on Poland in 1939. One phrase that the professor used—"We need space, but no Polish lice in our fur"—was echoed approvingly by other Eastern planners with whom he corresponded. We should not overlook the fact that the sweeping plans of the SS penetrated the universities. There were at least a few professors who were teaching their students, apparently with some success, to believe that arrogant treatment of other peoples was entirely acceptable. None of the students quoted below ever questioned that.

Already in the fall of 1939 (when many universities had suspended teaching), groups of students in Berlin, Vienna, and Prague set to work, drawing up ethnic population maps and reports on land ownership and use, which were of direct benefit to the implementation of SS plans. In fact the student leader coordinating this, Alexander Dolezalek, was quickly catapulted into a position as a leading adviser to Himmler on the master plan for the captured Eastern territories. He became head of the Planning Department of the Settlement Staff at Lodz, and later Poznan. In February 1940 a small group of students was seconded to the Labor and Settlement Staff offices in the East, which quickly led to the conclusion that these young people would be ideal in much larger numbers for advising the new settlers in many different areas, both technical and cultural. Reich Education Minister Rust was prevailed upon to count the work as a practicum that fulfilled part of the requirements for the course of study. Most of the students operated in occupied western Poland, the so-called Warthegau, where 3,000 of them were deployed in 1940. SS doctors who inspected all potential ethnic German settlers found a seriously high rate of trachoma, a contagious disease causing inflammation of the inner surface of the eyelids, especially among those from Volhynia. Medical students were called in to help, and handled some 1,200 patients, who each required an average of ten visits.

Students of pedagogy set up 101 new schools over the summer of 1940, catering to 3,389 children. So great was the disappointment of the settler parents, when the students headed back to campus in mid-September, that Reich Student Leader Scheel ordered new students to take their place in order to keep the schools open. Meanwhile in the last six months of 1940 some 140 students of civil engineering were brought in and given positions of precocious authority by each being placed in charge of a forced labor squad of some fifty to one hundred Polish and Jewish prisoners. In the first three months they repaired three thousand Polish farms and cottages to bring them up to a standard considered "habitable by Germans."[5] One of the nagging worries about the Nazi expansion to the East was whether German professionals would ever *choose* to spend their career in these often desolate areas. The experience with the initial batch of starry-eyed idealists among the students was encouraging, and one municipal civil engineer noted with satisfaction that not only had a number of very practical tasks been accomplished, but a way had been shown "of solving one of our chief concerns, namely the recruitment question for the East."[6]

Although the activities of students covered a wide range of tasks, from archival research on land titles to the construction plans for public toilets in Upper Silesia, the activities of female students, traditionally the real stepchildren of the education system of the Third Reich, are rather revealing of attitudes among the student body. One might not expect a particularly crass embrace of Nazi ideology from women students, who could have had no expectations of building a career in the man's world of the Party hierarchy. Yet an examination of the individual reports that have survived from some of these students shows a surprisingly successful assimilation of anti-Polish and anti-Semitic Party dogma.

The tasks that female students performed lay mostly in traditionally gender-separated areas of nurturing: caring for children in kindergartens, preparing cultural activities such as folk dancing for the villagers' leisure hours, and paying home visits to new settlers in order to inquire about any problems, to dispense housekeeping advice, and to ensure generally that all was well. The personal solicitude of such home visits naturally led to warm relations between the students and their ethnic German charges. This should not obscure the fact that the student leaders gave these women very precise guidelines as to their didactic tasks and even a kind of policing function. They were charged with reporting on the overall cleanliness and orderliness of the household.

The previous Polish owners of these farms had often been driven out of their homes only hours (in some cases, minutes) before the ethnic Germans arrived to "resettle" the property. Therefore the homes contained many traditional Polish decorations, wall hangings, pictures, and photos. The students were instructed to persuade the new owners that such objects, even as trivial as paper flowers, were contemptible and even sinister. If the inhabitants could not be persuaded to throw them out, then the student herself was to do so. Yet this was a potential mine field! The students' instructions added: "But take care! Often their own things look quite similar. Always ask first of all: 'Did you bring that with you, or make it yourselves?'" If such home decorations were strikingly similar, then it must have been rather hard in a practical way to persuade settlers that the Polish ones were somehow despicable, but that was left to the individual initiative of the student.[7] It must have been flattering to the German women students to be given this kind of responsibility. After all, at the same time some nine hundred women in the *Deutsche Frauenwerk* were simply working in factories to make clothing for the settlers, whereas the students were tasting real authority, and often enjoying real respect.

Like the male students, and other visitors to the East, they were first put through an orientation session, often in the city of Lodz (which was renamed Litzmannstadt). This city was an ideal location for indoctrination, because students could be shown in quick succession the contrasts between the achievements of the early German industrialists in the form of the great textile factories and their owners' villas, and the decrepitude of the poorer Polish areas, before indulging in some ghetto tourism to experience a real frisson of disgust.[8] For the three-day orientation "camp" the students lived out in the suburb of Grotniki in homes from which the owners had been forcibly expelled. This in itself was no doubt meant to give them a taste of the colonial rulers' life ahead of them if they chose to make their careers in the East. It provided for some a pleasant contrast to the downtown area. "The camp was an experience for us all. For the first time we got a feel for the East in all its mysterious novelty—yesterday still in Litzmannstadt, an ugly, typical, industrial town still with a Polish stamp, while today in Grotniki, a former Litzmannstadt suburb of villas, we were transformed into completely German countryside. Wide, open spaces, dotted with little hills, sandy soil, pine trees, and lakes."[9] Inge-Marie, a student from Rostock, proved more susceptible to the bombardment of negative propaganda in describing her impressions of Grotniki: "We lived in villas, that had previously belonged to Jews and Poles. For our taste almost all of them have to be described as pretty ghastly. Most of them were built of wood, had flat roofs and were painted in garish colors."[10]

The students were also deliberately taken into the ghetto, where some 250,000 Jews were crammed together under inhumane conditions. The German students were encouraged to think that the appearance of the inhabitants of this purgatory was a reflection of their character, and this seems to have worked. Ilse P. from Hamburg wrote in the summer of 1940: "The ghetto (the fenced-in Jewish quarter) made a great impression on us. Here we saw the genuine, filthy Eastern Jews just hanging around outside their shabby and dilapidated houses."[11] It is interesting that at this early stage of the war the student finds it necessary to define for others what a ghetto is ("the fenced-in Jewish quarter"). In the commercial and banking circles of her native Hamburg, Jews had been among the leaders of society, but the student accepts that these Jews must be more typical: their houses are run-down, and yet they just loaf about, rather than doing something about it. The fact that the Jews were deliberately kept on a starvation diet, leading to exhaustion and disease, has not occurred to her. I suspect that the verb used for "hanging around" (*umherlungern*) was part of the tour commentary, because it crops up in another student's description as well—and she also has to define the term "ghetto":

> The most alarming aspect of this town ... is the ghetto, an enormous section of the town blocked off with barbed wire, where the streets and squares are strewn with Jews hanging around, among whom there are some real criminal types. What on earth are we going to do with this riffraff? One is really glad to get out of there as quickly as possible, away from this sooty sea of houses with its prehistoric cobblestones.[12]

Inactivity and decay, the shocking opposites to German industry and order, lead here to thoughts of the pointlessness of these human lives, no doubt underlined by the Nazi tour guide. The contrasts were emphasized again and again, in a sort of hierarchy. A student from Berlin wrote of her arrival in Lodz: "Germans are here and have an open, determined look, then groveling Poles, and the ghetto."[13]

After the successful orientation, the Nazi leaders could feel confident that the students would react with the same disgust when out in the field. On arrival at her assignment in Gostynin, Anne R. from Jena reported: "The railway station, the street leading into town, and the town itself made a pleasant, friendly impression upon us, apart from the filthy, stinking Jewish quarter."[14] The students were quickly conditioned to believe that it was entirely proper to lock Jews away behind barbed wire, and were surprised when this was not the case. One kindergarten teacher assigned to Leslau, Irene K., wrote as follows:

> Whereas in Litzmannstadt and Kutno we observed with a certain abhorrence the ghettos in which the members of this hook-nosed race were assembled, it struck us in Leslau that the Jews were free to walk on any of the streets, not of course on the pavement, but in the roadway, and they all wear a yellow triangle on their back. We often came across a Jewess waddling along in the gutter while her Polish girlfriend tripped along beside her on the curb.[15]

In many of these reports, Jews do not simply walk, but some derogatory term is used to describe their gait, and confirm the stereotype.

In seeking to explain the attitudes of students through a theoretical framework, I am tempted to place them within a Marxian analysis and see economic, rather than political factors, as being uppermost here. Alarmed by graduate unemployment since the Depression a decade earlier, they were simply seizing a chance to improve their career prospects by volunteering for *Osteinsatz*. Opportunism was certainly rife in the Nazi student leadership, as I have written elsewhere. Yet here among the rank-and-file students there is little evidence of that. Most students did *not* talk about future careers in the East, or if they did, it was only in terms of a vague possibility to be considered among many. Their remarks about the subject peoples, while admittedly being mostly written for an official Nazi agency, the student leadership, have a ring of sincerity about them. I am not convinced that they were simply writing what they thought the recipient wanted to hear. The remarks, including the gratuitous anti-Semitism, appear to be genuine. The political education of the younger generation had made enormous strides in less than a decade. The constant hammering with Nazi ideology had, as Hitler and Goebbels had insisted all along, not failed to leave its mark.

The stated purpose of the volunteer activity of the students was to help the ethnic German settlers to help themselves. However, it emerges from the firsthand reports that Jewish and Polish slave labor was used, which provided a further opportunity for the students to compare their own work habits to those of the supposedly inferior races. Sometimes the work of renovating living quarters or the workplace had already been completed by the time the students arrived. The same Irene K. pronounced herself well satisfied with her accommodation, complete with servants:

> We felt really quite wealthy as we moved into "our new home." . . . "Our hardworking Jews" had painted the walls a nice yellow, and the Polish woman, who lived with her family in two rooms of the house, had made everything very tidy and clean. . . . The Jews had cut a path to the street through the wilderness in front of the house.[16]

Two other women, working together in Krozniewice to set up a kindergarten, also wanted a pleasant garden without doing the work themselves. They described how they went about the task: "Since there was more than enough work to be completed in and around the house, on the advice of our district leader we fetched 2–5 Jews every morning to work for us. . . ." They had very few tools to accomplish the jobs that needed doing, and a Jew sent to the mayor to fetch some came back empty-handed. So they sent him off again to the *Judenrat* with a list of demands. Literally scared for their lives, the members of the Jewish Council quickly produced the tools and materials. "On the one hand it was great fun to bring the garden into shape especially with the Jews, on the other it got on our nerves a bit because of all manual labor the Jews hate working with a spade most of all." Their solution to this lack of enthusiasm was revealed a little later: "Once when the Jews became too impudent, we had a sergeant sent to us to keep an eye on them."[17] The employment of slave labor in this way, not mentioned at all in published reports, puts a different complexion altogether on the keen voluntarism and idealism of these German students. They were not simply students acquiring some practical training in their specialist field, but were trying out their new roles as members of the master race, and being encouraged to imagine the pampered professional life that awaited them if they chose after graduation to work in the captured Eastern territories.

In theory the arrival of the students to assist the new settlers was meant to occur after the messy work of evicting the rightful tenants from their homes had taken place. Yet there were exceptions even to this. Six female students operating around Alexandrowo were granted "the opportunity to participate in an evacuation," as Eva P. proudly reported. With apparent concern for feminine sensibilities, the head of the Settlement Staff at first refused to allow this, with the argument that women would not be able to grasp "the necessary toughness of the operation." He clearly felt that the relentless violence of throwing Polish inhabitants at a moment's notice out of the home that had possibly been in their family for generations might spark sympathy among these female students. Nonetheless they managed to persuade him of their solid ideological credentials sufficiently for him to change his mind. Eva P.'s description of the event is worth quoting at some length, especially for what it tells us about the students' reactions:

> After most of the police had already left at 2 o'clock at night for the area to be evacuated, the six of us were split up among the vehicles

of the Settlement Staff and the responsible officers, and followed one hour later. . . . Meanwhile the police had already penetrated some of the villages and "cleared them out!" It turned out again and again that the Poles had heard about the imminent evacuation and had fled. In those cases there was nothing more to find in the squalid living quarters than a lot of dirt. The cattle, left unattended for days, were dead, presenting a pitiful sight in the cowsheds. But if the cows had been milked, and the beds or straw on which the Poles slept was still warm, one could assume that they were hiding not far away, in the corn stooks or in ditches. After a couple of warning shots they would crawl out trembling with fear, and would be loaded onto carts and taken to a collection camp. Most of them left their farm and the plot of land that had nourished them without any emotion. I saw just one woman out of many who was weeping. They packed the little that they were permitted to take with them, grabbing the few things from the cupboards and houses with much whining. What farmer in Germany would allow himself to be driven from his farm like that? The sun had already broken through the dawn with shining red, warm light, as we arrived at the collection camp. Men, women and children were assembled here in a barn with guards posted. They displayed no dejection, sorrow or concern for their future. We observed without exception a passivity, a mindlessness, a lack of emotion that were unfathomable, punctuated constantly by the impertinent attempt to still find some sly way of leaving the camp once again. Sympathy with these creatures?—No, at most a sense of horror that such people exist, people who in their whole being and essence are so infinitely alien and incomprehensible to us that there is no approach to them. For the first time in our lives, people whose life or death is a matter of indifference.[18]

To obtain a report like this, it had certainly been worthwhile from the Nazi point of view to allow these women to participate in the evacuation. The women displayed, even more than could possibly be hoped for, the precise reaction that the SS wanted. The victims were despised, rather than pitied. Because these Polish peasant farmers did not offer resistance to armed invaders in the dead of night, which would almost certainly have resulted in their being shot dead on the spot, they were condemned by the students as not displaying a proper love of their home and property, such as a German farmer certainly would. They were scorned because they complained about having to abandon their belongings, they were ridiculed because they trembled with fear when shot at, and they were despised because they did not weep. Although we are still in the summer of 1940, a year away from the decision to proceed with the "final solution," what a chilling testimony is presented here of the probable acquiescence of these future professionals in such an operation. If the life or death of these Poles had become a matter of indifference to the students, how much easier to foster such a reaction vis-à-vis the Jews, who were already more deeply disdained.

There are many examples throughout the Third Reich of Nazis, and especially SS men, boasting with a perverse pride of their toughness in suppressing their natural sympathy and human warmth for others in the name of carrying out some "tough, but necessary" action.[19] Yet it still comes as a surprise to hear student teachers talking in the same tones. Ruth D. from Dortmund reported the following incident, in which she forced herself to build up an antipathy toward a Polish girl, excluded from the village school because of her race:

> A blond, little Polish girl lived next to the school. She was the very opposite of the sly, Polish racial type, who are repulsive even to look at. She often came and watched our games in the open air longingly. And so I felt something like sympathy trying to creep in. I spoke with the district nurse about it. She herself hailed from Bromberg. Her father was murdered. Then she told me about all the distress that she had endured, and her anguish. No newspaper report and no radio report can describe that so grippingly as a person speaking from immediate experience. At that moment my rising sympathy disappeared completely.[20]

One should note that the student felt sorry for the little outsider *primarily*, it appears, because of the girl's blond, "Aryan" external appearance, the passing of a value judgment based on superficialities of this sort being central to the Nazi phenomenon.[21] Nevertheless the student then displayed the correct reaction in response to a report of Polish atrocities against ethnic Germans. Such reports about Germany's neighbors, which were deliberately exaggerated, when not entirely invented, by Goebbels' Propaganda Ministry, were meant to stigmatize the whole race, as has happened here even with an innocent and harmless young child. Evidently the orientation sessions had impressed upon the students that all Poles should be treated as dangerous and potentially violent.

Already by October 1941 Alexander Dolezalek noted in a lengthy memorandum on the resettlement operations being planned in ever more megalomaniacal fashion by his SS staff at Litzmannstadt that the continued close cooperation with the Reich Student Leadership was essential. Not only had the students' contribution been invaluable, but there were benefits for them too: "The outstanding political education, and further training in their academic field" made, in Dolezalek's words, "this marriage a particularly happy one."[22] The Old Fighters of the Nazi Party had never held a very high opinion of academics. This was an opportunity to put textbook learning to practical use, and at the same time drive home the wisdom and rightness of Nazi ideology. Here, I think, lies a clue to the genesis of this entire venture, which assigned several thousand students for fieldwork in captured territories. Was this a case of the all-powerful Nazi state instrumentalizing the students for its own malevolent purposes? I do not believe that to be so. I subscribe to a functionalist interpretation of the Third Reich, and I detect here the Reich student leadership grasping opportunistically at a means of improving the bad press from which the student body had frequently suffered in recent years. Soon after the war broke out, and it became clear that universities would not close down altogether for the duration, there was public criticism about the students leading a privileged life, while the ordinary man put his life on the line at the front. An expansion of *Osteinsatz* provided a way to improve the image of students (and by implication, their leaders!) in a practical, hands-on fashion. Positive reports from Party leaders in the East prove that the idea worked, especially in the short run. A short answer, then, is that *Osteinsatz* arose from the ambition, the striving to succeed, of the student leaders. It is not insignificant that at the Reich level, many of them were also SS officers, and were eager to advance in the ranks of that elite. Yet they could not succeed without an at least partially willing student body.

Alexander Dolezalek, thirty years later, struggled to convince his Polish interviewer that he did not believe that these fantastic plans for the East could ever be realized, that he retreated into "inner emigration" and almost joined German Resistance circles. His more famous colleague, Professor Konrad Meyer, author of the notorious *Generalplan Ost,* claimed that he was trying to slow down the harebrained schemes of Himmler, who thought that the colonization of the East could be achieved within a few months, by suggesting that it would take twenty-five years. The first task was to draw up precise surveys of roads, railways, villages, and towns, and to discuss development plans with a detailed cost analysis.[23] This is what the SS planners set out to do, and this is where successive wartime cohorts of students rendered sterling service. How would those students view their *Osteinsatz* today? I have not tracked down any of them, but I can guess their reaction from my interviews with Nazi student leaders in the 1970s, all of whom felt themselves to be idealists with nothing to apologize for. The head of the Ethnic German Liaison Office *(Volksdeutsche Mittelstelle),* Werner Lorenz, whose agency was centrally involved in the shifting of population groups and the reception of incoming ethnic Germans, was charged at Nuremberg with a long list of crimes against humanity. The historian Valdis Lumans noted recently that Lorenz "could not understand why he was being tried as a criminal for performing wartime tasks that he regarded as humanitarian and whose objective had been the welfare of the German *Volk.*"[24] Yet this was only one side of the coin. These German plans for the expansion of *Lebensraum* could not begin to operate without victims, who had to be expelled and were frequently killed or worked to death. *Vae victis,* woe to the vanquished, wrote the historian Livy two thousand years ago. But this was not war-as-usual, not simply a case of: "to the victor belong the spoils of the enemy," not even just a case of redrawing the map of Central Europe as had happened at Versailles. This was intended to be a *permanent* solution to Germany's unfulfilled aspirations, which entailed sweeping aside not merely national borders but whole populations in the quest for world-historical greatness. German students played their part in this, a part that, when seen in a wider context, one cannot help but consider sinister.

NOTES

1. Geoffrey J. Giles, "The Rise of the National Socialist Students' Association and the Failure of Political Education in the Third Reich," in *The Shaping of the Nazi State,* ed. Peter D. Stachura (New York, 1978), pp. 160–85.

2. Geoffrey J. Giles, *Students and National Socialism in Germany* (Princeton, 1985).

3. Cf. the Deutsche Studentenschaft's pamphlet *Student im Osten* (n.p., n.d. [1935]).

4. "Generalbericht vom studentischen Osteinsatz im Warthegau 1940–41," zusammengestellt von Claudine Takats (Einsatzleitung Ost der Reichsstudentenführung, Poznan), Bundesarchiv-Aussenstelle Potsdam (hereafter cited as BAP), R49 25/3057.

5. Facheinsatz Ost der deutschen Studenten, Sondernummer *Die Fachgruppe* 4, April 1941, p. 68.

6. K. Stadtoberbaudirektor [?] to Kubach, 4 September 1940, Lodz State Archives (hereafter cited as LSA), Stadtverwaltung Litzmannstadt 24.

7. Arbeitsanweisung für die Hausbesuche, *Die Fachgruppe* 4, April 1941, pp. 94–5.

8. These ghetto tours were an ongoing attraction for all kinds of visiting groups. There was, for example, just such a tour for members of the Nazi Lecturers' Association in July 1942. After a "good, very interesting speech" on Litzmannstadt by the mayor, the scholars set out in buses to see the city itself, including "the famous and infamous ghetto of L., the organization of which had already been described to us by the mayor." Götz Aly, "The Posen Diaries of Anatomist Hermann Voss," in *Cleansing the Fatherland: Nazi Medicine and Racial Hygiene,* ed. Götz Aly, Peter Chroust, and Christian Pross (Baltimore, 1994), pp. 145–6.

9. Report of Marianne F. from Heidelberg on participation in resettlement operations, Easter 1940, BAP R49 19/3051.

10. Report of Inge-Marie Sch., 1940, BAP R49 20/3052.

11. Report of Ilse P., ibid.

12. Letter, Gertrud to Ilse, 10 October 1940, ibid.

13. Report, Eva W., Studentinnen-Einsatz, BAP R49 19/3051.

14. Report, Anne R., ibid.

15. Report, Irene K., "Kindergartenarbeit in Leslau," ibid.

16. Ibid.

17. Report, Anni K. and Annerose E., ibid.

18. Report, Eva P., BAP R49 20/3052.

19. Notably, mass murder, and the most notorious example of this is Himmler's closed-door speech in Poznan in 1943, in which he claimed a special nobility for the SS on these grounds.

20. Report, Ruth D., BAP R49 19/3051.

21. Even Hitler was embarrassed by a similar incident, in which a little blonde-haired, blue-eyed girl he had taken under his wing turned out to be part Jewish. Professor Otto Reche, in the September 1939 report mentioned earlier, reflected this unswerving belief in the reliability of external appearances: "Anyone who knows the Polish rural population, knows how primitive, crude and often almost simpleminded the facial expressions of the people are and how crude their thought and behavior is." Quoted in

Michael Burleigh, *Germany Turns Eastwards: A Study of* Ostforschung *in the Third Reich* (Cambridge and New York, 1988), p. 169.

22. "Plan für die künftige Arbeit der Planungsabteilung der SS-Ansiedlungsstäbe Litzmannstadt und Posen, 18 October 1941," reproduced in *Vom Generalplan Ost zum Generalsiedlungsplan,* ed. Czeslaw Madajczyk (Munich and London, 1994), p. 36. See also extensive selections from the interviews by journalist Krzysztof Kakolewski with Dolezalek in the early 1970s in ibid., pp. 532–48.

23. Ibid., p. 548.

24. Valdis O. Lumans, *Himmler's Auxiliaries: The Volksdeutsche Mittelstelle and the German National Minorities of Europe, 1933–1945* (Chapel Hill, 1993), p. 261.

Jeffrey Lesser

Visions of the Other
Stereotypes, Survival, and the Refugee Question in Brazil

IN CONSIDERING THE SHOAH WITHIN A LATIN AMERICAN CONTEXT WE tend to think of Nazis first and Jews last, if at all. Certainly wild rumors, along with some truth, about the numbers of Nazis in the region has fueled such a perspective, and the popular idea that "the Boys from Brazil" actually exist has led many to forget that the United States was perhaps the country that most welcomed Nazis after the war. This tendency, I think, is only an exaggeration of more general trends in Jewry. Given that the World Jewish Congress *Dateline: World Jewry* report includes an entire section called "Nazi Legacy," I am not really surprised. Indeed, even on this panel on Jewish refugee communities, Nazis appear explicitly in the papers of two of my colleagues and are indeed appearing right now in my comments.

Today I would like to focus exclusively on Jews and their agency during the Holocaust. I would like to propose that through a sophisticated understanding of Brazilian social patterns and stereotypes— the dominant Brazilian discourse on race and society, if you will— Jews were able to save other Jews by opening the doors to a country that officially had shut them.

The story of Brazil and the Jews came to wide public notice only in 1947 when former Brazilian Foreign Minister Oswaldo Aranha, then president of the General Assembly of the United Nations, became a key bureaucratic player in the formation of Israel. Indeed, the vocal support of Aranha and the Brazilian representative to the United Nations, João Carlos Muniz, former director of Brazil's powerful Immigration and Colonization Commission, were critical in the establishment of the state.[1] Jews and Gentiles around the world viewed Israel's creation as a triumph of democracy in international politics. Brazil and Aranha, both crucial to the decision, were considered as friends of Israel, Zionism, and all Jews. In Tel Aviv a street was named after Aranha, as was a cultural center in a kibbutz settled by Brazilian Jews.

The honors accorded to Brazil following the United Nations vote might have been tempered if it had been widely known that fourteen years earlier Brazilian President Getúlio Vargas and his policymakers, including Aranha and Muniz, had proposed to prevent the entry of Jewish refugees. Following two years of informal restriction, on 7 June 1937, five months before the establishment of the fascist-inspired Estado Novo (New State), Brazil's Ministry of Foreign Relations (known as Itamaraty) issued a secret circular that banned the granting of visas to all persons of "Semitic origin." Jewish relief organizations, many of whose leaders were important UN lobbyists in 1947, knew of the secret circular. The British and United States diplomatic corps were also aware of its existence, but this was diplomatically ignored in the wake of Israel's creation. Even Aranha's reported comment that the creation of Israel meant that the Rio de Janeiro neighborhood of Copacabana, frequently referred to derogatorily as "Copacabanovitch," would be returned to the Brazilians, passed unnoticed.[2]

Why did Jews, a small part of a large immigrant stream from Europe, cause such consternation that they were eventually banned from entering Brazil?[3] And why, just one year after the ban was in place, did more Jews enter Brazil legally than at any time in the past twenty years? The answer to these two questions involves a change in the way a small but extraordinarily powerful group of intellectuals and politicians looked at Brazilian national identity and the role immigrants, and thus residents and potential citizens, would play in shaping it. This took place because the leaders of Brazil's Jewish community, along with influential members of international refugee relief organizations, successfully manipulated many of the stereotypes of Jews held by Brazilian policymakers and intellectuals so that past negatives became present positives. These foreign ministers, justice ministers, diplomats, journalists, and professors struggled to combine the pseudoscientific social categorizations so prominent among the educated in twentieth-century Europe and the Americas with a new nationalist sentiment. This fused with omnipresent traditional

Christian motifs so that attempts to engender devotion to *"a patria"* (patriotism) put non-Christian groups, and particularly those who had been attacked through the ages, in a precarious position.[4] Many in the Brazilian intelligentsia and political elite considered Jews culturally undesirable even while believing that they had a special, inherited relationship to financial power and could thus help Brazil to develop industrially. Jewish immigration therefore challenged policymakers who deemed Jews a non-European race but also wished to create a Brazilian society that mirrored the industry of the United States or Germany.

Beginning in the mid-1930s, Brazilian nativists regularly targeted Jews, whose economic success led to great visibility, as enemies of the urban middle class. Such bigoted attitudes, however, were not always mirrored by national leaders, who stereotypically viewed Jews as rich, intelligent, and industrially oriented. For the Vargas regime that had come to power in 1930, Jews were as economically desirable as they were politically inexpedient. This contradiction between economic needs and political wants was to take a number of surprising twists in the 1930s and 1940s. Jews, virtually ignored by federal policymakers before 1930, were simultaneously viewed in a positive and negative light.[5] As a result, during the late 1930s, Jewish immigration became an integral part of a political debate that sought to reconcile the growing movement for immigrant restriction with an awareness that some immigrants might bring much-needed skills and capital to Brazil.

Many influential members of the Vargas government believed that economic growth could be fostered by Jewish immigrants. Thus a tension existed between restrictive immigration policies deemed necessary for maintaining urban middle-class support and more open policies aimed at promoting economic development. This dialectic was resolved in 1938 when restrictions on Jewish immigration began to be systematically ignored or modified. By probing the contradictory ideological and political attitudes surrounding an immigration policy that simultaneously banned and permitted Jewish entry, I would like to suggest that notions about the desirability of Jewish immigration to Brazil were to change from anti-Semitism to philo-Semitism during the World War II era (Skidmore 1974; Degler 1971).

Few intragovernmental conflicts aroused as much passion, or drew as much attention, as Jewish immigration did during 1939. Over four thousand Jews entered Brazil in that year, more than in any year since 1929.[6] The marked increase should not suggest that prejudices against Jews and Jewish immigrants and refugees disappeared. Indeed traditional images of Jews—urban based, nonfarmers, financially oriented, and internationally powerful—that had been the basis for so much Jew hatred were, in late 1938 and early 1939, increasingly viewed as indicators of Jewish usefulness for Brazil's economic development.[7] In other words, stereotypes of Jews that had previously been judged as negative had come to be regarded by some important decision makers as positive attributes. The reasons for these changes were numerous. Jewish relief groups actively put positive twists on old stereotypes. The United States, itself unwilling to make a major commitment toward Jewish refugees, put pressure on others to do so. Furthermore, important federal politicians realized that Jewish refugees from Italy, Austria, and Germany did in fact have occupational experience needed in Brazil's industrializing economy and urbanizing society. The rejection of the absolute ban on Jewish entry thus did not signal so much a change in attitude as a change of interpretation. This reconceptualization of stereotypes gave almost ten thousand Jewish refugees a chance to survive.

From 1930 to 1937 Jewish stereotypes, when used by those making crucial decisions on immigration policy, worked to the disadvantage of Jewish immigrants and refugees. In 1938, however, this had begun to change. This was related directly to the appointment of the aforementioned Oswaldo Aranha, Brazil's ambassador to the United States, as foreign minister. Aranha, it must be emphasized, held many of the same anti-Jewish stereotypes as other politicians in the Americas and elsewhere.[8] He often tied Jews to an alleged world communist conspiracy, and believed they were "radically averse to agriculture" and that "en masse they would constitute an obvious danger to the future homogeneity of Brazil."[9] Aranha was not, however, a Judeophobe. There was an important philo-Semitic component in his conceptions. Jews, in the view of the new foreign minister, were rich, skilled, and influential and thus useful for Brazil's economic development. Moreover, Aranha recognized that the resolution of the Jewish Question in Brazil would have an impact on relations with the United States, a country he admired greatly.[10] As early as 1937 he had worried, as ambassador to the United States, that Brazil's ban on Jewish entry had to avoid provoking "the immense and powerful Jewish colony."¹¹ The notion of Jewish world influence played an important part in Aranha's attempt to present Brazil to the international community in a more liberal light.

A policy shift allowing Jews considered useful to enter Brazil seems, at first glance, simply rational. Since few Brazilians were trained industrial managers or skilled technicians, the undesirability of certain immigrants could be overlooked if they delivered needed economic or political benefits. Many German and Austrian Jewish refugees were in fact capitalists or industrialists, giving a factual basis to the stereotype.¹² Italian Jewish refugees, who often referred to themselves as the "colonia Mussolini," were almost universally administrators, academics, businesspeople, and members of liberal professions.¹³ Ethnic prejudice seemed momentarily to take a secondary role to development, but the desire to keep out Jews, who were deemed unable to guard "what is most sacred to us, the basis of our institutions: Country, Religion, Family," still remained.¹⁴ Something, however, had changed. Starting in 1938 influential politicians began implying that certain Jews did not carry the stain of being Jewish. This view helps explain why so many Jews were allowed into Brazil even while anti-Semitic images remained so preponderant. The change was not to ideas about Jews, but to ideas about who fit the category.

The most important reason that the images of Jews began to change in Brazil in the 1930s was related to the way Brazilian anti-Semitic stereotypes were conceived and discussed. By maintaining the traditional stereotypes and simply modifying the assessment of them, international relief organizations could turn accepted stereotypes to the advantage of refugees. One image of Jews, for example, involved money and economic success. Rich Jews could thus be seen as part of an international conspiracy to force national wealth to the exterior, or glorified for their ability to help domestic industrial development by injecting capital into Brazil. Influential Jews were hailed for the propaganda opportunities they represented, not the unassimilable foreign culture they had been accused of maintaining in the past. Negative stereotypes of "Jewish millionaires . . . [who] flee from their various European homelands, come to Brazil, and leave their capital in the United States or bring it to Argentina" were transformed into new ones of Jews as accountants, bookkeepers, and financial planners.¹⁵ Following this promotion of "Jewish" wealth and industriousness, past accusations of communist activity were dismissed. In a moment of crisis, Jews used anti-Semitic stereotypes against the anti-Semites. The haunting ghost of Theodore Herzl, who believed that he could count on anti-Semites to be rational in their desire to get rid of Jews and thus create a Jewish state, had arrived in Brazil.[16] Stereotypes of Jews helped refugees get visas.

Critical in convincing Brazilian leaders that some Jews were acceptable immigrants was both informal and formal U.S. influence. Old stereotypes took on new meanings when U.S. diplomats disingenuously overstated the leverage of Jews in U.S. political, economic, and journalistic spheres. Notions of Jewish influence were encouraged when financial schemes that would benefit Brazil's economy were offered by relief officials in exchange for visas. In March 1939 Oswaldo Aranha arrived in the United States to negotiate a series of trade and loan agreements with the U.S. government. While attending a dinner at New York's Council of Foreign Relations, the foreign minister was politely asked by a director of the stock firm of Bendix, Luitweiler and Co., if Brazil "was prepared to accept Jewish emigrants of a type and training to be readily assimilated and having sufficient financial resources."[17] Perhaps visas might be tied to reducing Brazil's debt. The foreign minister seemed interested and the following day was informed that an "American group interested in the problem of Jewish emigration from Germany" was prepared to accept a "substantial amount" of Brazilian currency as repayment for debt contracted in dollars. Deposits to a fund to help Jewish refugees would be accepted for debt obligations, which would have "a most salutary effect upon the standing and credit of Brazil." The plan appears never to have been acted on. Even so, it highlighted for Brazilian authorities a stereotype that they already held: that international Jewish power and wealth existed and was committed to helping refugees. Anti-Semitic stereotypes were turned on their heads.

Since influential policymakers held static images of Jews that could be positive, negative, or even both, those with the power to grant visas could easily shift between conceptions of Jews as useful to Brazil's economic development and harmful to its social development. Lindolfo Collor's published political diary *Europa 1939* shows one example of this dual image. In it he reports on the purge of Maxim Litvinov as People's Commissar of the Soviet Foreign Ministry. What was "picturesque," notes Collor, is that Litvinov's brother, a rabbi in Lodz, reportedly complained "of the detestable activity of my brother."[18] The story may or may not have been true. Either way, Collor's vision of "the Jew" as a communist and "a human symbol," as good and bad, is clear.

The tension between traditional anti-Semitic images and new positive judgments of Jews led some policymakers to simultaneously favor and oppose Jewish immigration. On any given day immediate political pressure, domestic or international, affected the implementation of policy. Correspondence sent by Oswaldo Aranha to various European diplomatic posts indicates the swings. On 9 August 1939 Itamaraty ordered H. Pinheiro de Vasconcelos, consul general in London, to give permanent visas to a number of Polish Jewish refugees.[19] These visas were issued a few months later. In mid-October 1939, on the other hand, the following orders were received by Brazil's legation in Helsinki: "The legation should stamp visas in passports of refugees as long as they are not Jews."[20] Seemingly contradictory memos granting visas to some refugees and denying them to others had an internal logic based on the dual images of Jews in Brazil.

Politicians in Rio were not the only ones revising their estimations of Jews; requests for exceptions to the anti-Jewish orders also arrived from Brazil's consulates and embassies in Europe. A diplomat in Paris, although believing in principle that Jews should not be allowed permanently into Brazil, wondered if it "would be prudent to persevere on the path" of absolute bans.[21] French Jews, he claimed, made up 75 percent of all French commercial interests and applied for Brazilian tourist visas only for business purposes. Pedro Leão Veloso, who considered himself "one of the few in our country who is not a declared enemy of the Jews," pointed out that "the Banco do Brasil can inform you that, thanks to the entrance of 70 capitalist Jews, the national economy benefited by 35 million milreis [U.S.$2 million]. Imagine what [all the others] brought?"[22] Jewish refugees, according to Leão Veloso, brought far more capital to Brazil than Argentine tourists, who were allowed to enter without question, presumably as long as they were not Jews.

Others wondered if visas for renowned Jews might promote Brazil's international image and help the country progress. Giorgio Mortara, the Italian Jewish editor of the prestigious *Giornale degli economisti e rivista di statistica* was dismissed from his post in 1938. Almost immediately thereafter he was invited to Brazil by IBGE (Instituto Brasileiro de Geografia e Estatística) director (and former foreign minister) José Carlos de Macedo Soares. Soon after arriving in Rio in early 1939 with his wife and four children, Mortara was appointed coordinator of the 1940 census.[23] The French playwright Hénri-Leon (Henry) Bernstein, living as a refugee in the United States, was rumored to believe that an extended visit to Brazil would inspire a new theater piece. In spite of Bernstein's well-known condemnation of anti-Semitism in his play *Isräel*, a diplomat asked, "What reasons could be invoked to refuse him a visa?" and worried that "our nation will lose an extraordinary propaganda opportunity."[24] Although Bernstein never pursued his desire for tropical inspiration, the Austrian Jewish novelist Stefan Zweig did. The granting of a life-saving visa to Zweig may well have influenced his decision to write the propagandistic *Brazil: Land of the Future*. Zweig's presence in Brazil indeed was used by the Department of Press and Propaganda to promote such unexpected areas as municipal government organization.[25] Zweig's claim that "wherever in our troubled times we find hope for a new future in new zones, it is our duty to point out this country and these possibilities" aroused the enmity of other intellectuals who recognized that anti-Semitism and visa grants for some Jewish refugees were not incompatible.[26]

In 1939 the number of Jews entering Brazil with permanent and temporary visas, according to Jewish groups, was 4,601, and according to the Conselho de Imigração e Colonização, 4,223.[27] Jews received more than 60 percent of the permanent visas and almost 45 percent of the temporary visas given to Germans and Poles.[28] Almost 9 percent of those with permanent visas and more than 14 percent of those with temporary visas were Jews.[29] One reason for the high numbers was the pressure the United States put on friendly nations to allow Jewish refugees to enter, a regular topic of correspondence between the Brazilian and U.S governments. The United States wished to "take an increased part in the establishment and settlement of Jewish immigrants in the Latin American countries," and regularly played on stereotypes of Jews by portraying refugees as having capital and skills.[30] Jews were also a hot topic in meetings of the Conselho de Imigração e Colonização, which tried to moderate between those who believed that some refugees should be allowed to enter if they would aid Brazil's economic development and others who viewed all Jews as social dangers and wanted the absolute ban reinstated.

The fears of an increase in the number of Jews in Brazil collided head-on with both new positive interpretations of stereotypes and U.S. diplomatic pressure. This left an impression on some foreign diplomats that the Brazilian Government, "while feeling sympathetic toward the plight of Jewish refugees, will continue to be extremely cautious about receiving additional numbers."[31] This gave Itamaraty officials the latitude to interpret visa regulations in light of their own opinions on Jewish immigration. Some individual consular officers gave visas to Jews in large numbers. In most German, Austrian, and East European consulates, however, visa applications were often rebuffed on the basis of the (now countermanded) first secret circular. Itamaraty sometimes approved visas directly from Rio de Janeiro and at other times rejected them.[32] While almost 4,500 refugees legally entered Brazil in 1939, many others were turned away.[33]

Nothing illustrates the shifting interpretations of policy more than a situation involving the famed scientist Albert Einstein, who visited Brazil twice in 1925. That voyage had been arranged by the Jewish Colonization Association, eager to "demonstrate to the people of Brazil that Jews are not only peddlers but that among them one may find world famous scientists."[34] The plan was a success. Brazil's most noted scientists formed a welcoming committee, important members of the Jewish community courted Einstein, and journalists printed long interviews with the scientist.[35] Over a decade later, Einstein's fame in Brazil and his warm feelings for the country encouraged him to approach Brazilian officials for help in getting visas for refugee Jews.[36] In 1938 an old friend of Einstein, Dr. Hans George Katz, a German Jew living in São Paulo with a permanent visa, contacted the scientist about his sister, Helene Fabian-Katz. Katz was desperately worried since Helene was in Nazi Berlin, frantic to leave and unable to get a visa. Einstein supported her application for a U.S. visa, but this was rejected. Finally the scientist suggested that Brazil might have visas available.[37] On 23 January 1939 Einstein wrote directly to Aranha, noting that there was "no risk of Mrs. Fabian-Katz ever becoming a public charge" and requesting that her visa application be approved.[38]

Aranha apparently never received the letter. In early February Dr. Katz again wrote Einstein, complaining that no action had been taken by Itamaraty and that the situation in Germany was becoming increasingly difficult.[39] Katz, however, had discovered that Aranha would be in the United States and wondered if Einstein could somehow contact the foreign minister while he was in Washington. The suggestion was a good one. Einstein wrote to Aranha in care of the U.S. State Department and had a copy delivered in person to Itamaraty in Rio by Cecilia Razovsky, the executive director of the National Coordinating Committee for Aid to Refugees and Emigrants Coming from Germany.[40] The request was received, held for three months, and then sent to the Conselho de Imigração e Colonização.[41] The visa for Fabian-Katz was then apparently granted as, some months later, Einstein again wrote to Aranha asking for a visa for another family friend, noting that "your kind assistance in a previous case encourages me."[42] Typed in the corner of the letter is a note from Einstein's secretary explaining that the "previous case" was that of Helene Fabian-Katz. Indeed she and the scientist were in correspondence between São Paulo and Princeton as late as 1953.[43]

In spite of its restrictions on Jewish immigration, Brazil established a relatively liberal attitude toward resident refugees. The refusal to institutionalize anti-Semitism in domestic policy was part of Brazil's continued desire to portray itself in a positive light to the world. Refusing entry to Jews on the basis of immigration law was much easier than attacking refugees already in Brazil. Furthermore, by blaming general immigration law for the refusal of visas to Jews, important politicians could still claim a willingness to make exceptions. In this regard, Brazil's policy was much like that of the United States. In 1940, for example, Vargas and Aranha met with a World Jewish Congress/American Jewish Congress study group traveling through South America.[44] The group also met with João Carlos Muniz, who, in spite of his regular attacks on Jewish immigrants and immigration, "expressed himself as highly gratified with the valuable contribution the Jewish community was making . . . [as] the refugees who had come in recent years had . . . brought new industries, supplementing their limited financial capital with large technical and intellectual capital [and provided] work opportunities for native Brazilians."[45] In late 1940 a firm in Pôrto Alegre requested diamond cutters, and a group of French Jewish refugees experienced in the trade were given visas as technical experts.[46] The almost 2,500 visas given to Jews in 1940 led refugee organizations to believe that "Brazil still continues to accept a great many [Jewish] immigrants."[47]

In January 1942, Brazil severed relations with the Axis and Japan; in August Brazil entered the war on the side of the Allies. This gave

Jews an opportunity to be "good" citizens and residents of Brazil, show solidarity with the plight of European Jewry, and battle anti-Semitism, all at the same time. Later that year a group of Jews presented five military training planes to Getúlio Vargas "as a gesture of solidarity in the war."[48] A few days later a fast day was observed in protest against the Nazi murders taking place in concentration camps.[49] Many young Jews joined the Brazilian armed forces, including, to the surprise of a journalist in Rio, a German Jew living in a city at the mouth of the Amazon (Belém do Pará).[50] Others contributed money to Brazilian relief organizations.[51]

With Brazil a member of the Allied camp, much of the antagonism directed at Jewish refugees seemed to subside. This was certainly related to a drop in Nazi propaganda in the Brazilian press. Furthermore, the resignations of three of the most powerful nationalist-authoritarians in the Vargas regime, Justice Minister Francisco Campos, Police Chief Folinto Müller, and Department of Press and Propaganda head Lourival Fontes, the latter two open Axis supporters, lowered the priority given to discussion of Jews. The press now glorified the position of those Jews in Brazil. The *Correio de Manhã* reported with excitement that Brazilian Jews and Jewish refugees attended a special religious service in Rio to "thank President Getúlio Vargas for saving their children."[52] Historical memory suddenly returned to the press as journalists began portraying Jews as successful farmers, and a *Diário de Notícias* editorial observed that "the activities of the Jews are not limited exclusively to city trade. Actually they are capable of engaging in other spheres of work that are certainly more useful to the country that did not deny them shelter."[53] Niteroi's *Diário da Manhã* echoed the praise, reflecting that Jewish children in the farming colony of Quatro Irmãos spoke Portuguese "and are masters of the history, geography and economics of Brazil (unlike) Aryan races where thousands of Brazilians do not speak their own language."[54] *O Globo* reported that Brazil's treatment of "Jewish victims of Nazi-Fascism" had led "a huge group of Israelites . . . to believe in our glorious flag" and volunteer for military service, an article even reprinted in *Nao Armada,* the military journal that had regularly attacked Jews since its inception in 1939.[55]

Why did the Vargas regime concern itself with writing secret circulars that were modified or left unenforced? The answer does not seem to be that one hand of the government did not know what the other was doing. Rather the shifting immigration policy reflected changing stereotypical notions about Jews and the role they might play in Brazil's industrial development. Asking the Jewish Question thus presented the government with an easy way to gain nationalist credentials and to quiet critics of its immigration policy. Nazi economic and ideological relations with Brazil prior to the outbreak of World War II certainly encouraged the Vargas regime to use Jews in this regard (Frye 1967). Yet negative international response to Brazil's denial of visas to all Jews coincided with Oswaldo Aranha's return from Washington and his new power as foreign minister. Aranha's philo-Semitic ideology, and absolute conviction that Jewish immigrants from Central Europe were essential to bringing capital and skills to Brazil and maintaining good relations with the United States, began to take hold among important Estado Novo policymakers, and soon absolute restriction no longer seemed viable. Pressure from the United States and Great Britain, Brazil's eventual diplomatic and military allies, and also the only war-year buyers of Brazilian cotton and coffee, influenced the Estado Novo to find other ways to use Jews to satisfy political and economic allies (Newton 1986, 567–9).

In retrospect the Estado Novo's Jewish immigration policy did exactly what it set out to do. Hard-line domestic critics were kept in line while Brazil garnered the benefits of an alliance with the United States and England. Moreover, in spite of the restrictions, Jewish immigrants brought skills and capital to Brazil and helped stimulate postwar industrial expansion. The seeming contradiction between policy and reality was just that. Both attitudes and policy changed between 1939 and 1942. The ups and downs of refugee admission, and the decision to legalize the status of refugees in Brazil, indicate the new dual image of Jews among policymakers. Jew hatred and philo-Semitism existed hand in hand, and this complicated and contradictory situation allowed some Jews to enter Brazil while still more were rejected. Even so, Jews were able to use the stereotypes that formed the basis of Brazilian anti-Semitism to save more than ten thousand lives.

NOTES

1. Jacob Robinson, *Palestine and the United Nations: Prelude to Solution* (Washington, D.C.: Public Affairs Press, 1947), p. 145; Edward B.

Glick, *Latin America and the Palestine Problem* (New York: Theodore Herzl Foundation, 1958); Ignacio Klich, "Latin America, the United States, and the Birth of Israel: The Case of Somoza's Nicaragua," *Journal of Latin American Studies* 20, no. 2 (November 1988): 389–432; Jorge García-Grandos, *The Birth of Israel: The Drama As I Saw It* (New York: Knopf, 1949), p. 247.

2. Cited in Ignacio Klich, "The Roots of Argentine Abstentionism in the Palestine Question, 1946" (unpublished manuscript used by permission of the author).

3. From 1900 to 1945 between 90 and 95 percent of the Jewish immigrants arriving in Brazil were from Europe. The others came from Turkey, the Ottoman Empire, Morocco, and Palestine.

4. Jeremy Cohen has expressed such a notion, perhaps anachronistically, in his *The Friars and the Jews: The Evolution of Medieval Anti-Judaism* (Ithaca: Cornell University Press, 1982), p. 254.

5. Commercial attaché to Octavio Mangabeira, 17 April 1930, maço 29.625/29 (1291), Arquivo Historico Itamaraty—Rio de Janeiro (hereafter cited as AHI-R).

6. Except where noted, all figures discussed in this chapter represent legal visas granted to Jews and accepted by Brazilian authorities.

7. Such stereotypes flowed directly from those that began in Europe in the mid nineteenth century. See Robert M. Seltzer, *Jewish People, Jewish Thought: The Jewish Experience in History* (New York: Macmillan, 1980), pp. 627–34; Lucy S. Dawidowicz, *The War against the Jews, 1933–1945* (Toronto: Bantam Books, 1976), pp. 29–62.

8. David S. Wyman, *The Abandonment of the Jews: America and the Holocaust, 1941–1945* (New York: Pantheon Books, 1984), pp. 178–92; Irving Abella and Harold Troper, *None Is Too Many: Canada and the Jews of Europe 1933–1948* (New York: Random House, 1982), pp. 101–26; Michael Blakeney, *Australia and the Jewish Refugees 1933–1948* (Sydney: Croom Helm Australia, 1985), pp. 101–21; Bernard Wasserstein, *Britain and the Jews of Europe, 1939–1945* (New York: Oxford University Press, 1979), pp. 1–39.

9. Aranha to Adhemar de Barros, 20 October 1938, maço 9601 (612), AHI-R. The anti-Semitic component to Aranha's thought has been examined briefly by Theodore Michael Berson, "A Political Biography of Dr. Oswaldo Aranha of Brazil, 1930–1937" (Ph.D. diss, New York University, 1971), p. 265, and more carefully by Maria Luiza Tucci Carneiro, *O anti-semitismo na era Vargas: Fantasmas de uma geração* (São Paulo: Brasiliense, 1988), pp. 258–95.

10. Aranha, for example, proposed that a U.S. public relations firm be hired and that journalists be paid for image-enhancing stories. Aranha to Vargas, 19 May, 4 June, 24 September, 27 November 1937, OA 37.19. 5,

OA 37.4.6, OA 37.24.9, OA 37.11.27, Centro de Pesquisa e Documentação de História Contemporânea do Brasil, Fundação Getúlio Vargas, Rio de Janeiro (hereafter cited as CPDOC-R).

11. Aranha to Vargas, 30 November 1937, EM/30/30/XI/37, maço 9857 (660), AHI-R.

12. Hirschberg, "The Economic Adjustment," p. 37.

13. Angelo Trento, *Do outro lado do Atlântico: Um século de imigração italiana no Brasil*, trans. Mariarosaria Fabris and Luiz Eduardo de Lima Brandão (São Paulo: Nobel, 1989), pp. 383–4.

14. Getúlio Vargas, 11 April 1939, attached to Scotten to Hull, 14 April 1939, 832.00/1253, National Archives and Record Center, Washington, D.C. (hereafter cited as NARA-W).

15. Rosalina Coelho Lisboa to Vargas, no date, GV 40.09.00/4, CPDOC-R.

16. Herzl was wrong. Most nineteenth-century national political leaders were unwilling to invest time, money, or land in the creation of a Jewish state. Amos Elon, *Herzl* (New York: Holt, Rinehart and Winston, 1975), pp. 195–212.

17. Illegible to Aranha, 8 March 1939, maço 10,561 (741), AHI-R.

18. Lindolfo Collor, *Europa 1939* (Rio de Janeiro: EMIEL Editora, 1939), p. 161.

19. 511.14 (547)/324, 9 November 1939, and 511.14 (547)/326, 13 November 1939, Maço 29.630 (1291), AHI-R.

20. Itamaraty to Legation in Helsinki, 13 October 1939, 558. (72), 511.14 (457), Maço 29.630 (1291), AHI-R.

21. Consul General (Paris) to Aranha, 13 June 1939, maço 10,561 (741), AHI-R.

22. Pedro Leão Veloso to Aranha, 26 January 1940, OA 40.02.01/1, p. 3, CPDOC-R.

23. Trento, 385.

24. Consul General (Paris) to Aranha, 13 June 1939, maço 10,561 (741), AHI-R.

25. Cândido Duarte, *A Organização Municipal no Governo Getúlio Vargas* (Rio de Janeiro: Departamento de Emprensa e Propaganda, 1942), p. 213.

26. Stefan Zweig, *Brazil: Land of the Future* (New York: Viking Press, 1942), p. 13; Dines; Leo Spitzer, *Lives in Between: Assimilation and Marginality in Austria, Brazil, West Africa, 1780–1945* (Cambridge: Cambridge University Press, 1989), pp. 170–1.

27. Figures from "Rapport d'activité pendant la periode 1933–1942," HIAS NY-Folder 1, Archives of the YIVO Institute for Jewish Research, New York (hereafter cited as YIVO-NY). Conselho de Imigração e Colo-

nização figures from *Diário Official*, 27 November 1940, 22135, and *Revista de Imigração e Colonização* 3, no. 1 (April 1942): 184–94.

28. *Revista de Imigração e Colonização* 1, no. 3 (October 1940): 123–4 (misprinted).

29. *Revista de Imigração e Colonização* 1, no. 3 (October 1940): 123–4 (misprinted).

30. Morris C. Troper (Joint) to HIAS-JCA Emigration Association. 11 January 1939, SCA (10–11 February 1939) II, p. 136, Archives of the Jewish Colonization Association, London (hereafter cited as JCA-L). Achilles to Robert Pell, 20 March 1939, 832.55 J/3; Achilles to Briggs, 13 March 1939, 832.55 J/2, NARA-W.

31. Scotten to Welles, 10 March 1939, 832.55 J/3, p. 4, NARA-W.

32. Raphael Fernandes to Aranha, 13 April 1939, OA 39.05.15/2; Aranha to Fernandes, 15 May 1939, OA 39.05.15/2, CPDOC-R.

33. Department of State—Division of European Affairs Memorandum, 13 March 1939, 832.55 J/2, NARA-W. In March 1939, for example, the steamship *San Martín,* carrying twenty-one Jewish refugees from Germany and Italy, requested permission to disembark at Recife after being refused at Montevideo. Telegrams of support from around the world were of no help since Itamaraty claimed, untruthfully, not to have received any visa requests until four days after the ship had left Recife in search of another port. Passport Division to Secretary of the President of the Republic, 24 March 1939. Fundo Secretaria da Presidência da República—Relações Exteriores (hereafter cited as PRRE), box 27.586, documents 7241 and 7341, Arquivo Nacional, Rio de Janeiro (hereafter cited as AN-R). Alfred Rothschild to Vargas 15 April 1939, PRRE, box 27.586, document 9768, AN-R.

34. Isaiah Raffalovich, *Tsiyunim ve-tamrurim be-Shiv'im shenot nedudim: Otobayografiya* (Landmarks and milestones during seventy years of wanderings: An autobiography) (Tel Aviv: Defus Sho-Shani, 1952), pp. 200–3.

35. *A Noite* (Rio), 21 March 1925; *O Jornal* (Rio), 22 March 1925.

36. Tucci Carneiro examined only Einstein's last effort in 1941. The unfilled request to Foreign Minister Aranha for a visa for a friend led to the erroneous conclusion that even the great scientist "was not sufficient to defeat the rigid Brazilian legislation." Tucci Carneiro, *O anti-semitismo,* 283.

37. Einstein to Katz, 12 December 1938; Katz to Einstein, 24 December 1938, Einstein Duplicate Archive, 53602, 53604, Seeley G. Mudd Manuscript Library, Princeton University Archives, New Jersey (hereafter cited as SMML-NJ); Falbel, *Estudos,* pp. 134–9.

38. Einstein to Aranha, 23 January 1939, Einstein Duplicate Archive, 53607, SMML-NJ.

39. Katz to Einstein, 4 February 1939, Einstein Duplicate Archive, 53608, SMML-NJ.

40. Einstein to Aranha, 14 February 1939; Einstein to Katz, 14 February 1939, Einstein Duplicate Archive, 53609, 53610, SMML-NJ; Einstein to Aranha, 24 February 1939, SP/SN/558./Anexo único, maço 9857 (660), AHI-R.

41. Itamaraty memo to CIC, 11 May 1938; Labienne Salgado dos Santos to Einstein, 11 May 1939; Salgado dos Santos to Razovsky, 11 May 1939, maço 9857 (660), AHI-R.

42. Einstein to Aranha, 3 December 1940, Einstein Duplicate Archive, 54769, SMML-NJ.

43. Fabian-Katz to Einstein, 18 September 1953; Einstein to Fabian-Katz, 25 September 1953, Einstein Duplicate Archive, 59627, 59629, SMML-NJ.

44. Cohen, *Jewish Life*, p. 3. In all the other nations the study group visited, they gained access to only low-level officials.

45. Cohen, *Jewish Life*, p. 12.

46. Dr. A. d'Esaguy (HICEM) to Mr. Baumgold (NY), 18 December 1940, HIAS/NY, folder 37, YIVO-NY.

47. Oungre to Gottschalk (HIAS), 28 November 1941, HIAS/NY, folder 10, p. 2, YIVO-NY.

48. *New York Times*, 24 December 1942.

49. *New York Times*, 29 December 1942.

50. *Diário de Notícias* (Rio), 27 October 1942.

51. Memorandum of D. Bloomingdale attached to Duggan to James W. Wise, 26 October 1942, 840.48 Refugees/3421, NARA-W.

52. *Correio de Manhã* (Rio), 5 September 1942.

53. *Diário de Notícias* (Rio), 27 October 1942.

54. *Diário da Manhã* (Niteroi), 24 November 1943.

55. *O Globo* (Rio), 18 September 1942; *Nao Armada* 35 (October 1942): 143–4.

Notes on Contributors

DORIS L. BERGEN (Ph.D., University of North Carolina, Chapel Hill) is Associate Professor of History at the University of Notre Dame. She is the author of *Twisted Cross: The German Christian Movement in the Third Reich* (1996) as well as numerous articles and essays on religion, ethnicity, and gender in the Nazi era. She recently completed a short textbook, *War & Genocide: A Concise History of The Holocaust* (2002).

RUTH BETTINA BIRN (Ph.D., Stuttgart) is Chief Historian, War Crimes Section, Citizenship and Immigration Legal Services, Department of Justice, Canada. She is the author of *Die Höheren SS- und Polizeiführer: Himmlers Vertreter im Reich und in den besetzten Gebieten* (1986) and, with Norman G. Finkelstein, *A Nation on Trial: The Goldhagen Thesis and Historical Truth* (1998).

RANDOLPH L. BRAHAM is Distinguished Professor Emeritus of Political Science at the City College and Doctoral Program at the Graduate Center of the City University of New York, where he is also the Director of Rosenthal Institute for Holocaust Studies. A prolific scholar, he is a specialist in comparative politics and is a recognized authority on the Holocaust. His monumental two-volume *The Politics of Genocide: The Holocaust in Hungary* (revised and updated in 1994) is considered the definitive work on the subject.

GEOFFREY J. GILES (Ph.D., Cambridge University) is Associate Professor of History at the University of Florida. His numerous publications include *Students and National Socialism in Germany* (1985). A specialist on higher education in the Third Reich, he is currently doing research on the role of university-educated personnel in the Holocaust.

ATINA GROSSMANN (Ph.D., Rutgers University) is Associate Professor of History at the Cooper Union in New York City. She is the author of *Reforming Sex: The German Movement for Birth Control and Abortion Reform, 1920–1950* (1995, 1997) and numerous articles on gender and modernity in interwar Germany as well as co-editor of *When Biology Became Destiny: Women in Weimar and Nazi Germany* (1984). She is writing a book on "Victims, Victors, and Survivors: Jews and Germans in Occupied Germany, 1945–1949."

MARION KAPLAN (Ph.D., Columbia University) is Professor of Modern European History at Queens College and the Graduate Center, City University of New York. She is the author of *The Jewish Feminist Movement in Germany: The Campaigns of the Jüdischer Frauenbund, 1904–1938* (1979); *The Making of the Jewish Middle Class: Women, Family, and Identity in Imperial Germany* (1991), which won the National Jewish Book Award in History and the American Historical Association Conference Group on Central European History Book Prize; and *Between Dignity and Despair: Jewish Life in Nazi Germany* (1998), which received the Fraenkel Prize from the Wiener Library, London. She is currently editing a history of Jewish daily life from the eighteenth century until 1945.

TOMASZ KRANZ is Senior Curator at the Majdanek State Museum. He is a specialist on the history of the Majdanek concentration camp and the Holocaust in Poland. He is the editor of *Unser Schicksal–eine Mahnung für Euch... Berichte und Erinnerungen der Häftlinge von Majdanek* (1994); *Zur Bildungsarbeit der Gedenkstätte Majdanek* (1997); and *Die Verbrechen des Nationalsozialismus in Geschichtsbewußtsein und in der historischen Bildung in Deutschland un Polen* (1998).

ROBERT A. KRIEG (Ph.D., University of Notre Dame) is Professor of Theology at the University of Notre Dame. He is a specialist in Christology and modern German Catholic theology. He is the author of numerous publications and has three books: *Story-Shaped Christology* (1988); *Karl Adam: Catholicism in German Culture* (1992); and *Ro-*

mano Guardini: A Precursor of Vatican II (1997). He is the editor of *Romano Guardini: Proclaiming the Sacred in a Modern World* (1995) and is the Associate Editor of *The HarperCollins Encyclopedia of Catholicism* (1995). He is currently conducting research on German Catholic theologians in the Third Reich.

LAWRENCE L. LANGER (Ph.D., Harvard University) is Alumnae Chair Professor of English Emeritus, Simmons College, Boston. He is the author of many books on the Holocaust. His most recent publications include: *Admitting the Holocaust: Collected Essays* (1995); *Art from the Ashes: A Holocaust Anthology* (1995); *Landscapes of Jewish Experience: Paintings by Samuel Bak* (1997); and *Preempting the Holocaust* (1998).

JEFFREY LESSER (Ph.D., New York University) is Professor of History at Emory University. He is a specialist in Brazilian ethnic and immigration studies. He is the author of *Welcoming the Undesirables: Brazil and the Jewish Question (1994)*, which won the Best Book Prize from the New England Council on Latin American Studies. *Welcoming the Undesirables* was subsequently published in Brazil and Israel. He is the co-editor (with Ignacio Klich) of *Arab and Jewish Immigrants in Latin America: Images and Realities* (1998). His latest work is *Negotiating National Identity: Immigrants, Minorities, and the Struggle for Ethnicity in Brazil* (1999).

ROBERT MELSON is Professor of Political Science at Purdue University and former Director of its Jewish Studies Program. He is the author of *Revolution and Genocide: On the Origins of the Armenian Genocide and the Holocaust* (1992). His and his family's memoir, *False Papers*, were published by the University of Illinois Press in 2000.

MICHAEL PHAYER (Ph.D., Munich) is Professor of History at Marquette University. He is the author of numerous publications on the Catholic Church during the Third Reich. His book, *The Catholic Church and the Holocaust, 1930–1945*, was published in 2000.

LARRY V. THOMPSON (Ph.D., University of Wisconsin, Madison) is Professor of History at the United States Naval Academy. He is a specialist on modern German history and the Third Reich. His publications include articles on the SS and German military influence in Argentina. His latest publication is "Friedrich-Wilhelm Krüger: HSSPF-OST" in *Die SS Elite,* ed. Ronald Smelser and Enrico Syring (2000).

PIOTR WRÓBEL (Ph.D., University of Warsaw, Poland) holds the Konstanty Reynert Chair in Polish Studies in the Department of History at the University of Toronto. He is a specialist on the national minorities of East Central Europe. A prolific scholar, he has authored or coauthored seven books and numerous articles. His latest publication is *Historical Dictionary of Poland, 1945–1996* (1998).